VOYAGES
IN
ENGLISH
8

LOYOLA UNIVERSITY PRESS

Chicago 1958

Nihil Obstat

AUSTIN G. SCHMIDT, S.J.

Censor Librorum

October 23, 1957

Imprimatur

✠ SAMUEL CARDINAL STRITCH

Archbishop of Chicago

October 24, 1957

LOYOLA UNIVERSITY PRESS

Printed in the United States of America

Library of Congress Catalog Card Number: 58-7184

T-RAP-NL-K

It is no doubt true that the child grows toward maturity and independence of thought as he progresses through the grades; but this growth is not as a rule a sharp and sudden one, nor does the psychology of the child undergo any great change during his years in the elementary school. Methods, general objectives, and, certainly, the fundamental principles that underlie the work of the school remain the same from year to year. The need in every grade is to bring about pupil growth by making good use of the experiences of the child and by providing new and broader experiences.

A child can grow in school only if he is active. He must therefore do something with or about his experiences. The first and most obvious thing that he can do is to tell others of them. We encourage his desire to tell about his experiences. We wish him to express himself naturally and joyfully. If we make him feel that we and all the group discover a value in what he has to say, he will wish more and more to express himself well and successfully. We give him models of written expression that will make him sensitive to the beauty of word and phrase. We teach him to use certain methods and to observe certain rules; and these he accepts because he finds that our methods and our rules are things that he can easily use or understand, and that they help him.

VOYAGES IN ENGLISH endeavors, insofar as a textbook can accomplish such a purpose, to create a classroom atmosphere conducive to a group spirit rather than to a selfish and individualistic spirit. Every child is made to feel that the entire group is interested in what others have to say. He is taught to listen courteously and to criticize in a kindly and constructive manner.

It is also necessary to supply the child with new experiences. Schools can do this by means of motion pictures, excursions, and other similar activities. A textbook can do so only by encouraging the reading of books and by the models and exercises it contains. VOYAGES IN ENGLISH studiously excludes from its model paragraphs and from the sentences in its exercises whatever is misanthropic, or destructive, or psychologically harmful. The world that it seeks to create for the child is a bright world, a happy world, a hopeful world, and a usefully busy world.

A child can tell of his experiences either orally or in written form. The authors accept it as a fundamental principle that oral expression should precede written expression. Expression, whether oral or written, should provide variety, stimulate the imagination, and inspire creative effort by taking different forms. Children can express themselves by telling the class of something they have read, by taking part in discussions, by class dramatizations of things read in books, by imaginary broadcasts, telecasts, and telephone calls, by writing a paragraph or by writing a letter. It has been the aim of the authors to make use of every form of expression that has been found to be practical and appealing.

The authors believe very wholeheartedly in the child-centered school, but only if that term is properly understood. The child is necessarily the center of the school's activity, for everything that the school undertakes, every activity in which it engages, has for its immediate object the doing of something to or for the child; nor can the school afford to forget, in any of its planning, what the child needs to achieve and what the child is capable of achieving. The school should be child-centered in the sense that it accepts child growth as something to be sought in everything that it does. But this growth need not be undirected; rather it should be planned by those whose broad experience has given them a vision of the heights to which children can rise when guided wisely and lovingly. This direction is something that children need, something that they desire, and something that they willingly accept if nothing has ever occurred to destroy their confidence.

Child growth has not only volume or quantity; it has what we may call direction. The child growth that is sought in VOYAGES IN ENGLISH is growth toward a Christian adulthood that is truly cultured, that accepts social service as a sacred duty, and that can render social service the better because it has been taught to think clearly and to express itself effectively.

Ahead of the child in the elementary school who is to arrive at this destination there does indeed lie a long, a very long, voyage. The authors cannot hope to have taken him many miles on his journey. It will be enough for them if they can feel that they have given him a seaworthy ship and started him on his way. To have done this much—even to have made a sincere attempt at doing it—is not a small thing in a day when for many children there is no sound vessel in which to sail, no known port of call, no provision for the journey, no compass, nor any stars visible through the ragged clouds by which to chart a course.

ACKNOWLEDGMENTS

The authors wish to express their thanks to the following for the use of copyrighted materials:

To Bobbs-Merrill Company for permission to use "The Name of Old Glory," from *Home Folks,* by James Whitcomb Riley; to Doubleday, Doran and Company, Inc., for permission to use the poem of Joyce Kilmer, "Trees," from *Trees and Other Poems;* to Houghton Mifflin Company for permission to use "The Singing Leaves," by James Russell Lowell; and to Dr. John McCrae Kilgour for permission to use "In Flanders Fields," by Colonel John D. McCrae.

Contents

CHAPTER SEVEN

Workshop for Future Citizens

PART TWO   **GRAMMAR**

CHAPTER ONE

Nouns

CHAPTER TWO

Pronouns

CHAPTER THREE

Adjectives

CHAPTER FOUR

Verbs

CHAPTER FIVE

Participles, Gerunds, Infinitives

APPENDIX

TO

CHRIST THE KING

THROUGH

THE IMMACULATE HEART

OF MARY

PART ONE

CREATIVE ACTIVITIES

The Speech
Laboratory

In which we experiment with the voice

According to the dictionary, a laboratory is a place devoted to experimental study in any branch of science. A *speech laboratory* is a classroom in which scientific experiments in *oral expression* are carried on. Every laboratory has its specific equipment. A speech laboratory has for equipment the God-given instrument of the human voice. Practical exercises in the form of experiments will help students to become efficient speakers at home, in school, and in business.

1. The First Experiment—at Home

Here speech takes the form of conversation. At the evening meal, for instance, we always chat with other members of the family. In a good home the conversation is both interesting and instructive.

MODEL: A FAMILY CONVERSATION

The Setting: A dining room. A family is seated around the dinner table.

FATHER. I received a telephone call this morning from your Uncle John.

MOTHER. Father John! I didn't know he was back from Rome.

EDWARD. O Dad! Tell us about him. Is he coming to see us?

FATHER. That's exactly why he called. He intends to spend the evening with us.

MOTHER. I'm delighted. Father John always has so many interesting stories to tell us.

MARY. Mother, may I please invite Dolores over this evening? She has always wanted to meet Father John.

MOTHER. You certainly may. Edward, if you wish, you may ask Vincent to come, also.

FATHER. I suppose you know how to introduce your friends to Father John.

MARY. Oh yes, Father, we practiced introductions in school. First we name the person we wish to honor. I'll say, "Father Hickey, I want to introduce my friend Dolores Mayer. This is my Uncle John, Dolores."

FATHER. Edward, you do the same. I know both of your friends will acknowledge the introduction by saying, "How do you do, Father Hickey."

EDWARD. Vincent will add, no doubt, "I've wanted to meet you for a long time, Father." He has often requested an introduction to Uncle John.

Were the members of this family interested in the conversation? Were the children respectful, and ready to listen as well as to take part in the conversation? The following questions can be used to judge conversations:

1. Is my courtesy unfailing?

   Do I always avoid interrupting a speaker?
   Do I always avoid changing the subject abruptly?
   Do I always avoid needless arguments?

2. Is my tone *clear* and *low?*

3. Is my grammar *correct?*

CLASS ASSIGNMENT

1. Dramatize the conversation of the Hickey family. Several pupils may be selected to take the various parts and the class may vote on the best performances.

> **IN CONVERSATION OBSERVE CAREFULLY:** *What you say*
> *How you say it*

2. Imagine that several students are eating lunch together. During the meal the conversation centers around the carnival on the grounds of Good Shepherd Church. Let five pupils dramatize this scene, each contributing comments on any phase of the subject which interests him.

3. Divide the class into groups and let each group plan a conversation that might take place at home when members of the family talk about:

1. A worth-while radio program
2. Plans for a trip to the beach
3. A Catholic book which the family has read
4. A baseball game
5. A church jubilee
6. A place studied in geography
7. A proposed vacation for Mother
8. The family's new car
9. A birthday party for a baby sister or brother
10. Plans for helping Mother and Father during the summer vacation

Introductions

When we bring home a guest whom our parents do not know we should introduce him to them. In introducing people we aim to make them known to each other. The following are rules of correct procedure. We should always be courteous, gracious, and cordial.

1. Introduce a man to a woman or a boy to a girl. We address the woman first, and then introduce the man. "Mrs. Connors, Mr. Buckley."

2. Introduce a lay person to a religious. "Sister Marie, may I present my sister Mary Alice?"

3. Introduce a younger person to an older or more distinguished person. That is, we say the name of the older person first. "Grandfather, this is Joseph Devlin, who has just moved into the house next door to us. My grandfather, Mr. Morris, Joseph."

4. When introducing two people of the same gender and about the same age, either name may be mentioned first. "Mary Kane, may I introduce Ella Sheehan?" "Ella Sheehan, my friend Mary Kane."

In acknowledging an introduction we simply say, "How do you do." We may add, if we wish, the person's name, "How do you do, Mrs. Bernard." When boys and men are introduced to one another they usually shake hands; girls and women do not. When a gentleman is introduced to a lady, she generally smiles and bows.

MODEL: AN INTRODUCTION

KATHLEEN. Mother, this is my new friend, Dorothy Coll. Dorothy moved here from Gesu parish.

MOTHER. How do you do, Dorothy. I hope you will be very happy in this neighborhood.

DOROTHY. How do you do, Mrs. Fries. If all the girls are like Kathleen, I know I am going to like it.

CLASS ASSIGNMENT

Practice the following introductions in class:

1. Imagine that Helen Gaul has just moved into the house next door to you. Take her to school and introduce her to the principal, Sister Paulita.

2. Introduce to your mother John Martin, whom you have brought home with you after school.

3. Walking on the street with your mother, you meet your friend Anita Gray, who is also with her mother. Introduce the two mothers.

4. Your cousin accompanies you to the children's Mass on Sunday. Introduce her to your teacher.

5. Gerard McCauley is a new pupil in your class. Introduce him to your pastor, Father Daly, whom you meet on your way into school.

6. Parents have been invited to inspect the newly equipped Scout rooms. Introduce to your mother and father the scoutmaster, Mr. Schwartz.

7. Introduce yourself to a girl who has just moved into your neighborhood and who has not yet made any friends.

8. Your father agrees to umpire a baseball game. Introduce to him your captain, John Manning, and the captain of the opposing team, Eugene Timlin.

9. Introduce two friends of yours who you feel should know each other because they have similar interests.

Telephone Calls

Telephone conversations are of frequent occurrence in the home. They may be *social* or *business calls.*

Social telephone calls include all the calls made to friends or acquaintances for the purpose of exchanging information, of extending, accepting, or declining invitations, of expressing our happiness because of the good fortune of a friend or our regret because of some misfortune, and in speaking of matters in which we are interested. We should avoid prolonged calls that may inconvenience others on the same line.

MODEL: A SOCIAL TELEPHONE CALL

(After dialing the number and receiving an answer)

Greeting   Hello, Mother. This is Sarah.

Message   Father Doyle came into class today and asked all the girls to go to the game at Eagle Field this afternoon to cheer the team on to victory. May I go? . . . The game should be over by five o'clock. . . .

Closing   Oh, thank you, Mother. I'll be careful. . . . Good-by, Mother dear.

CLASS ASSIGNMENT

1. Select a partner and dramatize the following telephone conversation between a young girl and a priest:

HELEN. This is Carr's residence. Helen is speaking.

FATHER CRAWFORD. Good afternoon, Helen. This is Father Crawford. Is Robert at home?

HELEN. No, he isn't, Father. He practices every afternoon with the track team. May I give him a message, Father?

FATHER CRAWFORD. If he returns before six o'clock, Helen, please tell him to call me at the rectory.

HELEN. I'll be glad to tell him to call you at the rectory before six o'clock, Father.

FATHER CRAWFORD. Thank you, Helen. Good-by.

HELEN. Good-by, Father.

CHECK YOUR TELEPHONE CONVERSATIONS:
Is your voice a smiling voice? Clear? Quiet? Musical?
Is your message brief?
Is your courtesy unfailing?

2. Divide the class into groups and let each group prepare and present one of the following telephone conversations:

1. You have an extra ticket for the football game. Extend an invitation to your friend to accompany you.

2. A friend is visiting you from out of town. One of your classmates and your guest are interested in music. Invite the classmate to dinner.

3. Call your Aunt Lucy to thank her for a birthday gift.

4. Call the home of Elizabeth Lane, who is recovering from an operation. Inquire about Elizabeth's health.

5. One of your classmates invited you to go skating with him. Call him and tell him that you have planned to go away and will not be able to accept the invitation.

Business Calls

We should know exactly what we wish to say before we take up the telephone to make a business call. A thoughtful and considerate person does not waste the time of busy people by asking needless questions. When placing an order or making an appointment by telephone, we should first give our name and then transact our business briefly and clearly.

MODEL: A BUSINESS TELEPHONE CALL

Good morning. This is Ellen Discher.

I should like to have a dental check-up. May I have an appointment with Dr. Gray on Thursday afternoon? . . .

Thank you. I shall be in the office on Thursday afternoon at four o'clock. Good-by.

When emergencies arise and we must make telephone calls for assistance, we should try to keep cool. Once we have made up our mind as to what should be said, we should state clearly who and where we are and the reason for our call.

MODEL: AN EMERGENCY TELEPHONE CALL

Dr. Perry, this is Michael Collins, 5346 Catharine Street.

My mother fainted about ten minutes ago and has just regained consciousness. She complains of a severe pain around her heart. Can you come at once? . . . We gave her aromatic spirits of ammonia, Doctor, nothing else. . . .

Thank you, Dr. Perry. We'll tell her to lie still and that you will arrive within thirty minutes.

CLASS ASSIGNMENT

1. Dramatize the following telephone call:

NURSE. Good morning. Dr. Gray's office.

ELLEN. Good morning. This is Ellen Discher. I have an appointment with Dr. Gray for this afternoon at four o'clock, but it will be impossible for me to be there at that time as my mother is ill. May I please come next week?

NURSE. I'm very sorry. Dr. Gray is to attend a dental meeting in Cleveland next week and is making no appointments. Will you be able to come on Monday, November 8, at four o'clock?

ELLEN. Yes, thank you. I will come on that date. I'm very sorry I was forced to cancel today's appointment. Good-by.

2. Place an order for groceries to be delivered before twelve o'clock.

3. Call the grocer to report that the groceries your mother ordered early in the morning have not yet been delivered.

4. Telephone a local store to ask about the price of radios of certain types.

5. Your father is returning from Miami, Florida, by air. Call the airport and ask the time of arrival for Flight 156.

6. Make an appointment by telephone with any of the following persons:

1. A doctor
2. A music teacher
3. Your mother's hairdresser
4. A priest

2. The Second Experiment—in School

There are very many opportunities for conversation in the ordinary exchange of courtesies in school. For example, we may be called upon to direct a stranger whom we meet in the corridor of the school.

MODEL: GUIDING A STRANGER

STUDENT. Good morning. May I help you?

STRANGER. Yes, thank you. I should like to see your principal if she is not too busy.

STUDENT. I shall be very glad to take you to her office. Do you have an appointment?

STRANGER. Yes, Mother said she would be free at ten o'clock. *(They walk off together.)*

STUDENT. This is Mother's office. *(He raps gently.)* Please pardon me, Mother. This gentleman wishes to see you.

STRANGER *(bowing)*. I appreciate your kindness in directing me. Thank you very much.

STUDENT *(bowing also)*. You are welcome.

CLASS ASSIGNMENT

Divide your class into groups and dramatize conversations that would arise from the following incidents:

1. The superintendent of schools arrives at your school during recess and asks to be directed to the principal's office. Offer to take him there.

2. Take a visitor to the school library and introduce him to the librarian.

3. You meet a teacher carrying a large number of books to the school building. Offer to carry the books for her.

4. Explain to a new pupil the qualifications for membership in the Safety Squad.

5. Discuss with your teacher new books that might be purchased for the school library.

6. A group of eighth-grade boys call on the pastor to ask his permission to organize a basketball team. Explain that an older brother of one of the boys has offered to coach the team.

Group Discussions

Very much of our happiness in life will depend upon our ability to work with others. No matter what our occupation may be, we shall be a member of some group, club, association, or union. Decisions will be made that affect our own welfare. Shall we be silent while questions are being discussed, or shall we have ideas and present them in such a way as to command respect?

In school we learn to think in a group, to pool our bit of knowledge with that of others for the common good, to sift differences of opinion, to change our own opinion gracefully when we see that the arguments on the other side are stronger, and to defend our own view courageously if we are certain that we are right, especially if the opposite opinion should be against faith or morals.

Informal Discussions

Informal discussions are those in which the class is not organized with elected officers. The teacher or someone appointed by the teacher presides as chairman or leader. A day in advance of the time set for the discussion the teacher may announce: "Tomorrow at oral-expression period we shall hold an informal discussion on the qualities of a true sportsman. I should like the members of the class to come prepared to take part in the discussion by offering helpful suggestions. Paul Curran, will you please act as leader of the discussion?"

MODEL: AN INFORMAL DISCUSSION

(The oral-expression period is in progress. Paul Curran acts as leader or chairman.)

PAUL. In this meeting let us discuss the qualities of a true sportsman. Which do you think ranks first among the traits a good sportsman should possess?

EDWARD. I think loyalty heads the list, Mr. Chairman. A loyal sportsman puts forth his best efforts at all times and under all circumstances, however trying they may be.

GERALDINE. Don't you want to put being a good loser very high on this list? I like to see defeat acknowledged with a smile.

PAUL. Of course, Geraldine. Everyone likes to see the loser sincerely congratulate the winner.

MICHAEL. I always remember a quotation Sister gave us. It was this, "Not failure, but low aim, is crime."

FRANCES. That reminds me that a true sportsman never stoops to anything low, never cheats to win. It would seem to be better to lose every time than to try anything underhand to win.

JAMES. That's a good point, Frances. All the great sports leaders loathed cheating as they would a disease. My father told me that Knute Rockne used to say that our Lady would not be proud to see her boys win if they had to sacrifice honesty to do it.

PAUL. Will somebody else express his opinion?

GEORGE. A true sportsman should be courteous at all times. There is no place in a game for a fellow who can't treat the other players with the respect he'd like shown to himself.

PAUL. That's a good thing to remember, George. It seems to me that we could sum up this discussion by condensing all these qualities under one heading, courage. If the sportsman has the courage to do the right thing, he will find that all these traits follow. Everything we mentioned calls for courage in some degree. Let's hope that from this talk we will all determine to possess these qualities and so be really true sportsmen!

Notice that it is the leader's duty to keep the discussion moving in an orderly fashion and to sum up the suggestions at the end. Was the discussion lively? Did a number of pupils participate and express their ideas? Did the leader state any conclusion arrived at by the group?

CLASS ASSIGNMENT

Choose a leader and hold a group discussion. Select from the following list the topic you would like to discuss in class:

1. The true meaning of school spirit
2. Types of aircraft
3. How farming has changed in America
4. The value of an extensive vocabulary
5. The proper manner of displaying the flag
6. The qualities a public official should have
7. The importance of fair play
8. The meaning of a vocation

Speaking to the Class

It is only a step from group discussions to reports and formal talks to our classmates on subjects of general interest. Our talks before the class will be more interesting if we plan in advance what we are going to say. The speaker will arouse interest in his audience if he has an effective opening sentence. The details that follow this good beginning sentence must likewise be carefully organized. As we learned in earlier grades, the best way to keep to the topic is to make an outline.

Blanche Owens decided to give a talk on schools, but this subject was too general. She therefore limited her talk to one topic, why we have Catholic schools. The following outline aided her in making the talk:

WHY WE HAVE CATHOLIC SCHOOLS

I. Maintenance of Catholic schools
   A. Sacrifices entailed
   B. Willingness of Catholic parents
   C. Reason for making sacrifices

II. Advantages of Catholic education
   A. Doctrinal instruction
   B. Preparation for sacraments
   C. Religious atmosphere and influence

III. Results of Catholic education
   A. Good general foundation
   B. Equipment for life

MODEL: WHY WE HAVE CATHOLIC SCHOOLS

To measure the tremendous sacrifices which Catholic parents make to send their children to Catholic schools would be a difficult task. Why is it that men and women feel themselves well repaid for the effort and the expense of building and maintaining parochial schools? The answer lies in the satisfaction they find in knowing that their children are enjoying the many advantages of a religious education.

"What are these advantages which the Catholic school claims to give?" someone may ask. Here are a few of them. All through the grades the children are under the influence of religious teachers who strive earnestly to instill in their hearts a love of God and a desire for goodness. At the same time these teachers give accurate instruction in the truths of the faith and the duties and obligations of Catholics. The sacraments are carefully explained, and children are encouraged by word and example to receive them frequently. Moreover, religion is not confined to the catechism period; its influence is felt in every subject taught during the day. The entire atmosphere of the school is Christlike. Pupils learn how to live as Christians.

As the school years pass, the parents realize that all the subjects of the curriculum are well taught and that their children have an adequate grasp of all the fundamentals. When the time comes for boys and girls to take their places in the world, parents are confident that these children go forth well equipped for the battle of life. Catholic education has put into their hands a sword and a shield.

Did the speaker explain why we have Catholic schools? Did she follow her outline? Was the beginning sentence interesting? Was it evident that the speaker had given some thought to her subject; that is, did she have ideas to be expressed?

The Four-Leaf Clover of Good Speech

The good speaker has both mental control and physical control. The qualities of a good speaker are sometimes compared to the leaves of a four-leaf clover:

1. IDEAS. *What* we say is of the most importance. Ideas are acquired from four sources: observation of life about

us; conversation with experienced talkers; reading; our own reflections on what we see, hear, and read.

2. STYLE. *How* we say it also requires attention. Our speech should be grammatically correct, and it should also show careful diction (choice of words) and varied sentence structure.

3. VOICE. Let it be low in pitch, musical, flexible. Speak distinctly, so that everyone understands what is said.

4. POSITION. Stand with body erect, head not too high, eyes holding the audience, hands relaxed.

CLASS ASSIGNMENT

1. Prepare a short talk on any one of the following topics. You may use the beginning sentence, the details to be developed, and the ending sentence suggested for each topic, or you may alter them to suit your own speech:

1. PASTEUR'S SCIENTIFIC ACCOMPLISHMENTS

Beginning sentence	Few scientists can look back over a lifetime as full of accomplishments as that of Louis Pasteur.
Details	Process of pasteurization; principle of inoculation; isolation of various disease germs; treatment of hydrophobia
Ending sentence	The world we live in today is a better one because of the tireless work of this great man.

2. BASEBALL TECHNIQUE

Beginning sentence	Since baseball is our national sport, American children should have more than a superficial knowledge of the game.
Details	Playing field; position of players; object of game; method of scoring
Ending sentence	Whether you are a player or a spectator of this great American game, accurate knowledge should help you to enjoy it more thoroughly.

3. WATER RESOURCES OF THE UNITED STATES

Beginning sentence Water, which has always played an important role in the drama of human existence, is one of the most widely developed resources in the United States.

Details Used for drinking, power, transportation, irrigation, mineral content

Ending sentence We see, then, that the water supply is a vital element in the social and industrial development of our land.

2. Prepare an original talk to be given in your classroom. These are the important steps to be followed: (1) Choose a subject. (2) Limit the subject to one topic that can be covered in a short speech. (3) Make an outline. (4) Prepare an interesting beginning sentence. (5) Follow the outline in developing the topic. (6) Think of a strong ending sentence. The purpose of the speech and the object you have in making it will help you compose this ending sentence.

3. The Third Experiment—Formal Discussions

Formal discussions differ from informal discussions in several ways. Formal discussions are conducted under officers elected by the class. The laws of parliamentary procedure are observed. Only one person may speak at a time, and to do so he must be recognized by the chairman. If any action is to be taken, a motion must be made, seconded, and approved by a majority of the voters.

The officers necessary for conducting the first formal meeting of a class are (1) a temporary chairman, appointed by the teacher or elected by the class, and (2) a temporary secretary, appointed by the chairman. The following is a report of the first formal meeting held by a class of students of your own age.

A FORMAL DISCUSSION: "SHALL WE ORGANIZE A
CATHOLIC ACTION CLUB?"

CHAIRMAN *(standing at desk or table).* The meeting will please come to order. Let us rise and say the prayer. *(The pupils recite a short prayer.)* Elizabeth Doyle, will you kindly act as temporary secretary? *(Elizabeth sits down on the right of the chairman.)* The purpose of this meeting is to organize a club. Does anyone wish to make a suggestion?

JANE BRESCH *(rising).* Mr. Chairman, Jane Bresch. *(If the speaker is known to the chairman, she need not give her name.)*

CHAIRMAN *(seated).* Jane Bresch. *(This "recognizes" Jane, giving her the floor, or empowering her to speak.)*

JANE. I move that we form a Catholic Action Club.

JOSEPH FRIEL *(not rising).* I second the motion.

CHAIRMAN. It has been moved and seconded that this class form a Catholic Action Club. Is there any discussion?

CARL CONNOR *(rising).* Mr. Chairman—

JOSEPH WAGNER *(also rising).* Mr. Chairman—

CHAIRMAN *(recognizing the first speaker to rise).* Carl Connor.

CARL. Mr. Chairman, perhaps a Catholic Action Club would be hard for an eighth grade to handle.

JANE. Mr. Chairman, Jane Bresch.

CHAIRMAN. Jane Bresch.

JANE. Mr. Chairman, I think the eighth grade can manage a Catholic Action Club if the organization is kept simple.

CHAIRMAN. Is there any further discussion?

MARGARET DONAHUE. Mr. Chairman, Margaret Donahue.

CHAIRMAN. Margaret Donahue.

MARGARET. Mr. Chairman, I'd like to know just what Catholic Action means.

CHAIRMAN. Will Jane Bresch please tell us what Catholic Action is?

JANE. Mr. Chairman, Catholic Action is an apostolate or mission for the salvation of souls. Its activity begins with trying to make one's own life holy and then trying to win other souls for Christ.

HELEN BOWE. Mr. Chairman, Helen Bowe.

CHAIRMAN. Helen Bowe.

HELEN. Mr. Chairman, how can we carry out this activity?

CHAIRMAN. Your question is out of order now, Helen. We shall discuss it later. Are you ready for the question?

VOICES. Question! Question! *(When a discussion is too long or is out of order, or when speakers wander from the subject, the chairman and members obtain a vote on "the question before the house" in the above manner.)*

CHAIRMAN. It has been moved and seconded that we form a Catholic Action Club. All those in favor say *aye. (The majority say* Aye.*)* Those opposed, *no. (Only a few say* No.*)* The motion is carried. Shall we call the club the Catholic Action Club, or do you prefer another name?

JAMES HANNA. Mr. Chairman, James Hanna.

CHAIRMAN. James Hanna.

JAMES. Mr. Chairman, I think Catholic Action Club is a good title. We might shorten it to CAC. I move we call it the Catholic Action Club.

CHAIRMAN. Will someone please second the motion?

JAMES LYONS. Mr. Chairman, I second the motion.

CHAIRMAN. It has been moved and seconded that we call our club the Catholic Action Club. All those in favor say *aye;* opposed, *no.* The motion is carried.

CHAIRMAN. There remains other business to be transacted. We need a constitution in order that we may have a standard of conduct. Will someone please move that the chairman appoint a committee to draft a constitution to be presented at the next meeting? *(The motion is made, seconded, and carried.)* Thomas Malone, Elizabeth Joyce, and John Rafter will kindly serve on this committee. *(The members whose names are called rise and bow to the chairman.)*

CHAIRMAN. Is there any further business?

WILLIAM MYERS. Mr. Chairman, William Myers.

CHAIRMAN. William Myers.

WILLIAM. I move to adjourn.

RAYMOND COLLINS *(not rising).* I second the motion.

CHAIRMAN. It has been moved and seconded that we adjourn. All those in favor say *aye;* opposed, *no.* The *ayes* have it. The meeting stands adjourned.

The constitution defines the purpose of the club, the qualifications for membership, the duties of the officers, the manner of their election, provisions for amendments, the payment of dues, and the order of business for the meetings. The following model should be of interest to the committee appointed to draw up the constitution.

CONSTITUTION

ARTICLE I.—NAME

This club shall be called the Catholic Action Club (CAC).

ARTICLE II.—AIM

The aim of this club is to foster holiness, first in oneself and then in others.

ARTICLE III.—MEMBERSHIP

Any student of eighth grade is eligible.

ARTICLE IV.—OFFICERS

The officers shall be: a president, a vice-president, a secretary, and a treasurer.

ARTICLE V.—DUTIES OF THE OFFICERS

Section 1. The president presides over all meetings and appoints all committees.

Section 2. The vice-president presides over the meetings in the absence of the president.

Section 3. The secretary calls the roll, keeps the minutes, and takes care of all correspondence.

Section 4. The treasurer keeps the funds of the club and pays all expenses.

ARTICLE VI.—ELECTION OF OFFICERS

The officers shall be elected by a majority of the votes cast. They shall hold office for two months.

ARTICLE VII.—MEETINGS

Section 1. The regular meetings shall be held every Friday morning at eleven o'clock, during the oral-expression period.

Section 2. The president may call other meetings for special purposes as the need arises.

ARTICLE VIII.—AMENDMENTS

This constitution may be amended upon approval of two thirds of the members, provided due notice of the proposed amendment and the date on which it is to be considered is given.

BY-LAWS

ARTICLE I.—ORDER OF BUSINESS

The order of business shall be: call to order, prayer, reading of minutes, unfinished business, reports of committees, new business, entertainment, adjournment.

ARTICLE II.—COMMITTEES

The president may appoint standing committees to take care of different phases of Catholic Action. He also has the power to appoint special committees when the occasion arises.

THE SECOND CLUB MEETING

(The temporary chairman presides. After the prayer he calls on the temporary secretary to read the minutes, or the record of the first meeting.)

SECRETARY *(reading)*. A meeting of the eighth-grade class was called to order on November 18 at eleven o'clock for the purpose of organizing a club. Robert Harris, temporary chairman, presided. It was moved and seconded that a Catholic Action Club be formed. After some discussion this motion was passed.

A motion was made and seconded that the club be called the Catholic Action Club. This motion was carried. The chairman appointed a committee to draft a constitution to be submitted at the next meeting. The members of the committee were Thomas Malone, chairman, Elizabeth Joyce, and John Rafter.

The meeting was adjourned at 11:40.

> Respectfully submitted,
> Elizabeth Doyle, *Secretary*

CHAIRMAN. You have heard the minutes. Are there any corrections? If not, the minutes stand approved as read. The purpose of this meeting is to elect officers for the Catholic Action Club. Nominations are now open for the office of president.

KATHLEEN CAMPBELL *(rising)*. Mr. Chairman, Kathleen Campbell.

CHAIRMAN. Kathleen Campbell.

KATHLEEN. Mr. Chairman, I nominate Robert Bresch.

CHAIRMAN. Are there any other nominations?

GEORGE EBERWINE. Mr. Chairman, George Eberwine.

CHAIRMAN. George Eberwine.

GEORGE. Mr. Chairman, I nominate Joan Haggerty.

JOHN RAFTER. Mr. Chairman, John Rafter.

CHAIRMAN. John Rafter.

JOHN. Mr. Chairman, I move that the nominations be closed.

CLAIRE McCASSON *(not rising)*. I second the motion.

CHAIRMAN. It has been moved and seconded that the nominations for president be closed. All those in favor say *aye;* those

opposed, *no*. The *ayes* have it. We will therefore proceed to the election of a president. Will the secretary distribute the ballots? Please write on the paper the name of the nominee for whom you wish to vote. It is always courteous for a nominee to vote for a nominee other than himself. *(When all the ballots have been written, the chairman proceeds.)* The secretary will kindly collect the votes. Will Mary James and John Curran act as tellers to count the votes? *(The votes are counted.)* There should be forty votes. The result of the voting is twenty-five votes for Robert Bresch and fifteen votes for Joan Haggerty. Robert Bresch is elected president of the Catholic Action Club. *(Robert Bresch takes his place in the chair and conducts the election of the other officers.)* [1]

PRESIDENT. The officers elected will kindly take their places up front. Will the chairman of the committee appointed to draft a constitution please make his report? *(The one first appointed to a committee becomes the chairman of that committee.)*

THOMAS MALONE. Mr. President, members of the Catholic Action Club, we submit the following draft of a constitution for the club, subject to the approval of the club. *(It is wise to make cop-*

---

[1] The election of officers may also be conducted by having those who wish to vote for a certain candidate raise their hands.

*ies of the constitution, so that every member may have a copy.
If this cannot be done, each article and by-law must be read and
voted on separately.)*

PRESIDENT. The members will kindly take home the copies of
the constitution. We shall discuss the proposed constitution at
our next meeting. Thank you, Thomas. The business for today is
now concluded. Is there a motion for adjournment?

EDWARD DACEY. I move we adjourn.

ELIZABETH JOYCE. I second the motion.

PRESIDENT. It has been moved and seconded that we adjourn.
All those in favor say *aye;* opposed, *no.* The motion is carried;
the meeting is adjourned.

At the third meeting the same order of business is followed. Under "unfinished business" comes the adoption of
the constitution, voted upon in the usual manner. A discussion may reveal different phases of Catholic Action to
be investigated by various committees; such as Catholic
Action in the home, Catholic Action in foreign missions,
Catholic Action in leisure, and so forth. The president then
appoints standing committees—that is, permanent committees—to take care of these phases. An entertainment
committee may also be appointed at the suggestion of
any member.

Committee Reports

A committee report may be read by the chairman of the
committee or by a secretary appointed by him. It should
pass the following test:

CONTENT. Does the report cover the problem referred to the
committee? Does it express honest opinion? Are the proposals
practical for the group?

STYLE. Is the report grammatically correct? Is the expression
interesting and forceful?

A COMMITTEE REPORT ON CATHOLIC ACTION IN LEISURE TIME

As chairman of the Committee on Catholic Action in Leisure Time, I beg to submit to the president and members of the Catholic Action Club the following report:

The committee suggests, first of all, charity toward our neighbor as a means of advancing Catholic Action in our leisure time. How can this be done concretely by our members? (1) By being kind in the home to all the family; (2) by visiting sick children in homes or in the hospital; (3) by visiting children in their homes, bringing them toys, fruit, candy; (4) by writing letters to lonely children.

In these four ways the committee feels that the members of the CAC (Catholic Action Club) may advance Catholic Action through the wise use of our leisure time.

Respectfully submitted,
Genevieve McBrearty, Chairman

Many clubs open their meetings with the singing of the Catholic Action song, "For Christ the King." This song can be obtained from The Queen's Work, St. Louis, Missouri.

PROJECTS FOR A CATHOLIC ACTION CLUB

Campaigning for Catholic Action:

1. Publicity on main and classroom bulletin boards
2. Notices in the school paper, the local paper
3. Talks by members on different phases of Catholic Action
4. Talks by students from other schools on what their schools are doing for Catholic Action
5. Lecture at a club meeting by a guest speaker: (a) a priest of the parish, (b) a missionary, (c) a member of a Catholic organization, (d) a city official

CLASS ASSIGNMENT

1. Discuss the possibilities of organizing a club in your classroom. Decide upon the type of club to be organized and the name. The teacher may lead the first discussion.

2. Elect the officers of the club, following the procedure in this chapter.

3. Suggest other activities for a Catholic Action club.

4. The Fourth Experiment—Choral Speaking

There is no better way in which to experiment with the voice than through choral speaking.

Choral speaking is not a new discovery, but a revival of the old Greek manner of reading poetry. By means of choral speaking moderns have rediscovered the beauty of rhythm, and have thus recaptured not only the melody of poetry, but the thought itself singing in the lines.

A choral-speaking group may be likened to an orchestra. The human voices are the instruments which bring out the music, interpreting the thought. The dark or heavy voices are the brasses; the light voices, the flutes and violins; and the medium voices, the oboes and clarinets. Separately and in chorus, these voices blend to interpret the measures of poetry, in much the same fashion as the instruments interpret the measures of a sonata, a symphony, or a simple rondeau or chanson. Many of the principles of music may be used in choral speaking.

Time and Pitch

A choral-speaking group or choir is governed, as is the orchestra, by time and pitch. In lyric poetry, ringing with joy and gladness, the time is quick; in dirges or solemn poetry, slow and measured. Nonsense rhymes are read in quick time and in a higher pitch, to indicate the merriment that is the basis of their rhythm. Elegies, or songs that mourn the dead (a person or an ideal), are read in slow, measured time and low pitch. Descriptive poems are read in conversational tone, time, and pitch.

The Director

Every orchestra has its conductor, who blends the instruments into one beautiful whole. So every choral-speaking group has its director, who blends the different voices into one melody.

The director should be a lover of poetry. He should possess a keen appreciation of rhythm, a delicate sensitivity to the effect of the pause, of the inflections of the voice and the relation of these to the interpretation of the lines. For example, a simple, stressed word takes a *falling slide* or *inflection* of the voice:

> Fallen cold and dead \

Words that ask a question take a *rising slide* or *inflection* of the voice:

> How old are you, friend? /

Words used in pairs take a *rising* and *falling inflection* to avoid monotony of tone:

> Blow, / bugle \

Words that are contrasted in meaning, sarcastic, or of double meaning, take a *double slide* or *inflection* of the voice. After a little practice you will learn how to vary the inflection of your voice so as to produce the best possible effect.

Finally, a good orchestra conductor must see that all his instruments are in tune. Likewise, a good director in choral speaking sees to it that the human voices of his choir are in tune. For this purpose he gives tuning-up exercises before every lesson.

TUNING-UP EXERCISES

Breathing is essential to the correct use of the voice.

Exercise. Inhale through the mouth or the nose, inflating the diaphragm, the chest wall, and the ribs; exhale through the sound box or larynx.

Test. Place the hands on the ribs just above the waistline. Feel the expansion and the recession of the ribs with the incoming and outgoing breath.

Correct vowel formation is essential to correct speech. The production of good tone depends upon the position of the mouth. Watch your teacher while she forms the vowel sounds and try to imitate the position of her lips. The following suggestions will help you to pronounce each vowel correctly:

1. Form the vowels with the lips in the correct position.

2. Say the vowels first in low pitch, slow time; then repeat in quick time, high pitch; in conversational time and pitch.

3. Sing the vowels on different notes. Scale work is very valuable for acquiring a musical tone.

You may find it helpful to practice before a mirror until you feel that you are pronouncing the vowels correctly. Many prominent speakers began their training in this way.

Enunciation:

Exercises in vowel practice—*oo* and *woo:*

oo   oo   oo   woo   woo   woo

Exercises in enunciation are an excellent preparation for all speech work and especially for choral speech.

Nonsense jingle spoken in unison:

Coo, coo, coo,
Turtle dove, coo
Moo, moo, moo,
Jersey cow, moo!
Ow, ow, ow; bow, bow, bow
How now, brown cow,
Why do you moo down town?

GROUP WORK: "BLOW, BUGLE, BLOW"

Song from "The Princess," by Alfred Lord Tennyson

First Voice
The splendour / falls on castle walls //
  And snowy summits \ old in story; //
The long light shakes across the lakes, //
  And the wild cataract / leaps in glory. //

Refrain (Unison)
Blow, \ bugle, / blow, \ set the wild echoes \
  flying, //
Blow, / bugle; \ answer, / echoes, \ dying, /
  dying, \ dying. //

Second Voice
O hark, / O hear! / how thin and clear //
  And thinner, / clearer, / farther going! //
O, sweet \ and far / from cliff \ and scar //
  The horns of Elfland \ faintly blowing! //

Refrain (Unison)
Blow, \ let us hear the purple glens \ replying, //
Blow, / bugle; \ answer, / echoes, \ dying, /
  dying, / dying. //

Third Voice
O love, they die \ in yon rich sky, //
  They faint on hill / or field \ or river; //
Our \ echoes / roll from soul \ to soul, //
  And grow / for ever \ and for ever. //

Refrain (Unison)
Blow, \ bugle, / blow, \ set the wild echoes \
  flying, //
And answer, / echoes, \ answer, \ dying, /
  dying, / dying. //

PREPARATION FOR CHORAL SPEAKING OF "BLOW, BUGLE, BLOW"

1. Read the poem very carefully at least three times until you have made its beautiful pictures your own: the sun shining on the craggy walls and turrets of the old castle, on the green waters of the lakes, and the cataract leaping over the rocks. Hear the bugles echoing and re-

THE SPEECH LABORATORY 31

echoing over field and waters, and gradually dying off behind the hills.

2. Notice the phrasing as it is marked in the poem; feel the beat of the measure as you say the poem for yourself.

    \\ is used to indicate a falling slide or inflection.

    / is used to indicate a rising slide or inflection.

    // is used to indicate a pause in the rhythm.

3. Do you know the meaning of the last stanza? Make a list of the words you do not know and find their meanings in the dictionary.

4. The whole class should read the poem in unison, then separate into groups, each group trying the three parts marked *First Voice, Second Voice,* and *Third Voice.* Go a step further and choose the very best speakers for the

different stanzas, the class taking the refrain as a kind of accompaniment. Be sure not to break the rhythm in the words "dying, dying, dying."

Caution. Avoid slovenly enunciation. Be careful of your mouth position for the vowels, of crisp articulation for consonants. Avoid loudness. Keep your voice soft and low, especially in the refrains.

5. Chapter Challenge

Show that you have mastered this chapter by filling in the blanks in the following statements:

1. A speech laboratory is a place that is devoted to ....

2. Conversations in the home and elsewhere should be marked by unfailing ...., clear and low ...., and correct ....

3. In introducing a younger person to an older person we should say ....

4. Men and boys usually .... when introduced. Women and girls ....

5. There are two types of telephone calls, ... calls and .... calls.

6. In answering the telephone we should give our .... or .... first.

7. .... discussions are those in which the class is not organized with elected officers.

8. The discussion leader should see that: (1) the discussion is ....; (2) the discussion keeps to ....; (3) he .... the points discussed.

9. The best way to keep to the topic in making a speech is to prepare ....

10. The four-leaf clover of good speech includes: (1) ...., (2) ...., (3) ...., (4) ....

11. Formal discussions are conducted by .... and the laws of .... are observed.

12. The .... of a club presides over all meetings and appoints all ....

13. The vice-president presides at the meetings in the absence of ....

14. The duties of the secretary are ....

15. The .... keeps the funds of the club and pays all bills.

16. A club member gains the floor by ....

17. To make a motion a member .... and says: ....

18. The records of the meetings of a club are called ....

19. .... is a revival of the old Greek manner of reading poetry.

20. .... wrote "The Princess."

CHAPTER TWO

Studying the
Paragraph

*A paragraph is a group of related sen-
tences developing one topic*

A paragraph, whether it is long or short, develops *one
main idea.* Every sentence in the paragraph must relate
to that one main idea or *topic.* Notice how the sentences
in the following paragraph develop the topic.

MODEL: GATEWAYS TO THE FUTURE

The future of the young people of today is studded with gateways to fame and service. Atomic energy stands restlessly waiting
to be directed into constructive peacetime channels. The infant
science of electronics solicits further exploration and development. The almost daily discovery of new drugs continues to make
the field of medicine a scene of exciting adventure. Stronger-than-
steel plastics invite investigation of their limitless possibilities.
Problems of world cooperation challenge solution from tomorrow's citizens. Looking through these doorways into the world
of the future, do you not see an important place for every boy
and girl of today?

1. The Parts of a Paragraph

A good paragraph can be divided into three parts: (1) a
beginning sentence, (2) middle sentences, and (3) an
ending sentence. The beginning sentence begins the paragraph, attracts attention, and gives a hint of what is to
follow. It may also express the central thought of the

paragraph. The middle sentences develop the thought introduced in the beginning sentence. The ending sentence gives the last detail, sums up the paragraph, or makes a personal comment.

MODEL: OUR LADY OF LITTLE ONES

Beginning sentence How happy the boys and girls of today should be to realize that the apparitions of our Lady which have attracted the greatest attention have been those in which she appeared to children!

Middle sentences Bernadette was still an immature girl when she beheld the Immaculate Virgin in the grotto at Massabielle. When France and the world needed the stern warnings of Our Lady of La Salette, it was to a youthful shepherdess and her companion that the message was given. In later years three young children of Portugal were the chosen ones to whom she revealed the power of the rosary in moving the heart of God. Because the world continues to need our Blessed Mother, perhaps she

Ending sentence will visit us again. Could she confide to you a secret or a mission?

The Beginning Sentence

To win a race you must get a fast start, and to write a good paragraph you must have a good beginning sentence. The beginning sentence must do what its name implies, *begin* the paragraph. It must be so interesting as to attract the attention of the reader immediately. Likewise, a good opening sentence must give a hint of what is to follow in the paragraph. Study the beginning sentence in the paragraph that follows.

MODEL: A NEW HORIZON

Beginning sentence   Have you ever seriously considered what will follow the doffing of your high-school mortarboard? Pupils who are planning careers for themselves should not overlook the tremendous possibilities in the field of radio. These opportunities are so broad in their scope as to attract students of various aptitudes. The class orator might be interested in becoming a successful announcer, or the prize-winning essayist may seek employment in writing scripts. For the mathematically inclined pupils there is always the technical side, while experience gained in school plays may make a future director of broadcasts. Investigate the realms of radio for an interesting, worth-while career.

A GOOD BEGINNING SENTENCE:
1. *Begins the paragraph*
2. *Attracts attention*
3. *Gives a hint of the content of the paragraph*
4. *Often arouses curiosity*

CLASS ASSIGNMENT

1. Examine the beginning sentence in the following paragraph and tell why it is a good opening sentence:

LIFE ON A STAIRCASE

The worst punishment of my life was administered by my grandmother, a lovable but strict guardian who believed in suiting the penalty to the crime. Because I had tracked up her shining front stairs with my muddy shoes in spite of numerous warnings, I received the unique sentence of spending the rest of the day on those same steps. With an armful of playthings I staggered to my place of exile and settled down for a long stay. A full hour had not passed before I grew tired of my toys. The kitten I had brought along deserted me shamefully, so I turned to my books. The light on the stairs was poor, however, and reading soon became more of a burden than a pleasure. Even the welcome diversion of a midday lunch was spoiled by Grandmother's unsmiling silence as she set it down. I shifted uneasily from one step to another and wisely resisted a strong impulse to slide down the slippery rail. At last, overcome by weariness and self-pity, I laid my head down and slept through the rest of those miserable hours. Was it really my worst punishment? Perhaps it was my best, for since that time I have never trailed through any house with mud on my shoes.

2. Test the following sentences by the standards of good beginning sentences. What thoughts do they suggest?

1. Teen-age students are mirrors of the latest fads.

2. On the football field a quick brain is worth more than powerful shoulders.

3. Collecting stamps is a fascinating way to study geography.

4. Learning to ride a bicycle is not so easy as it appears.

5. Girls are ornamental, not useful.

6. China, the land of the flowery kingdom, is beautiful and enchanting.

7. In our back yard we have a plot of ground which my mother proudly refers to as "Our Garden."

8. My twin sister Mary has many charming idiosyncrasies.

9. In many ways a small town is an attractive place in which to live.

10. There is a house which I pass on my way to school that is different from other houses.

3. Copy the following paragraphs in your notebook, supplying a good beginning sentence for each paragraph:

1. DANCING DILEMMA

.... Why had I never heeded those endless advertisements with their guarantees of ten, only ten, easy lessons? I seemed to have as many legs as an octopus; my number concepts about one, two, three failed me, and the music blared at me from every direction. Why I didn't trip Rose will be added to my long list of unsolved mysteries. Finally the torture was over, the orchestra stopped, and I found myself escorting my brave young sister to her place. Was she only being her usual good-natured self when she assured me that I had the makings of a real dancer?

2. FOOTBALL PREVIEW

.... Thousands of multicolored pennants gaily wave above the heads of the eager spectators. On either side of the huge gridiron are agile cheerleaders, whose lusty shouts reverberate through the stadium as they leap and toss, confident of victory. Down the white-chalked field majestically marches the high-stepping drum major, skillfully twirling his gleaming baton. He is followed by a spirited and colorfully attired school band. The polished instruments flash beneath a radiant sun. To me, this brief period of pregame activity tops even the most spectacular moments of the game.

3. QUEEN OF THE WORLD

.... Each picture shows Mary as queen of some foreign land where zealous priests and religious labor to bring souls to her Son. The silent sphinx surveys her from a background of pyramids and palms in her setting as "Patroness of Africa." "Our Lady of China" is a lovely Chinese maiden framed in the delicate cherry blossoms of the East. A Mexican panorama surrounds her as the "Virgin of Guadalupe." Enthroned among the frozen wastes of the North, "Our Lady of the Snows" receives graciously the homage of kneeling Eskimos. Mary seems most familiar as "Our Lady of the Near East," for in this picture she sits and spins at the door of her little Nazareth home. Gazing at these portraits of God's Mother, we realize that her maternal protection extends to all nations and that her widespread mantle covers the earth.

The Topic Sentence

A sentence which states the main idea or the theme of the paragraph is called the *topic sentence*. Frequently the beginning sentence does more than give a hint of the content of the paragraph; it expresses the central thought of the paragraph. Such a sentence is called the topic sentence. In the following paragraph the beginning sentence is the topic sentence.

Model: A Perilous Pursuit

Topic sentence   Down into the cool depths of tropical waters go dauntless men whose dangerous occupation is pearl diving. These indomitable explorers, in their subsurface search for pearls, are subjected to all forms of exposure. In the fathomless abyss of the ocean floor they encounter many horrible denizens of the deep. In addition to these living dangers, there is always the fear of rapidly changing ocean currents and beds of quicksand. Can we not see how clever must be the men who courageously face these perils of the sea? We should pay tribute to their spectacular deeds and recognize the risks they take to give the world new wealth.

Although the topic sentence is often the beginning sentence, it may be one of the middle sentences, or even the ending sentence.

Model: The First Christmas Renewed

Topic sentence   An air of quiet expectancy permeates our church on Christmas morning. As silent worshipers we realize that we can participate, through the Mass, in all the glory and joy of Christ's first coming. At the Gloria, that clear echo of the angels' song, we are transported to Judea's starlit hills. The Gospel then bids us follow wandering shepherds in their journey to a lowly cave. Hear the Sanctus bells! They remind us that we have reached the threshold of a divine abode and suggest a prayerful pause. The awesome words of the Consecration bring God to earth once more, and with the shepherds we lift adoring eyes to Mary's Son, elevated above the head of the priest. Consummate joy is ours when, at the

> Communion, we receive the Babe of Bethlehem into our hearts. What an exalted privilege it is thus to relive the first Christmas!

The first sentence, *An air of quiet expectancy permeates our church on Christmas morning,* gives a hint of the subject, but does not state the topic, *that through the Mass we can participate in all the glory and joy of Christ's first coming.* The second sentence, therefore, is the topic sentence. All the other sentences explain or tell more about the idea expressed in the topic sentence.

We must remember that the topic sentence tells both the subject (the general idea) and the particular aspect (the theme or main idea) of our paragraph. We may, for example, decide to write a paragraph about butterflies. How will this subject be limited? If we wish to write a paragraph about the activity of butterflies, the topic sentence might be: *The butterfly is a good example of perpetual motion.* Thus we not only mention the subject, *butterflies,* but we tell the reader that we intend to discuss the ceaseless activity of these insects. The topic or the particular aspect of the subject is indicated in the words *perpetual motion.*

In the following sentences the subject has been underlined once and the words that indicate the topic of the paragraph have been underlined twice:

Each autumn the trees surrounding our house present a veritable riot of color.

Nature can boast of no creature more industrious than the intrepid beaver.

There are few instruments whose mechanism is as intricate as that of an ordinary watch.

CLASS ASSIGNMENT

1. Point out the subject and the topic or particular aspect of the subject in each of the following topic sentences:

1. Mr. Harper, my father's employer, is a man of commanding appearance.

2. The cool and competent manner with which the surgeon entered the room and issued orders inspired the confidence of all his patients.

3. Amid all the luxury and splendor of the court the young prince sat silent and unimpressed.

4. My first diving lesson was interesting and exciting.

5. Even at that early hour the harbor was humming with activity.

6. The deserted mansion, with its banging shutters and broken windows, was shrouded in mystery.

7. Nothing but old-fashioned flowers are permitted to bloom in my grandmother's garden.

8. Surfboard riding is a dangerous but fascinating sport.

9. The newsroom of the city paper was by this time in complete disorder.

10. The person who perfectly fits the title "friend in need" is Lillian, our maid.

2. In each of the following paragraphs name the topic sentence and point out the subject and the topic:

1. A Soaring Servant

High above crowded cities and deserted towns giant silver planes whiz by with amazing frequency. Each huge transport is manned by a crew of expertly trained individuals, among whom is the flight stewardess. The importance of the work of an air hostess may be gauged by the numerous duties which she must perform. This young woman meets many different types of people and she must handle all with talent, tact, and courtesy. Her role calls for the possession of even more than a dual personality; she must be a combination of nurse, mother, waitress, companion, and good-will agent. Boredom never enters this winged servant's realm, for her responsibilities often multiply with each soaring hour. Rarely does she become confused, tired, or irritated. For an occupation that demands of a woman training, courage, and stamina, that of an air stewardess heads my list.

2. WOODLAND PRAYER

As I reached the high rocky shelf, I paused and turned for a better view of the beautiful valley through which I had come. Far below, a little creek pushed insistently past its banks. Wild ducks moved swiftly through the clear water, their blue-green plumage gleaming with an almost metallic brightness. Warm sunlight laid a hand in benediction upon the earth. Shining through the trees it cast lacy patterns of light and shadow on the ground. The trees themselves stood proud and tall, conscious of their riotous coloring, and paid to every passing breeze a gracious tribute of drifting leaves. God had surely blessed this lovely valley, and its beauty offered Him in return a mute prayer of thanksgiving and praise.

The Ending Sentence

Just as a good beginning sentence is a necessary part of a well-developed paragraph, so, too, is a good *ending* or *concluding sentence*. The ending sentence, as its name implies, must end the paragraph. It may be the last detail in the paragraph, a summing up of details, or a personal comment. It should be written in such a manner that it leaves the reader or the listener satisfied and lets him know that the paragraph is finished.

Does the concluding sentence of this paragraph have the qualities of a good ending sentence?

MODEL: THE OUTER SANCTUM

It seems to me that the mental agony accompanying a visit to the dentist does not begin when I am confronted with his terrifying equip-

ment, but in the waiting room. Fellow sufferers occupy the chairs, bearing their aches and pains in grim silence. Hanging triumphantly on the walls are numerous diplomas certifying the dentist's proficiency. The magazine pile, one potential oasis in this desert of anguish, is topped by a pamphlet setting forth the latest scientific methods of torment. From under the office door slip ominous sounds, and the attendant nurse flits back and forth casting sympathetic glances at **Ending sentence** the next victim. Nothing can possibly happen in that eerie, inner room to equal the excruciating pangs of "just waiting."

CLASS ASSIGNMENT

1. Examine the ending sentences in the following paragraphs and tell why they are good:

1. MASS COMES TO GRANDMOTHER

To thousands of people the telecast of the solemn high Mass from Holy Name Cathedral on New Year's Eve was just another program. To my invalid grandmother, resigned to the fact that never again would hers be the privilege of assisting at the Holy Sacrifice, it was an almost incredible miracle. Ten minutes before the beginning of the Mass this dear little lady was seated in her wheel chair, her gaze fastened intently upon the television screen.

Her entire countenance fairly glowed with quiet expectancy as she eagerly awaited the beginning of the sacred drama. Several times her vision blurred and from two soft brown eyes I saw tears of joy splash unashamedly upon the flushed cheeks. Though the slightly parted lips formed no words, they told me of my grandmother's sincere amazement that the honor of witnessing Calvary's renewal was hers once again. The usually firm chin quivered a bit, and snatches of a fervently whispered prayer of thanksgiving reached my ears. I needed no announcer to inform me when the priest made the initial sign of the cross. The news was revealed by the beautiful, almost unearthly radiance that flooded the wrinkled face. As I reverently drew nearer to the screen, I murmured my own gratitude for the Mass, for Grandmother, and for our new television set.

2. SLIPPER SHOW

Mary Jane, my three-year-old sister, always manages, without a word, to acquaint the family with the fact that she is wearing new shoes. Skipping blithely into the living room, she performs several nimble antics, all calculated to draw our attention to her shining footwear. This ruse failing, she seats herself in a prominent position and swings her feet rapidly, stopping now and then to gaze fixedly at her toe or to brush an imaginary speck from the glossy surface. If this trick brings no response, she goes to a far end of the room where there is no carpet. Back and forth she walks, her slippers tapping on the hardwood floor. At last someone relents and asks casually, "New shoes, Mary Jane?" She flashes us a grateful smile and sallies forth to exercise her wiles on the unsuspecting neighbors.

2. Examine the following ending sentences suggested by pupils. Discuss each sentence and tell whether it meets the standards of good ending sentences listed on page 47:

1. That day I learned that great men often have humble beginnings.

2. The poor old clock never knew the trouble he caused the morning he decided to take a rest.

3. No, our home life is never dull when the twins are awake.

4. What a charming little black-and-white thief he turned out to be!

5. Now I am thoroughly convinced that one never knows what may happen in a moment of excitement.

6. Because he is faithful, because he serves them well, the safety-patrol boy is a true friend to all boys and girls.

7. I realize now the truth of the statement, "Success grows out of struggles to overcome difficulties."

8. Never again will I dread soliciting advertisements for our school paper.

9. Good books may be lifeless objects to you, but to me they are intimate companions.

3. For each of the following paragraphs supply a good ending sentence:

1. SAFETY SENTINELS

Invaluable are the services rendered by the school Safety Squad. As prompt as the dismissal bell, a safety patrolman is at every classroom door, ready to conduct the lines to an orderly exit. Other members of the squad are stationed at strategic points in corridors and passageways, to assure safety on the stairs. Still others, regardless of the weather, stand faithfully at their posts on busy street corners in order to bar the reckless dash of thoughtless little children. The schoolyard, too, comes under the supervision of these guardians of safety, who care for minor injuries and enforce rules of fair play. Finally, we must not forget the boys of the Safety Squad in their roles of bus marshals, lunchroom inspectors, and ushers in any emergency. ....

....

2. THE PRETZEL'S PAST

Every American boy and girl has probably enjoyed eating the crisp, brown delight known as a "pretzel." It is doubtful, however, whether many of them know that they owe the origin of this delicious tidbit to the priests of southern Europe. When the small children who were being instructed by the monks had mastered their prayers, they were given a little reward in the form of a biscuit which was called a pretzel. The priests did not coin the word but simply took it from the Latin *pretiola,* meaning "little gift" or "reward." If the tiny ones adopted a particularly devout position in reciting their prayers, a twisted pretzel was given them. The twist was designed to represent the folded arms one should display when addressing God. ....
....

2. Characteristics of a Paragraph

Every paragraph has a beginning sentence, middle sentences, and an ending sentence. There is also a topic sentence, in which the main idea of the paragraph is stated. This may or may not be the first sentence in the paragraph. A good paragraph has two additional qualities: (1) it deals with one main idea or topic, and (2) it holds together because the sentences follow one another in logical order.

Unity in a Paragraph

Every paragraph must have *unity;* that is, it must keep to the topic or one main idea. All the middle sentences of a paragraph should help to develop the topic; they should give more information about the central idea. There must be no misfit sentence in a paragraph.

The following paragraph has unity. It develops one idea or one thing only—the power in the hands of a priest. All the sentences exhibit this quality of unity because they relate to the topic and contribute something important to the paragraph.

MODEL: POWER UNPARALLELED

What sublime power lies within the anointed hands of a priest! Time and again they pour the regenerating waters of baptism, and a soul springs to supernatural life. Raised in absolution over modern Magdalenes and prodigal sons, they snatch sinners from the very brink of hell. These hands, human yet charged with divinity, reach even into eternity and bring God Himself to earth again. Their potency is especially felt each morning when, Calvary renewed, a sinful world is spared. How often the exquisite joy of Holy Communion is ours because these consecrated hands may handle the sacramental body of Christ! When death stealthily closes in, they are again ready, at a moment's notice, to prepare us with the strengthening oils of extreme unction for the journey to eternity. Do we adequately esteem and sufficiently thank God for the priestly hands that minister to us?

CLASS ASSIGNMENT

1. Does this paragraph discuss one and only one topic? Does it have unity?

ROCKING-CHAIR SAGA

Household furnishings often occupy a prominent place in the memories of a child. Many of the recollections of my early years are built around a comfortable old rocker which stood in the corner of my mother's room. What opportunities it offered for juvenile amusement! Disguised by a blanket and turned on end, it became a smugglers' cave inhabited by buccaneers who were a constant menace to the pantry shelf. The covering removed, a patient steed groaned under the weight of three sturdy riders. If other pieces of furniture could be pressed into service, the rocker was transformed into a locomotive hauling a train of startling appearance. The rocker in its natural position, however, holds the dearest memories of all. Then it became a little house of comfort and love in which Mother soothed her tired children and rocked away the cares of a weary day. Pirates' cave to Mother's throne —could anything but a rocking chair have stood the strain?

2. Read carefully each of the following paragraphs, then answer the questions that are asked:

1. White Magic

In spite of keen competition from a variety of newly invented materials, cotton continues to hold its own as a most versatile product. Many who appreciate the usefulness of ordinary cotton cloth are unaware of a lengthy list of other uses ranging from explosives to mayonnaise. Yes, it is true; the oil from the cotton seed is employed in the making of salad dressing, and the cotton linters become the powerful guncotton so necessary in quarrying and in mining. The canvas from which sails and tents are made is woven from cotton. Books are bound with it. Cotton forms the basis for most of our waterproof fabrics. Treated with acids and other chemicals, the once useless short fibers of the plant become cellulose acetate, from which rayon is made. Glue, paint, and varnish also come from cotton, as well as a plastic material which is light and strong. In this country cotton has long been king of fibers and for the present it seems to be in no danger of losing its throne.

1. What is the main idea expressed in the topic sentence?
2. Do the middle sentences tell you anything about the topic of the paragraph? Do they add details?
3. Does the paragraph have unity? Why?
4. Can you improve the paragraph?

2. The Age of Innocence

Kathleen, appearing in the doorway, might have stepped out of a page of Grimm's *Fairy Tales*. At any moment I expected her to perch on a leaf or a flower and be fanned by butterflies' wings. Instead, she toddled toward me, carrying her thirty inches of babyhood unassisted. Dainty white socks and patent-leather slippers covered her pattering feet. Her chubby little hands toyed with the skirt of her sprigged dimity dress, as if seeking a complimentary appraisal. An elfin face, which boasted of eyes that matched the blue of the sky, peeped out from beneath a white poke bonnet. When she deigned to smile, two entrancing dimples appeared and then coyly withdrew. I gasped in delight at one of the most beautiful of God's creations, a baby girl.

1. What is the main idea stated in the topic sentence?
2. Do all the middle sentences relate to the main idea?
3. Does the ending sentence add another detail or does it express the writer's feeling about the baby?
4. Does the paragraph have unity?

Coherence

Another quality of a good paragraph is *coherence*. When one sentence leads to the next sentence in natural and logical order, so that the main idea of the paragraph is easy to follow, the paragraph has coherence. Coherence means "sticking together." The sentences of a coherent paragraph stick together because every sentence is in its proper place.

The paragraph that follows is unified and coherent. All the sentences relate to the main idea stated in the topic sentence. The expressions *once, this, after, next, finally,* join the sentences, so that one idea follows another in a definite order.

MODEL: SUGGESTIONS FOR SPEECH STRIDES

A lively interest in words will do wonders to enlarge your vocabulary. Once you have decided to acquire new words, you will be amazed to find the many ways in which this can be accomplished. Learning synonyms and antonyms of the words in your present stock will give you an excellent start. This will entail exploring the dictionary, that storehouse of information about words. After the initial spurt, try competing in word quizzes or vocabulary tournaments. Next, endeavor to gain a knowledge of the fine shades of meaning attached to each word. Finally, keep your ears wide open for choice phrases used by eminent speakers, famed radio commentators, priests, and teachers. The variety of words which you are able to master in a short time will surprise you. In addition, you will soon find that new words are like new acquaintances; the better you know them, the more friendly you will feel toward them.

Disorderly Paragraphs

Frequently the sentences of a paragraph refer to the topic, but they are so arranged that the relationship of one thought to the other is not clear. The sentences are jumbled together in such a way that they fail to develop the main idea in a satisfactory manner. Care must be taken to avoid *disorderly sentences* in paragraphs.

Read the two paragraphs that follow. The topic is the same in both paragraphs. In the paragraph on the left all the sentences relate to the topic, but they do not follow one another in proper order. Do you find it easier to understand the paragraph on the right? Do you like the sentences when they are arranged in logical order? Which paragraph is coherent?

MODEL: ETHER ENTHUSIASTS

The reception room of any local broadcasting company is an excellent setting for a study in diverse personalities. In another section of the room tense amateur actors stage a last-minute rehearsal as they prepare to go forth in the cause of drama. Of course there is a singer, a tall, lean-looking young man, from whose throaty depths snatches of sweet mellow tones glide forth. The very walls and furnishings must chuckle as they view the daily gathering of hopeful audition seekers. The nervous tapping of his foot belies his confident pose. Beside her sits a natty sports announcer, convinced of his ability to give the baseball results in a really unique way. Mrs. Gavin waits patiently, recipes in hand, prepared to tantalize the ether waves with new suggestions along culinary lines. Amused as we may be at these would-be artists, we must nevertheless salute them for the fire of ambition that burns within each waiting heart.

The reception room of any local broadcasting company is an excellent setting for a study in diverse personalities. The very walls and furnishings must chuckle as they view the daily gathering of hopeful audition seekers. Mrs. Gavin waits patiently, recipes in hand, prepared to tantalize the ether waves with new suggestions along culinary lines. Beside her sits a natty sports announcer, convinced of his ability to give the baseball results in a really unique way. The nervous tapping of his foot belies his confident pose. Of course there is a singer, a tall, lean-looking young man, from whose throaty depths snatches of sweet mellow tones glide forth. In another section of the room tense amateur actors stage a last-minute rehearsal as they prepare to go forth in the cause of drama. Amused as we may be at these would-be artists, we must nevertheless salute them for the fire of ambition that burns within each waiting heart.

CLASS ASSIGNMENT

Rearrange the middle sentences in each of the following disorderly paragraphs:

1. PROPELLING PERSONALITIES

Have you ever considered how many different ways there are of performing an ordinary action? One man gives an aggressive shove, carrying with him three or four beneficiaries who follow in his wake. If you wish to see a practical illustration, stand some day inside a large department store and observe the hordes of shoppers that pass through the revolving door. Occasionally a mercenary character, bent on conserving his fast-waning strength, places himself in the glass-bound opening and rides in on the wings of a generous assault from the rear. Another contents himself with a measured thrust, precisely calculated to bring him and no one else safely indoors. A whole army of varied personalities will pass before you in just a few minutes spent in watching this passing parade.

2. HOLIDAY HERALDS

The Christmas season is ushered into our city each year by a gigantic parade, a spectacle that delights the hearts of thousands of children. Last of all rides Santa in his roomy sleigh, drawn by eight splendid reindeer. These stout guardians march fearlessly, unaware that they are followed by fierce dragons that breathe out smoke and fire and move threateningly from side to side. A battalion of wooden soldiers leads the way. Next come the beloved storybook friends, prancing along the street and playing all the pranks so familiar to their faithful readers. His appearance brings a smile to every face and a sigh of regret, for with his arrival comes the end of this bit of Fairyland for another year.

GOOD MIDDLE SENTENCES:
  1. *Relate to the main idea (unity)*
  2. *Are arranged in proper order (coherence)*

3. Types of Paragraphs

The paragraphs that we read in books, newspapers, and letters are usually of three types. One paragraph may tell a story, another may describe something, and a third paragraph may explain something.

Narration

Paragraphs that tell a story are narrative paragraphs, and this kind of writing is known as *narration*. Narrative paragraphs tell about interesting events, perhaps in the life of some famous person or even in our own lives. They tell when, where, and how the incident occurred. The events in the story usually lead up to a climax, and the paragraph is then brought quickly to an end.

In the following paragraph an eighth-grade student tells of an embarrassing experience.

MODEL: AN UNWILLING HERO

On the evening of our school play I made my theatrical debut before a record-breaking crowd packed into the auditorium. Lacking the budding genius of my talented classmates, I had assumed the lowly role of stagehand. As the curtain fell at the end of the first act, a floodlight above the center of the stage slipped from

position and dangled precariously on a single wire. Seizing a ladder, I lumbered onto the stage, moored the offender, and informed the attendants in the wings that the play could go on. Hearing my shout, the boy in charge of the curtains gave the ropes a mighty jerk. The draperies swept apart, revealing to the expectant onlookers a grimy figure in overalls perched high in the air. Scrambling down, I bowed awkwardly, shouldered the ladder, and made a hasty exit while the hall rocked with laughter. I had left the stage never to return.

Does the writer tell you when this incident occurred and how it happened? What is the climax of the story? Do you know what the victim's reactions were?

CLASS ASSIGNMENT

1. Read this paragraph and answer the questions on page 57:

DAISIES BRING DISASTER

I am really very fond of my sister Jane, although recently I had reason to wish that she were suddenly transported to some uninhabited island. On the afternoon of the high-school dance I was drafted to act as manikin for her. Of course I offered what seemed to my masculine mind very logical arguments, but all too soon I found myself enveloped in yards of blue silk. For what seemed like hours I stood in various ridiculous positions while innumerable daisies were sewed on me or on the dress. At last a satisfied sigh on the part of my seamstress sister indicated that each dainty flower had assumed its rightful place. Before my services were dispensed with, however, one final turn was demanded of me. Adopting an anything-to-please attitude, I executed an exaggerated pirouette. Suddenly the sound of muffled laughter reached my ears. Whirling around, I beheld five of my classmates heartily enjoying the performance. I assure you that I immediately scrambled out of the dress. The damage was done, however, but not to the new gown. To this day I am forced to give unwilling response to the nickname "Daisy."

1. What kind of paragraph is this?
2. Does the beginning sentence arouse interest?
3. Which is the topic sentence?
4. Is the ending sentence satisfactory?
5. Does the paragraph have unity? Coherence?

2. Supply a good beginning sentence for the following narrative paragraph. Be sure that it fulfills the requirements mentioned on page 37:

A MUSICAL ENTRANCE

.... My friend and I mounted the steps proudly, enjoying the envious glances of a few stragglers. With heads held high we proceeded up the middle aisle to our places. The solemn stillness that pervaded the vast auditorium was broken by a shrill squeak, then another and still another, each one louder than the first. Every step became an agony, for whether I walked on my toes or my heels the dreadful sounds continued, and the audience seemed to hold its breath so that everyone might hear. With a gasp of relief I reached my seat and hid my crimson face. No one, I was determined, was going to move me from that spot until the auditorium was empty and my shoes and I could depart unobserved.

3. Review the qualities of a good ending sentence, page 47, then write one for this narrative paragraph:

AN ADDED EXPENSE

We no longer question our frisky puppy's ability as a watchdog, for he proved it yesterday. Mother had secured a workman to repair the damaged parts of our fireplace. After Trixie had performed the usual sniffing act by which he is accustomed to catalogue a person as friend or enemy, he retired to his favorite corner. Sleep was out of the question, however, for here was an intruder recklessly banging and hammering within view of Grandfather Dillon's picture on the mantel. While the dog carefully feigned sleep he kept a vigilant eye on the suspected individual. All went well until the workman removed the photograph so that it would not be broken. With one wild leap Trixie bounded from his corner and in a second had a sizable portion of the man's sleeve in his teeth. ....

Description

In our everyday conversations we tell others what we have seen, what we have heard, how we feel, or how certain things taste or smell. We are artists who are continually painting pictures, but we are painting with words instead of with brush and paints. We call this type of writing *description*.

Descriptive paragraphs must have unity and coherence, just as other paragraphs do. All the sentences must refer to the particular person or scene that is being described in the paragraph, and they must help to describe the subject. In addition, the details are arranged in some order, very likely in the order in which they are naturally observed. The most striking detail is probably mentioned first. A word picture of a person very often starts with the face and moves downward. The description of a landscape or outdoor scene may start with the ground and move gradually upward, or it may start with the sky and

move down. Did the writer of the following paragraph obtain coherence by following a definite plan?

MODEL: MY CHESTNUT CHUM

Prince we've named him, and no horse was ever more worthy of such a title. He stands fifteen hands high and bears himself like a champion. Delicately pointed ears crown a well-shaped head, while the intelligent look in his spirited eyes is matched by the regal arch of his neck. Every inch of his reddish-brown satin coat gleams with careful attention. His color is uniform except for tiny patches of white on one of his hind feet. Do you wonder why Prince is my pride and joy?

CLASS ASSIGNMENT

1. Read the following descriptive paragraph and then answer the questions that follow:

MORNING VISITOR

Early every morning the doorway of our kitchen frames a unique picture, the strong and sturdy figure of the paper boy. His hair is a peculiar red, and when not discouraged by a disreputable cap of undetermined color, it stands high on his head like the flame of a candle. The eyes beneath are blue, an honest friendly blue. A little flock of freckles stand like a group of impudent children at the bridge of his nose, waiting to slide down merrily to its upturned tip. Several battle scars in the shape of missing teeth are revealed by his wide grin, but the determined chin below testifies to the fact that they were not lost without a struggle. His hands, though thin, are strong and brown. The dark green sweater he usually wears is patched at the elbows, and baggy corduroy trousers miss his scuffed shoes by several inches. All in all, he looks just what he is, an "all-American newsboy."

1. Which is the topic sentence? What is the general idea expressed in this sentence?

2. What details are mentioned in the middle sentences? Are these details arranged in a logical order?

3. Does the ending sentence add another detail to the picture? Does it express the writer's thought or feeling? Does it end the paragraph in a satisfactory manner?

2. In the column on the right are details that might be mentioned in describing the topics listed in the column on the left. Arrange these details in the order in which they should be described if the paragraph is to have coherence:

TOPIC	DETAILS
1. Beauty of a country estate	drive, house, gateway, surroundings
2. Fury of a snowstorm	end, break, gradual cessation, warnings, approach
3. The majestic outline of a tree	limbs, leaves, boughs, trunk
4. A novel birthday party	varied decorations, new games played, attractive invitations, unusual refreshments
5. An attractive face	eyes, hair, cheeks, mouth, teeth
6. Courage of an aviator	descent, gains in altitude, take-off, landing, progression
7. Colors of spring	ground, sky, flowers, trees
8. A friendly squirrel	size, tail, teeth, head, color

3. Enumerate details which may be used to develop each of these topic sentences:

1. The main altar in our church always impresses me.

2. As I gingerly took my place in the dentist's office, everything I saw tended to increase my nervousness.

3. Rare and beautiful flowers grew in the remote garden.

4. How handsome Richard looks in his new uniform!

5. Candles twinkling in the semidarkness cast a soft, amber light upon the loveliest shrine of our Lady I had ever seen.

6. Between the velvet-curtained windows at the upper end of the room stood a gigantic Christmas tree.

7. On a summer day Crystal Lake presents many interesting sights.

Exposition

When we give explanations or directions we use a form of composition known as *exposition*. Explanations and directions must be clear, accurate, and complete. In this type of writing, as well as in narration and description, it is essential that all the sentences of the paragraph pertain to the topic. The necessary and important details must be included, and these details or instructions must be given in the proper order so that the paragraph will have both unity and coherence.

MODEL: HOW TO FIND THE MASS OF THE DAY

If we wish to hear holy Mass by following the exact words of the priest, we must learn how to find in our missal the Mass of the day. How do we know what Mass the priest will say? If the day is Sunday, he says the Mass of the Sunday. We find what Sunday it is in the Catholic calendar. If a saint's feast day falls on Sunday, we say in addition the prayer of the saint. In the case of a very solemn feast, a double of the first or second class, the Mass of the feast is said. The second prayer is that of the Sunday, but the Gospel of the Sunday is no longer read at the end in place of the usual Last Gospel. On weekdays we read the Mass of the saint or the feast. When no feast is given, we use the Mass of the preceding Sunday or, if the priest wears black vestments, the requiem Mass. By using the missal at Mass we become familiar with the official prayers of the Church and participate in the offering of the Holy Sacrifice.

CLASS ASSIGNMENT

1. Read the following paragraph and then answer the questions that follow:

AN UNWILLING PUPIL

When a kitten reaches the age of four weeks, the time is ripe to teach it the art of drinking milk. Little effort will be needed

to lure your pussy to the saucer, but forcing her to partake of the white substance is a real problem. Gently press her mouth into the liquid. She will probably resent this mistreatment and swiftly turn around, ready to dart in any direction. Firmly grasp the retreating form and immerse her lips once more into the milk. If her mouth is tightly closed, force it open and permit a few drops of the liquid to fall from your fingers into her mouth. The sensation will be pleasing and before long she will be feverishly consuming the contents of the saucer. This procedure won't have to be repeated, for you will always be a welcome person in her domain when you are carrying the familiar dish.

1. What is the topic of this paragraph?
2. Does the beginning sentence introduce the topic?
3. Are all important details included?
4. Are they mentioned in logical order?
5. Is the ending sentence satisfying?

2. Write beginning sentences for paragraphs on these topics:

1. How to assemble a model airplane
2. How to salute the flag
3. Why I like collecting stamps
4. How to give artificial respiration
5. How to protect the passer in a football game

3. Examine the following topics. Decide whether a paragraph on each topic would be narration, description, or exposition:

1. How to baptize a baby
2. A canoe ride on Pine Lake
3. The steel mills of Pittsburgh
4. A decision that required courage
5. Why I think the Chinese Exclusion Act was unfair
6. The sanctuary in our church
7. The transportation posters in our classroom
8. John Swoboda becomes an American
9. How to take care of our eyes
10. In the early days of our parish
11. How salmon are caught in the Columbia River
12. A glimpse at a Brazilian coffee plantation
13. How to make a free throw
14. The cheering section at a football game
15. What a forest ranger does when he discovers a fire
16. My favorite wild flower

4. Choral Speaking

The poems that we read for choral speaking are paragraphs in verse. Some tell stories, others paint pictures in words. The nonsense jingles merely amuse us. Reading poetry in unison helps to bring out more clearly the meaning of the verses.

TUNING-UP EXERCISES

Breathing:

Inhale, hold breath for ten counts, then exhale, at first slowly, then all at once explosively.

Exercises for clean t:

Tip of the tongue   tip of the tongue   tip of the tongue

> Zinty Tinty, Two penny Bun!
> The cock went out to have some fun,
> He had some fun, he beat the drum—
> Zinty Tinty, Two penny Bun!

GROUP WORK: "THE NAME OF OLD GLORY"

By James Whitcomb Riley

First
Group,
Light
Voices

Old Glory! \ say, // who, //
　　By the ships \ and the crew, //
And the long, blended ranks of the gray \ and the
　　blue,— //
Who gave \ you, Old Glory, // the name // that you
　　bear
With such pride \ everywhere //
As you cast yourself free to the rapturous air //
And leap out full-length, // as we're wanting you
　　to?— //
Who gave \ you that name, with the ring \ of the
　　same, //
And the honor \ and fame / so becoming to
　　you? //
Your stripes \ stroked in ripples of white \ and of
　　red, //
With your stars \ at their glittering best / over-
　　head— //
By day \ or by night //
Their delightfulest light
Laughing down // from their little square heaven of
　　blue!— //
Who gave you / the name of Old Glory?— / say,
　　who— //
　　Who gave you the name of Old Glory? //

Refrain
(Unison)

The old banner lifted, \ and faltering then //
In vague lisps \ and whispers / fell silent again. //

Second
Group,
Heavy
Voices

Old Glory: // the story \ we're wanting to hear //
Is what the plain facts of your christening \ were,— //
For your name— \ just to hear it, \
Repeat it, \ and cheer it, / it's a tang to the spirit //
As salt \ as a tear ;— //

And seeing you fly, // and the boys \ marching by, //
There's a shout / in the throat \ and a blur / in
    the eye //
And an aching to live \ for you always— // or die, //
If, \ dying, / we still keep you \ waving on high. //
And so, // by our love \
For you, // floating above, //
And the scars \ of all wars // and the sorrows \
    thereof, //
Who gave you \ the name of Old Glory, // and why
  Are we \ thrilled // at the name of Old Glory? //

Refrain   *Then the old banner leaped, like a sail in the blast, /*
(Unison) *And fluttered an audible answer at last.*

Unison   And it spake, with a shake of the voice, and it
       said:— /

Solo   "By the driven snow-white / and the living blood-red
Of my bars, // and their heaven of stars overhead— //
By the symbol // conjoined of them all, // skyward \
     cast, //
As I float from the steeple, / or flap at the mast, //
Or droop o'er the sod \ where the long grasses nod,— //
My \ name is as old as the glory of God. //
. . . So // I came by the name of Old Glory." //

Unison   [Repeat last line very softly like a signature.]

STUDY OF "THE NAME OF OLD GLORY"

1. Read the poem over carefully three times, so that you may thoroughly understand its meaning.

2. Picture the Stars and Stripes flying in the breeze. Recall how the national anthem was written.

3. Think of what the colors and the stars stand for: blue for loyalty and faith; white for purity; red for love and sacrifice; the stars for hope.

4. Are there any lines which puzzle you? Find out their meaning before you try to read the poem aloud.

5. Read the poem in unison now, first deciding on the time and the pauses. Observe the pauses marked in the poem as here printed.

6. Divide the class into two groups, one of light voices and the other of dark voices. Let each group read the poem as marked. Both groups read the lines marked *Unison*. Strive for a clear interpretation of the lines, appreciation of the beauty and thought of the poem, and crisp enunciation and articulation.

7. After you have learned the poem, it may be put on reserve for such occasions as Armistice Day, a patriotic holiday in February, or other suitable occasions.

5. Chapter Challenge

1. A paragraph is a group of .... developing one ....

2. A sentence that states the main idea or theme of the paragraph is called the .... sentence.

3. The parts of a paragraph are: (1) ...., (2) ...., and (3) ....

4. An ending sentence sometimes tells what the author .... or ....

5. A paragraph has unity when ....

6. A sentence that has nothing to do with the topic of the paragraph is known as a .... sentence.

7. When the sentences of a paragraph do not follow one another in a reasonable way the paragraph is said to lack ....

8. Three types of paragraphs are ...., ..., and ....

9. Paragraphs that tell a story are .... paragraphs.

10. .... paragraphs paint a picture of a person, a place, or a thing.

11. When we give explanations or directions we use a form of composition known as ....

12. "The Name of Old Glory" is a poem about ....

CHAPTER THREE

Writing Paragraphs

In which we follow definite steps in writing paragraphs

In Chapter Two we studied many model paragraphs and found that every paragraph has a beginning sentence, middle sentences, and an ending sentence. The main idea or topic of a paragraph is stated in a topic sentence, which may or may not be the first sentence of the paragraph. We learned, too, that every paragraph must have unity and coherence. By unity we mean that all the sentences in the paragraph relate to the main topic. By coherence we mean that the sentences must be arranged in logical order.

Paragraphs that tell stories are known as narrative paragraphs; those that paint pictures or describe things are called descriptive paragraphs; paragraphs that explain or give directions are expository paragraphs.

1. Writing a Class Paragraph

In this chapter we shall apply the knowledge gained through the study of paragraphs to the writing of our own paragraphs. Let us begin by working together to write a group paragraph. Our experience in conversations and group discussions has shown us how much information and help can be gained from sharing our ideas with our classmates. We shall obtain a better knowledge of the skills to be mastered in paragraph writing if we work together and all follow the same plan.

We can write the best paragraph about a subject which interests us. Everyone seems to enjoy telling about the incidents or experiences in his life that stand out because of the joy or pleasure that they have brought. Let us write a group paragraph, one to which all the pupils in the class will contribute, about some pleasant incident in our life. This will be a narrative paragraph.

The first step in writing a paragraph is to select a subject. Who of us has not enjoyed a day at an amusement park? Shall we use this as the subject of our class paragraph? Of course it would be impossible to tell in one paragraph everything that happened on this eventful day. We must limit the subject to a single incident, to *one topic*. If a day at an amusement park is the subject of the paragraph, the topic may be a ride on the roller coaster. Can you think of other ways in which the subject could have been limited?

We have found out in preceding years that our paragraphs are much easier to write and that they are more interesting to the reader if we have a good command of words. Before we commence to write, then, we shall build a vocabulary of words and phrases that will help us in relating our experiences on the roller coaster.

APPEARANCE OF ROLLER COASTER	SYNONYMS FOR ROLLER COASTER
gaudily painted	chariot
gleaming brightly	coach
gaily daubed	Thunderbolt
riotously colored	rocket car
silver-toned	express train

Actions of Roller Coaster		My Actions	
swoop	glide	gasp	tremble
soar	crawl	stiffen	cling
careen	zip	huddle	slide
swerve	plunge	cringe	jerk
chug	whiz	slouch	squirm
lurch	rocket	grasp	shudder

The Ride Itself	My Sensations and Reactions	
downward plunge	soaring spirits	excitement
breath-taking descent	palpitating heart	fear
mad rush through time	mounting terror	trepidation
and space	wildly pounding heart	relief
crawling ascent	breathless joy	gratitude
perilous curves	reeling head	regret

We are now ready to put in order the various ideas that have occurred to us as we gathered words and phrases for our vocabulary. We all know the value of an outline in writing a paragraph. It is the framework upon which the paragraph is built. An outline is to an author what a blueprint is to a builder. In the outline we arrange the thoughts we had about our ride on the roller coaster in a clear and logical manner.

TOPIC: A RIDE ON THE ROLLER COASTER

Beginning sentence A. How we felt as we stepped into the car
Middle sentences B. Impressions during the ride
        1. The ascent
        2. At the summit
        3. The first descent
        4. The repeated ups and downs
Ending sentence C. Final reaction to the ride

The purpose of the beginning sentence is to attract attention and arouse interest in what is to follow. In this sentence we begin the narrative and take the reader into the story. The beginning sentence may or may not be the topic sentence of the paragraph.

The outline tells us that in the beginning sentence of our class paragraph we are to tell how we felt as we stepped into the roller coaster. Of course this will not be the same for every person. Several members of the class will undoubtedly suggest beginning sentences, such as:

I felt ready for anything that could possibly happen as I courageously stepped into the chariot that gleamed like silver in the morning sun.

Mingled emotions of fear and regret clashed within me as I settled myself in the Thunderbolt that July afternoon.

Dauntlessly and with soaring spirits I stepped into the riotously colored roller coaster.

Sporting an air of bravado that was ninety-nine per cent feigned, I took my place among the fun seekers in the gaily painted roller coaster.

A satisfying ending sentence is essential to a good paragraph. It lets the reader know that we have completed our story of the incident. Very often it expresses the writer's feelings or reactions. Any one of the following sentences suggested by eighth-grade pupils could be used as an ending sentence in the paragraph on the roller coaster:

I am sure that even a trip around the world would not be so thrilling as that five-minute ride on the roller coaster.

The sight of the exit sign was most welcome, and I firmly resolved to keep my feet on the ground in the future.

All kinds of rides fascinate me, but for breathless excitement the Thunderbolt is king of them all.

Smiling bravely for the benefit of my friends, I assured them that this mad rush through time and space was truly "the greatest ride on earth."

Every pupil in the class now has the pleasant task of writing a paragraph telling of his experience on the roller coaster. He may select the beginning sentence he likes best. In the middle sentences he will present details of the ride, one after the other in logical order until he reaches the climax of his story, the most exciting part of the ride. In writing these sentences he has a large choice of words which his classmates have suggested. From this vocabulary he selects those words and phrases that are suitable for his story. The climax is the highest point of interest in a story. Once the climax has been reached, he quickly ends the paragraph.

Naming a paragraph is very important, for many people are attracted by a clever title. The topic of the paragraph, a ride on the roller coaster, is not a good title. It fails to attract attention and is too general. We want a title that arouses interest and one that particularly suits the paragraph we have written. Let the class suggest good titles. Each pupil will select one that fits his paragraph. Are the titles listed on page 74 good titles?

A Thrill a Moment	The Ride of a Lifetime
Invading the Clouds	The Sky's the Limit
A Maze of Hills	Hurtling through Space
Solar Expedition	Eventful Journey

The advantages to be gained when a class works together on a group paragraph are well illustrated in the following model paragraph:

MODEL: EVENTFUL JOURNEY

Mingled emotions of fear and regret clashed within me as I settled myself in the Thunderbolt that July afternoon. The strident shouts of the gruff operator cut across the air as the screeching of released brakes noisily announced the initial ascent. With palpitating heart I stiffened myself against the back of the brightly gleaming car. For one thrill-packed second I was conscious of being unwillingly poised on a gigantic hill, then down, down I plunged at breath-taking speed. Before I had even a grim chance of retrieving my composure this mad rush was repeated with terrifying rapidity. Desperately I clung to the steel bar of the chariot as it careened and whizzed around each perilous curve. Suddenly, as I shuddered and cringed in my place, the rocket car gave a wild, uncontrolled lurch, then with an asthmatic cough wheezed to a full stop. Head reeling, I staggered out of the coach, relieved and grateful for the feeling of solid ground. I am sure that even a trip around the world would not be so thrilling as that five-minute ride on the roller coaster.

CLASS ASSIGNMENT

1. Read the following paragraph and then answer the questions that follow:

WHIZZING THROUGH SPACE

Dauntlessly and with soaring spirits I stepped into the riotously colored roller coaster. Before me stretched two shining parallel rails along which the Thunderbolt, on a seemingly peaceful ride, glided. The bravery of the previous minutes fled as we approached the summit of the first incline. When the chariot swooped head-long into an abyss my courage also took a downward plunge. While I was trying to control the fear that was encompassing me, the miniature train whizzed smoothly along. Close, oh too close, however, were two more gigantic crests. Frantically I grasped the handle bar, wishing that someone had devised a tunnel in this series of ups and downs. My heart pounded wildly, the very air choked me, when with a zip and a jerk we went low, then high into the air. This time my spirits refused to rise again. The sight of the exit sign was most welcome, and I firmly resolved to keep my feet on the ground in the future.

1. Does the beginning sentence arouse interest and give a hint of the content of the paragraph?

2. Do the middle sentences present the details of the ride in logical order?

3. Does the ending sentence satisfy the reader?

4. Does the paragraph have unity? Why?

2. Using the outline and the vocabulary given in the preceding pages, write an original paragraph relating your experience on a roller coaster.

2. Steps in Building a Paragraph

We found that the writing of a class paragraph was very easy if we had a plan and followed a definite procedure. In addition, the paragraph was very interesting and gave evidence of all the qualities of a good paragraph. Let us now examine in greater detail the steps to be taken in writing a paragraph in order that we may apply all these principles to our own writing.

Selecting and Limiting the Subject

After we have decided that a certain subject interests us and that we would like to write a paragraph about it, we must first limit that subject to a topic that can be treated in a single paragraph. Thus we found it impossible to write a paragraph about a day at the amusement park, and for this reason we limited the subject to one topic, a ride on the roller coaster. We could have chosen other topics, such as the appearance of the park as we entered the gate, a journey through the fun house, or how to be a great weight lifter.

Study the following list of subjects and topics. Suggest other topics for some of the subjects. Would a pupil find it easier to write a paragraph based on a subject or one based on a topic?

SUBJECT	TOPIC
Our library	The children's corner in the library
The Panama Canal	How the Panama Canal has increased our trade
A trailer trip	My first night in a trailer
The ocean	Sunset on the ocean
Nurses	The duties of a nurse
Animals	Learning to ride a horse
Policemen	The traffic officer at our school
Fire engines	The race to a fire
Basketball	A shot that won the game for our team

CLASS ASSIGNMENT

1. In the following list of subjects and topics one or the other is missing. Supply a subject or a topic in the blank space:

SUBJECT	TOPIC
....	How to make a telephone call
National figures	....
....	A busy pier
A clown	....
Autumn	....
....	A picturesque road
....	Why I like baseball
Grandmother's house	....
....	The advantages of the airplane
....	The willow tree in our yard

2. Limit each of the following subjects to a topic that you could discuss in a paragraph:

Trains	Modern inventions	Christmas
The flower show	Birds	Pets
Flags	Statues	Nurses
A concert	The art exhibit	Vehicles

3. Study the topics chosen for each of the subjects in the preceding assignment and tell whether the paragraph based on that topic would be classified as narration, description, or exposition.

Building a Vocabulary

After the topic of our paragraph has been decided upon, we will want to make a list of words and phrases that may be used in the paragraph. Words are the tools that we use to express our thoughts. In building a vocabulary we must first think about the ideas that we wish to include in our paragraph.

A student who decided to write a paragraph describing a campfire built the vocabulary on page 78. Do you think

that these vivid and action-flashing words would help you
to write such a paragraph?

FLAMES	LOGS	SPARKS
blazing	sputtering	like fireflies
leaping	popping	little twinkling stars
roaring	hissing	glittering diamonds
dancing	snapping	flickering lights
dazzling	crackling	dancing moonbeams
darting	spitting	shimmering specks
shooting	glowing	dots of gold

WOOD	ACTIONS OF SPECTATORS	SHADOWS	
fragrant	singing	creeping	ghostly
spicy	telling stories	hovering	fading
balmy	dancing	darting	shifting
sweet-smelling	playing games	flitting	gloomy

CLASS ASSIGNMENT

1. Read this paragraph carefully and then answer the questions
that follow:

THE SPELL OF THE CAMPFIRE

Deep in the gloom of the forest the gypsies gather around the
blazing fire, presenting a scene of haunting beauty. Sweet-smell-
ing pine twigs, snapping like giant firecrackers, perfume the air
with a spicy fragrance. Dancing flames dart high into space,
hover overhead, and fade quickly into the gloomy blackness.
Showers of sparks leap skyward like fireflies, leaving behind the
sputter of crackling logs. Under the spell of the flickering lights
the gypsies sway rhythmically and chant the ancient songs of
their race. A fiddler steps into the glowing circle. Flitting shadows
play upon his face as the sobbing melodies of his violin pierce the
silence of the night. Forgotten are the cares of a busy day as one
and all succumb to the deep enchantment, the magic mystery of
a gypsy campfire.

1. What is the subject of this paragraph? The topic?

2. Did this writer use any of the words from the suggested vocabulary? Name them.

3. Is the beginning sentence the topic sentence?

2. Build a vocabulary that will help you to write a paragraph describing any of the following:

An unusual person	A new automobile
A priest	An artist
A book character	A modern steamship
An animal at the zoo	Our living room

Making an Outline

As we limited the subject to the topic that we wished to discuss in our own particular paragraph and as we gathered words and phrases for our vocabulary, we were forced to give considerable attention to the ideas that we intended to express. Now we are ready to put these ideas into order; to make a plan for the paragraph. We call this plan an outline.

In the outline we include the topic, the beginning sentence, the middle sentences, and the ending sentence. It is not necessary that we repeat beginning, middle, and ending sentences as we grow older. These parts of a paragraph are so firmly fixed in our minds that we can substitute the letters A, B, C, or numbers, for these parts.

TOPIC: THE SQUIRREL NICKY

A. Introducing our summer boarder
B. His characteristics
    1. Cocky
    2. Greedy
    3. Proud
    4. Scrappy
C. Our feeling about him

CLASS ASSIGNMENT

1. Read the following paragraph and decide whether the writer followed the outline which has been suggested:

OUR SUMMER BOARDER

"Here, Nicky," we call each morning to the squirrel who has rented our maple tree for the summer, and down the rough trunk of his leafy home he comes. He is not the bashful squirrel of the picture books, peeping shyly from behind a tree in some woodland glen, but a cocky fellow who calls for his daily rations with an air of bold assurance. Nicky does not scamper; he swaggers. He does not take the nut we hand him and dart away timidly to consume it in seclusion. No, he gobbles it complacently on the doorstep with a wary eye on us lest we go away before he is ready for a second helping. There is the distinct look of a victor enjoying the spoils of a hard-fought campaign as he accepts our offering. His very name and appearance testify to his warlike character, for he has lost a generous portion of his left ear in defending his exclusive right to our bounty against another squirrel who dared to challenge his supremacy. His impudent ways have captivated us completely, and our garden will never be quite the same without this summer boarder.

2. Prepare an outline for a paragraph on each of these topics:

The approach of a storm	An old-fashioned clock
Our May procession	A scene from a hilltop
My first corsage	A movie I enjoyed
Fun at camp	The ideal nurse

Writing the Paragraph

After we have made the outline we know what thoughts are to be presented in the beginning or topic sentence, how the story will follow in the middle sentences, and what we have decided to express in the ending sentence. We remember that a beginning sentence must attract the reader's attention and must give at least a hint of the topic of the paragraph. The details presented in the middle sentences enlarge upon the topic sentence. We must take care that all the sentences pertain to the topic and that they are presented in a natural order, an order that the reader can follow easily. The ending sentence may present the last detail or it may tell the reader what we think or feel.

Christening the Paragraph

After we have written the paragraph we must select a good title. In this title we wish to attract the reader's attention, arouse his curiosity, and perhaps give a hint of the contents of the paragraph. Study the following topics and titles. Are the titles appealing?

TOPIC	TITLE
The flower show	Blossoms on Parade
A snow scene	Winter Wonderland
An airplane in flight	Silver Swallow
My first day at school	Adventure Story
Burning autumn leaves	Pungent Pastime
A spring storm	April's Tears

CLASS ASSIGNMENT

1. Using the suggested topic and ending sentences, complete the following paragraphs by filling in the details mentioned:

1. Topic sentence: With hearts filled with sadness we gazed upon the once beautiful forest land which the finger of fire had transformed into a scene of horror and destruction.

Details: Trees blackened and burned; ground scorched; streams dried up; no signs of animal life

Ending sentence: How many years of nature's patient healing will be necessary to erase the scars of human carelessness?

2. Topic sentence: The city square near our home is always a scene of activity.

Details: Romping children; spraying fountain; agile squirrels; singing birds

Ending sentence: From morning until night this little spot presents a panorama of unsuspecting actors.

2. Write an attractive title for each of the paragraphs in the first part of the assignment.

3. Write an interesting title for a paragraph based on each of the following topics:

The guest room	Helping the missions
An enjoyable party	My most embarrassing moment
The meaning of the	How to prepare for an examination
paschal candle	Learning to skate

4. Build a paragraph in your classroom. Be sure that the following steps are taken: (1) Select a subject; (2) limit the subject to a particular topic; (3) build a vocabulary; (4) make an outline; (5) suggest beginning and ending sentences; (6) write the paragraph; (7) select a title. Any of the following subjects may be used for your class paragraph:

A day at the seashore	The church carnival
A birthday gift	A visit to a dairy
Earning money	A boat ride on Lake Michigan
A sunrise	A basketball game
Swimming	Atomic power

Writing Conversations

In some of the compositions that we write we may wish to report the exact words of the speaker. We know that for this purpose we use quotation marks. It is also customary to begin a new paragraph each time the speaker changes. Study the following composition, which contains direct quotations. It is concerned with one topic, *the different methods of saying "No."* To show that different persons are speaking, the writer begins each person's words on a separate line and indents the first word.

MODEL: FAMILY REFUSALS

Each member of our household has a different method of saying "No" to me.

"Positively no!" growls my father in a fiercely determined voice. In other words this means, "I'll think it over."

"No, dear," says Mother quietly, and she means it.

"Not now," decides Grandmother after serious consideration. This is ambiguous, signifying either "Later" or "Never."

"Oh, no," protests my sister weakly, but she is really saying, "You'll have your own way anyhow."

"No!" explodes the junior member of our household. His eyes add, "And don't try to coax me either."

To be denied a request is often discouraging, but my disappointment is usually lightened by the novelty of being refused in so many different ways.

CLASS ASSIGNMENT

1. The following conversation is punctuated correctly, but it is written as one paragraph. Rewrite it in correct form:

A SUDDEN RELIEF

As Jane prepared to pack her suitcase for a long-awaited vacation trip, she discovered that her key was not in its usual place. "I've looked everywhere and cannot find the key to my suitcase," she said to her mother. "Have you seen it, Mother?" "No, dear, I haven't," answered Mother. "I remember that Edward used your bag not long ago. Have you asked him?" "Oh, thank you, Mother," said Jane. "I recall now that Edward did say that he would leave the key in my desk drawer. Now I will not hesitate to use my suitcase." Thus relieved, Jane rushed to her room to begin packing for the journey.

2. Write an original short conversation, being careful to paragraph it and punctuate it correctly.

3. Writing Longer Compositions

Once we have mastered the art of writing paragraphs, it is a simple matter to write longer compositions containing several paragraphs. We remember that a paragraph is a group of sentences developing one topic, and that we develop the topic by giving details concerning it. Sometimes we have so much to say about these details that we need a separate paragraph for each detail. The relationship between the paragraphs, however, must be made clear, so that the reader can easily follow the writer's thoughts from the beginning of the composition to the end. The composition as a whole must have both unity and coherence.

In the following composition the subject is the virtue of humility. The topic is the nature of humility. Observe how the writer develops this topic by means of three details: what humility is, how our Lady possessed perfect humility, and how we can strive for this virtue in our own lives.

MODEL: A NOBLE PATH

What is humility? Perhaps you have at some time had a picture taken that was an exceptionally good likeness. The photograph may not have pleased you entirely, but because it did not exaggerate either your good points or your bad points it was unmistakably you. To have in the mind's eye such a picture of yourself, with all your faults and virtues, is to be humble, for it has been accurately stated that humility is truth.

No creature ever traced a clearer mental portrait of herself than did our Lady. "Behold the handmaid of the Lord," she said as she trembled in an angel's presence. Conscious of her great dignity, however, the same maiden could say with calm certainty, "All generations shall call me blessed." Here was her true image, distorted neither by pride nor by insincerity. Her acceptance of herself as she was and as God wanted her to be made humility one of the brightest gems in Mary's crown of virtues.

In giving us His Mother as a model God placed humility within our reach. To grasp it and make it our own we must stand in the strong spotlight of truth. There we shall see ourselves as we are and as God sees us. This candid view must lead each of us to attribute the good that we find in ourselves to God's grace and the evil that we discover to ourselves. Doing this, we shall begin to walk the way which has led so many saints to a heavenly reward, the path of humility.

In the first paragraph of this composition the virtue of humility is defined by comparing it to a photograph of ourselves. The second paragraph calls our attention to examples of this virtue in our Lady. The third paragraph urges us to acquire this virtue and reminds us of the reward it brings. Notice how the paragraphs are tied together. The last sentence in the first paragraph says that we are humble if we have in our mind a clear picture of ourselves, with all our faults and virtues. The first sentence of the second paragraph reminds us of the clear mental picture which our Lady had of herself. The third paragraph is linked to the second paragraph by repeating the subject of the second paragraph, God's Mother, who has been given to us as a model.

When we write compositions of our own, our outline will tell us just what details are to be covered in the various paragraphs. There are several methods of tying the paragraphs together. Among these are:

1. The first sentence of one paragraph may contain a reference to the preceding paragraph.

2. The last sentence of a paragraph may indicate the detail to be treated in the next paragraph.

3. A word from one paragraph may be repeated at the beginning of the next paragraph.

4. Transitional expressions may be used.

By transitional expressions we mean words or phrases that serve as a bridge connecting one sentence or paragraph to the next. Some transitional expressions are:

now	from that day	in the same way
but	in the meantime	at once
moreover	before long	in order that
presently	in addition	on the other hand
consequently	without delay	for example
furthermore	in the next place	inasmuch as
however	at last	in like manner
although	somewhat later	by means of

CLASS ASSIGNMENT

1. Read the following composition and then answer the questions that follow:

A ROSARY REMINISCES

The earliest memory I have is of being laid on a counter before the shining eyes of a dear little eight-year-old girl. A rosary was to be her first Communion gift and she had been brought to the store by her parents so that she might choose the one she desired. I held my breath as she examined one by one the beautiful sam-

ples which the salesman presented for her inspection. Lovely pearl beads and expensive silver rosaries were all returned to their boxes when she whispered shyly to her father that she would like the little blue rosary. At last I belonged to someone, and my life was really about to begin.

From that day on time went swiftly by, and every passing year brought me closer to my little friend. I went to school in her pocket and to church in her purse. I shared in her smiles and joined in her tears. My blue Hail Marys were the last familiar objects her fingers touched at night and with my tiny silver crucifix she traced her first morning sign of the cross. Her joys and sorrows, her hopes and fears, were all mine.

Now we have grown old and the years have left their marks upon us both. No longer is my silver bright, and the blue beads that were once smooth and new are nicked and worn with prayer. The hands that hold me are wrinkled with age and the eyes that were once so merry are growing dim. What a comfort it has been for two dear friends to have lived an entire lifetime together!

1. What is the topic of the composition?

2. How many paragraphs are there? Are these paragraphs all about one thing?

3. What detail in the life of the rosary does the first paragraph describe? The second paragraph? The third?

4. How does the writer show the relationship of the second paragraph to the first? The third paragraph to the second?

2. Divide the following composition into paragraphs:

IDENTICALLY DIFFERENT

From the window seat of our library I have an excellent opportunity to study closely the amazing differences in my twin brothers. Peter, unmindful of the discomforts of a hard stool, is avidly devouring the contents of a new book of modern inventors. Even in his cramped position the neatness of his general appearance is apparent. Well-brushed hair above a high forehead is but one indication of his orderly habits. Behind his thoughtful brown eyes I know that ideas are being born and catalogued for future use. The grave, almost grim set of his mouth betrays the earnestness with which he approaches even the most insignificant task. Peter, I muse lovingly, is the ideal student. Paul, on the other hand, presents a vastly different picture. Unaware of my intense scrutiny, he is crouched before the television watching a football game. With an impatient gesture he brushes aside the blond, wavy hair which insists upon shading his twinkling eyes. Beneath these pools of mischief highly colored cheeks give evidence of the hours spent outdoors. Sparkling white teeth flash from between lips that are constantly parted in gay laughter. As he leaps impetuously to his feet to cheer the winning team, I smile in delight at Paul, the ideal sportsman. What a study in contrasts my twin brothers present!

3. Write a composition of two or more paragraphs on any one of the following:

An autobiography of a clock	A place of historic interest
The lumber industry	The adventures of a wallet
The life cycle of a coin	My favorite saint
The president's Cabinet	Experiences on a hiking trip

4. Choral Speaking

The poems we read for choral speaking may often suggest subjects for our compositions. The exercises on page 89 will aid us in enunciating clearly.

TUNING-UP EXERCISES

Breathing:

Inhale, hold breath for ten counts, exhale with *ah,* then with *hah,* then with *ou,* keeping the mouth very round as in *o.*

Enunciation:

Exercises in the use of the long simple sounds *ah* and *er:*

Laugh, clown, laugh, down the moonlit path
Whir, whir, whir
The earth whirs along—
Work, world, work, mirth be your song!

Let us study Monsignor Benson's "Christmas Carol" with a view to dramatizing it for a classroom celebration.

INDIVIDUAL AND GROUP WORK: "CHRISTMAS CAROL"

By Robert Hugh Benson

First Speaker	There went a merry company //
Chorus	On the road to Bethlehem, //
First Speaker	Going all to taxèd \ be
	By the governour's decree //
Chorus	On the road to Bethlehem— //
First Speaker	Would I \ had been there to see. //
Chorus	*Would I had been there to see*
	On the road to Bethlehem; //
	Mary, \ Joseph, / pray for me! //
Second Speaker	Coldly / blew the wind and snow //
Chorus	On the road to Bethlehem. //
Second Speaker	Two \ there were that walkèd slow, //
	All / that day / so long ago, //
Chorus	On the road to Bethlehem; //
Second Speaker	Would I \ had been there also. //
Chorus	*Would I had been there to see*
	On the road to Bethlehem; //
	Mary, \ Joseph, / pray for me! //

Third Speaker	One, \ a maid of high degree, //
Chorus	On the road to Bethlehem, //
Third Speaker	Walking, walking / wearily;— //
Mary	"Joseph— \ Joseph, / wait for me
	On the road to Bethlehem!" //
Third Speaker	Would I \ had been there to see. //
Chorus	*Would I had been there to see*
	On the road to Bethlehem; //
	Mary, \ *Joseph,* / *pray for me!* //

Fourth Speaker	Thus they came the town within, //
Chorus	To the town of Bethlehem; //
Fourth Speaker	Sought they straight the public inn, //
	So they might a shelter \ win //
Chorus	In the town of Bethlehem; //
Fourth Speaker	See them tirling at the pin. //
Chorus	*Would I had been there to see*
	On the road to Bethlehem; //
	Mary, \ *Joseph,* / *pray for me!* //

Innkeeper	"Get you gone— \ the night is late //
	In the town of Bethlehem." //
Fifth Speaker	Hear them chapping at the gate, //
	Richer \ folk both small / and great, //
Chorus	In the town of Bethlehem— //
Fifth Speaker	When *they* \ knock the poor must wait. //
Chorus	*Would I had been there to see*
	On the road to Bethlehem; //
	Mary, \ *Joseph,* / *pray for me!* //

Sixth Speaker	Sought they straight the stable door //
Chorus	In the town of Bethlehem. //
Sixth Speaker	Mary \ dropped upon the floor; //
	Wearied \ was she—wearied / sore //
Chorus	In the town of Bethlehem. //
Mary	"Joseph dear— \ I can no more." //

Chorus	*Would I had been there to see*
	On the road to Bethlehem; //
	Mary, \ Joseph, / pray for me! //
Joseph	"Cheer thee, \ cheer thee, / Mary Maid, //*
Chorus	In the town of Bethlehem— //
Joseph	See the straw \ is smoothly laid." //
Seventh Speaker	Poor folks' wages, \ poorly paid, //
Chorus	In the town of Bethlehem! //
Seventh Speaker	Would \ I had been there to aid. //
Chorus	*Would I had been there to see*
	On the road to Bethlehem; //
	Mary, \ Joseph, / pray for me! //
Eighth Speaker	What a lodging, cold / and bare, //
Chorus	In the town of Bethlehem. //
Eighth Speaker	Bring me wrappings fine \ and fair, //
	Silk / and satin \ rich / and rare, //
Chorus	In the town of Bethlehem— //
Eighth Speaker	Lay Our Lady softly \ there! //
Chorus	*Would I had been there to see*
	On the road to Bethlehem; //
	Mary, \ Joseph, / pray for me! //

Ninth Speaker	Nay, no silk \ or satin bright //
Chorus	In the town of Bethlehem! //
Ninth Speaker	Think \ ye on this wondrous sight
	Soon to see : / The Lord of Light
Chorus	In the town of Bethlehem //
Ninth Speaker	Comes in lowliness \ tonight. //
Chorus	*Would I had been there to see*
	On the road to Bethlehem ; //
	Mary, \ Joseph, / pray for me! //

Tenth Speaker	Ox \ and ass / with patient pace, //
Chorus	In the town of Bethlehem, //
Tenth Speaker	Mark the Maiden \ full of grace //
	Lying by the manger-place //
Chorus	In the town of Bethlehem— //
Tenth Speaker	Lying in such sorry case. //
Chorus	*Would I had been there to see*
	On the road to Bethlehem ; //
	Mary, \ Joseph, / pray for me! //

Eleventh Speaker	Ere the night \ had passed to morn, //
Chorus	In the town of Bethlehem, //
Eleventh Speaker	Rose the Sun \ on us forlorn ; //
	In the manger old \ and worn, //
Chorus	In the town of Bethlehem, //
Eleventh Speaker	Jesus Christ \ our Lord / was born. //
Chorus	*Would I had been there to see*
	On the road to Bethlehem ; //
	Mary, \ Joseph, / pray for me! //

Twelfth Speaker	Eastern Kings \ are on their way //
Chorus	To the town of Bethlehem ; //
Twelfth Speaker	Shepherds \ run ere break of day //
	At His Feet their vows \ to pay //
Chorus	In the town of Bethlehem, //
Twelfth Speaker	Where a God Incarnate \ lay. //

Chorus	*Would I had been there to see*
	On the road to Bethlehem; //
	Mary, \ Joseph, / pray for me! //
Chorus	Christian souls, \ with one accord //
	Come to Holy Bethlehem; //
Right Side	Meet Him \ at His Holy Board; //
Left Side	Praise the Saviour, \ praise the Lord,— //
Chorus	In the town of Bethlehem //
Right Side	Who on us \ His glory \ poured! //
Left Side	*Would I had been there to see*
Chorus	*On the road to Bethlehem; //*
	Mary, \ Joseph, / pray for me! //

Study of the Poem

1. Read over the poem very carefully, and in silence, in order to picture the events of the birth of Christ as told by the English poet.

2. Let the students who are tellers of the story be divided into two groups, on either side of the classroom or stage, about ten in each group. These represent the narrators and the chorus. The entire class may act as narrators or chorus if circumstances permit.

3. Lines marked "Chorus" are *refrains*—that is, repeated lines—and should be said by the two groups in unison. Each refrain re-echoes the feeling of the lines preceding it.

4. As the class reads the poem, the actions may be pantomimed if desired.

5. The characters for the pantomime are: our Lady, Saint Joseph, the innkeeper, the shepherds, the kings, and men and women going to Bethlehem for the census ordered by the Roman governor.

6. The scenes for the first five stanzas are laid *before* the curtain, on the road to Bethlehem. There should be two exits or openings in the curtain: one in the middle, the entrance to the stable, and the other the inn door to the right of the middle.

7. The scenes for the other stanzas are laid behind the curtain to represent the stable. Our Lady and Saint Joseph pass through the middle opening to get ready for the Nativity group when the curtain is drawn back. If a curtain is lacking, let the children in the last row of the chorus form a human curtain, coming together from each side while the scene is being laid behind, and stepping back into the chorus formation when the scene is ready.

8. Try to follow the grouping in some famous picture of the Nativity scene. Correggio and other famous artists have painted scenes of the Nativity.

5. Chapter Challenge

1. We can write the best paragraph about a subject that .... us.

2. In a group paragraph all the pupils write on the same ....

3. The first step in paragraph writing is to select a ....

4. The second step is to limit the ....

5. We .... in order to have a list of words and phrases that will help us express our ideas to others.

6. We put our thoughts in order by making an ....

7. After a paragraph has been written we must give it ....

8. When we write the exact words of several speakers, we not only use quotation marks, but we ....
....

9. If a composition has two or more paragraphs, all the paragraphs deal with .... topic. The individual paragraphs take up different ....

10. To link the paragraphs of a composition together we may use .... expressions.

11. The last sentence of a paragraph may indicate the .... to be treated in the .... paragraph.

12. A .... from one paragraph may be repeated in the succeeding paragraph.

13. The first sentence of one paragraph may contain a .... to the .... paragraph.

14. The words *consequently, in addition, on the other hand* are ....

15. In the last section of this chapter suggestions are made for dramatizing the poem ....

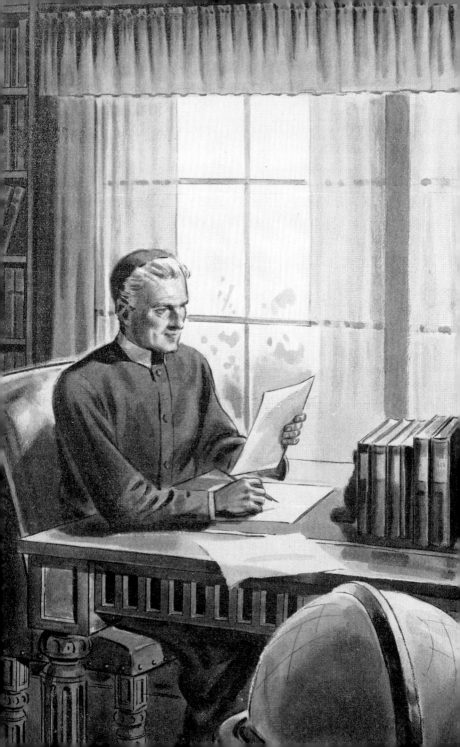

CHAPTER FOUR Polishing a
Paragraph

*In which we learn how to improve our
paragraphs*

It is said that Cardinal Newman, the great English
scholar, once sent a book to a friend with a message of
greeting inscribed on the flyleaf. His friend, charmed with
the beauty of the inscription, said to himself, "How I wish
that I could express my thoughts as beautifully and readily as Newman does!" He consoled himself by thinking
that only a genius like Newman could write such a gem.
While reading the book this man came upon a scrap of
paper upon which was written, in seven or eight different
ways, the thought expressed by Newman on the flyleaf.
The great prose writer wrote, rewrote, polished, and re-
polished his sentences before he obtained the effect which
he desired.

Can we not do this also? We may never be a Newman,
but we can acquire correctness of expression, clearness of
thought, and beauty of diction if we carefully read, improve, and rewrite the paragraphs that we compose. Per-
fection requires earnest and sustained effort. If Newman
rewrote phrases seven or eight times, we will not consider
it too much trouble to rewrite our paragraphs until they
are as perfect as we can make them. In perfecting our
paragraphs we examine both words and sentences.

1. Polishing Words

We employ words effectively when we make use of vivid, expressive, action-flashing, picture-making words to convey to our readers the exact ideas we wish to express. Our spoken or written word is the vehicle through which our intellect communicates thoughts to others.

How do we receive impressions? Does our brain have messengers or servants? Five sturdy messengers, our senses, carry sensations to our brain and relay its messages to alert organs. Words that appeal to our senses of hearing, sight, taste, smell, and touch are very useful.

Through our ears we receive sensations of sound. Let us review some of the words that can be used to describe these sounds to others.

voices	moan, whisper, shriek, roar, bellow, croak, yell, shout, murmur, hum, screech, gasp, mumble, laugh, snicker, snort, yodel, scream, wail, sigh
water	roars, splashes, bubbles, gurgles, murmurs, sings
animals	squeal, neigh, grunt, whine, chatter, purr, moo, howl, squeak, whimper, growl, roar, yelp, bay, mew, cackle, bellow, bleat, yap, bark
birds	sing, squawk, chirp, warble, coo, twitter, call, crow, scold, caw, hoot, gobble, quack, squeak
bells	jingle, tinkle, chime, clang, bang, toll, clatter, peal
airplanes	drone, purr, hum, buzz, sputter, zoom

Through our eyes we receive the sensations of sight. Some words that can be used to tell what we see are:

people	saunter, lurch, stroll, strut, march, hike, tramp, jaunt, ramble, rove, skip, rush, plod, trudge, wobble, shuffle, limp, falter, totter, sprint, tread, amble
animals	trot, canter, gallop, lope, jog, scamper, creep, stalk, pad, slink, crawl, lag, waddle, hobble, prance

birds	fly, swoop, flutter, soar, glide, wing, flap, dart, flit, dive, hover, hop
leaves	whirl, flutter, tremble, scurry, twirl, dance, tumble, dangle, swirl, twist
waves	roll, tumble, toss, dash, rush, surge, swell, billow, ripple, gush
lights	flicker, flash, glow, shimmer, shine, twinkle

Through our mouth we get taste sensations. We use such words as the following to tell others how our foods and drinks taste:

foods	sweet, tart, bitter, sour, tangy, spicy, piquant, mellow, mild, savory, delicious, luscious, peppery, creamy, sharp, flat, gritty, sugary
beverages	sweet, sour, mellow, creamy, biting, rich, tart, tangy, flavorful, insipid

Through our nose we perceive various odors. Note the words that can be used for such odors:

forest	pungent, pine-scented, aromatic, spicy
flowers	fragrant, sweet-scented, perfumed, honey-sweet
air	salty, tangy, exhilarating, invigorating, damp, acrid, balmy, refreshing

Through the skin sensations of touch come to us. Do you make use of such words as the following in the paragraphs that you write?

water	cold, hot, warm, tepid, icy, tingling
cloth	soft, rough, coarse, flimsy, downy, silky, bristly, starchy, crisp, limp, velvety, smooth, woolly, heavy, sleazy, firm
fruit	smooth, fuzzy, firm, prickly, downy, squashy
wind	cold, scorching, piercing, moist, biting

Our sentences can easily be improved by using words that appeal to the senses in place of dull, commonplace words. Note how the use of such words has improved the sentences that follow:

The tired man slept quietly by the side of the burning fire.	*The weary man dozed complacently by the side of the blazing fire.*
From the kitchen came a faint smell that filled the house with a promise of good things to come.	*From the kitchen was wafted a delicate aroma that filled the house with a tantalizing promise of delicious things to come.*
We walked through a garden smelling of flowers and filled with the singing of many birds.	*We sauntered through a garden fragrant with flowers and filled with the warbling of many birds.*

CLASS ASSIGNMENT

1. Point out the vivid, expressive words in these sentences:

1. The lanky young messenger jauntily entered the room.

2. The pony cantered through the pine-scented forest.

3. A chubby little urchin darted eagerly across the rickety wooden bridge.

4. Hanging from the rod of the exhausted fisherman was an enormous struggling pike.

5. Rich, creamy milk was set before us and a gentle voice bade us drink.

6. We entered a tranquil forest where a friendly little brook splashed and gurgled to the accompaniment of the soft whisper of rustling leaves.

7. Shining, white-capped waves surged majestically toward a distant shore.

8. She had a high, shrill voice that reminded us of the harsh jangle of a bell.

9. The blazing sun beat down upon us mercilessly as we dragged ourselves along the dusty road.

10. Grunts and squeals issued from the barnyard when the farmer appeared.

2. Write a sentence describing the sound, feeling, taste, smell, or appearance suggested by each of the following:

a motor	steam	the fire siren	green apples
spices	a skyscraper	pine needles	a creaking gate
burning leaves	feathers	a bobolink	thunder
a rose	turkey roasting	an alarm clock	frogs croaking

3. Improve the following sentences by substituting picture words for plain words:

1. We were surprised that the building was so large.
2. The happy child ran to her mother.
3. The ruler gave nice gifts to his loyal servant.
4. In the distance stood a dark mountain, plainly outlined against the bright sky.
5. The horse ran quietly along the curved path.
6. The gum came out of a little slit in the tree.
7. All day we worked in the small office.
8. I could not do a hard puzzle like that.
9. Along the road stretched a kinglike carpet of many colors.
10. Small sandpipers flew back and forth as the waves flowed onto the beach.
11. The missionaries worked hard.
12. Our guest told us about funny happenings at camp.

Synonyms

Synonyms are words that have the same general meaning. Each word, however, has a definite and specific meaning which makes it more suitable in one sentence than in another. Note the many synonyms for the word *weak* that have been used in the following paragraph.

A Strange Reception

At a *rickety* antique table in the dimly lighted dining room sat a *frail* old lady pouring tea into *fragile* cups. Her hand under its *flimsy* covering of lace was *shaky* and she seemed even older than the *tottering* servant who hovered nearby. Only when the ritual had been completed did she raise her head to indicate that she had heard my *timid* knock.

CLASS ASSIGNMENT

1. For the italicized word in each of the following sentences substitute from the suggested list a word that has the same general meaning and that is particularly suited to the sentence:

1. With an *impetuous* gesture Saint Peter cut off the ear of the man who came to apprehend Jesus.

cruel   slow   careful   impulsive   well-aimed

2. The *calmness* of the ocean impressed him more than a sermon.

noise   tranquillity   magnitude   depth   color

3. It is *foolish* to think that the team will win.

preposterous   wise   intelligent   correct   right

4. She was by nature an extremely *reserved* person.

happy-go-lucky   careful   youthful   reticent   handy

5. During the pause that followed, John made an *apt* remark.

foolish   impudent   pertinent   wise   unnecessary

6. He faced a *fearful* enemy.

formidable   large   well-informed   treacherous   weakened

7. The quality of his work suggested *hidden* ability.

sufficient   excessive   latent   unusual   needless

8. It was an *important* decision for a boy of fourteen to make.

imprudent   unnecessary   strange   momentous   foolish

9. An *able* young woman was given the position.

severe   competent   pretty   hard-working   interesting

10. He had a *particular* plan to follow.

clever   foolish   brief   surprising   specific

2. Rewrite the following sentences, using synonyms for the italicized words:

1. Much of the *hostility* among the Indian tribes ceased with the coming of the missionaries.

2. The old general's voice *quavered* as he spoke the words of surrender.

3. As her terror mounted her voice rose to a *shriek*.

4. He strolled through the old house, lost in *reveries* of a dim past.

5. Her *vivacious* manner drew the attention of many.

6. He was accused of *duplicity* in his methods of dealing with his men.

7. A severe *reprimand* was administered to the defendants by the judge.

8. His death was caused by a mysterious and *potent* poison.

9. He admitted being a *tyro* at the game of golf.

10. The leaders hoped to avoid any *enmity* between the two countries.

3. In each of the following groups of sentences tell what ideas the italicized words bear in common and what differentiates one word from another:

1. Children who neglect to study during the year have *difficulty* at examination time.

John tried to overcome his speech *impediment*.

The wide river was an *obstacle* to the campers, who were trying to reach the cabin before the storm broke.

2. *Conversation* lags when there are few good listeners.

A business *conference* was held at the end of the week.

In the lives of some saints we read of frequent *colloquies* with our Lord.

4. Use the synonyms *reprimand, reproach, admonition, reproof, criticism,* and *disapproval* to fill the blanks in these sentences:

Mother sends us to school each morning with the .... to be good and to do nothing that will meet with the .... of our teachers. She allows no .... of authority, and by a glance of .... or a stern .... she shows her displeasure at a .... we have received in class.

5. Use the synonyms *important, decisive, significant, essential, influential, considerable,* and *momentous* to fill the blanks in the following sentences:

To win the Revolution it was .... that Americans receive help from abroad. Through the efforts of .... citizens we had obtained .... aid from the French, but it is .... to note that they did not help us openly until a .... victory had been won at Saratoga. The battle was .... because it brought about the .... decision on the part of the French.

6. Use the synonyms *sin, evil, misdeed, offense, transgression,* and *guilt* in filling the blanks of the following sentences:

Every .... of the law of God is a ...., either mortal or venial according to the seriousness of the .... Although circumstances may lessen the .... of the offender, he should remember that there is .... in even a slight ....

2. Polishing Sentences

We have found that our sentences can be improved by changing plain words to words that appeal to the senses or to words that express exact meanings. Let us now study other ways of improving sentences.

Adding Colorful Pictures and Comparisons

In many cases our sentences may be improved by adding words or phrases that present a clearer picture of the scene we have in mind. Study the phrases that may be used in sentences describing ships, a stormy sky, hair, or eyes. Do they help to form a picture in one's mind?

SHIPS	A STORMY SKY
glided with sails unfurled	rain-filled clouds shedding tears
skimmed the blue waters	threatening black clouds
plowing the choppy seas	a flaming streak of lightning

HAIR	EYES
shining red hair	green and sparkling
wavy blond ringlets	piercing brown eyes
raven tresses	warm blue-gray eyes

Very often the words that we add to sentences take the form of a comparison. We may say, for example, that the grass was *as smooth as velvet* or that the babbling brook sounded *like a happy child singing a merry tune*. When-

ever we use the word *like* or *as* in comparing two unlike things, we are using a figure of speech called a *simile*.

The frost on the window was like a delicate lace curtain.
The storm raged like an angry giant.

In other sentences we may compare two unlike things by saying that one thing *is* another; that is, we imply the comparison instead of expressing it definitely with the word *like* or *as*.

Books are keys to the doors of the past.
Her voice was a soothing lullaby.
Habit is a cable.

In these sentences we mean that *books are like keys,* her voice was *as soothing as a lullaby,* and that *habit is like a cable.* An implied comparison of two objects or ideas is called a *metaphor.*

CLASS ASSIGNMENT

1. Use each of the following phrases in a sentence:

WAVES	HANDS
tossing their briny manes	chubby, dimpled hands
tumbled onto the beach	with strong and flexible fingers
with foaming white crests	expressive, sensitive hands

RAIN	VOICE
descended with muffled beat	musical, lilting voice
tumbling little waterfalls	deep, gruff voice
drizzling quietly	firm and convincing tone

2. Study the following figures of speech and tell whether each is a simile or a metaphor:

1. Fireflies glowed in the dark like tiny stars.
2. He hoarded his wisdom as a miser does his gold.
3. The pine trees stood on the mountaintop like lonely sentinels.

4. The meadow in early morning was a field of sparkling diamonds.

5. The judge's eyes were daggers of relentless steel.

6. The clouds chased across the sky like a flock of woolly sheep.

7. Each new year is a blank copybook spread open before us.

8. He was as agile as a deer leaping through the forest.

3. Use these comparisons in sentences of your own:

SHIPS	HAIR
like birds on the wing	bright as a copper penny
like a warrior meeting the foe	like burnished gold
swaying like graceful dancers	black as ebony

4. Complete these comparisons to form a simile:

1. feet like
2. tired as
3. eyes like
4. deep as
5. tinkling like
6. white as
7. sparkling like
8. peaceful as
9. music like
10. daffodils like

5. Polish the following sentences by adding colorful pictures or comparisons:

1. The squirrel, huddled in the tree, looked small and gray.
2. The lost cub whimpered.
3. The field lay before us.
4. The falling rain obstructed our view.
5. The sergeant gave the order in a loud voice.

Varying the Length of Sentences

Experienced writers vary the length of their sentences. The first drafts of our paragraphs may contain a series of short, choppy sentences that are very monotonous to the reader. In polishing we combine such sentences to form longer sentences. We do not, however, make the mistake of using the overworked conjunction *and* in combining all our sentences. Instead we make use of such connectives as *when, where, as, who, although, because, which, while, since, after,* and so forth.

SHORT SENTENCES	COMBINED SENTENCES
Marco Polo entered the court of Kublai Khan in 1275. There was great rejoicing.	*When Marco Polo entered the court of Kublai Khan in 1275, there was great rejoicing.*
The Philippines are sometimes called the isles of treasure. They are the largest group of islands in the Malay Archipelago.	*The Philippines, the largest group of islands in the Malay Archipelago, are sometimes called the isles of treasure.*
Hilaire Belloc is a noted historian. He has also written many outstanding poems.	*Although Hilaire Belloc is a noted historian, he has also written many outstanding poems.*

Another common fault in writing is rambling, or the stringing together in a single sentence of a number of different ideas concerning the thing about which we are writing. Should we find that our compositions contain a number of long, involved sentences, we improve them by dividing the sentences into shorter ones that discuss related ideas.

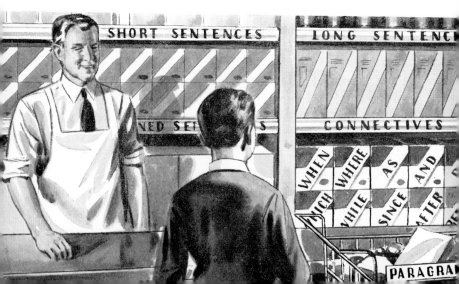

Long Sentences	Improved Sentences
Caesar had a cruel manner and therefore he was greatly disliked and he could not count many true friends among his acquaintances.	*Because of his cruel manner Caesar was greatly disliked. He could not count many true friends among his acquaintances.*
A small child was playing on the sidewalk when her ball suddenly bounced into the street, and the little girl ran after it because she did not notice the car which was careening wildly down the street after having just skidded around the corner.	*A small child was playing on the sidewalk when her ball suddenly bounced into the street. Not noticing an approaching car, the little girl ran out after her ball. The automobile, having skidded around the corner, was careening wildly down the street.*

Changing the Order of Words

If we follow the same sentence pattern of subject followed by predicate, our readers are likewise bored. We can add variety to our paragraphs and make them more interesting by occasionally inverting the word order.

Natural Order	Inverted Order
We walked triumphantly across the stage.	*Triumphantly we walked across the stage.*
The songs of a thousand birds came from every bush and tree.	*From every bush and tree came the songs of a thousand birds.*
Dad discovered that the gasoline tank was leaking before we had gone very far.	*Before we had gone very far Dad discovered that the gasoline tank was leaking.*

Another method adopted by good writers to obtain variety in sentence structure is the use of questions or exclamatory sentences where they are appropriate.

CLASS ASSIGNMENT

1. Combine each of the following groups of short sentences into one clear sentence:

1. Mother Catherine Drexel has done much for the Negro. She founded the Sisters of the Blessed Sacrament.

2. I built the campfire according to the scoutmaster's directions. It did not burn well.

3. "Gallegher" was written by Richard Harding Davis. It is the story of a newsboy who overcame many obstacles to deliver copy to the office of the newspaper.

4. Great numbers of immigrants have settled in America. America has been called the Melting Pot.

5. Saint Paul was one of the greatest missionaries in history. He preached the gospel of Christ to the gentiles.

6. The Lateran Treaty was signed in 1929. The conflict between the Church and the Italian state was brought to an end by it.

2. Improve the following sentences:

1. Peary tried for nearly twenty years to reach the North Pole and finally he succeeded and discovered it in 1909.

2. Excitement danced in the eyes of the happy little children and they were delighted when they saw the colorful circus parade and it continued its merry tour of the village.

3. Once a year the West Point hockey team plays the Royal Canadian Military College in a game which has become a shining example of good sportsmanship because half the West Pointers root for the Canadian team and the trophy stays in possession of the team that loses.

4. In Gloucester, Massachusetts, there is a monument erected in memory of fishermen who lost their lives at sea and I saw that statue last summer when I went on my vacation with my mother and father who had decided to go there instead of going to New Jersey as we usually do.

5. There are eleven players on a football team and they must keep physically fit by eating good, wholesome food and getting

plenty of sleep so they will always be ready to do their best on the gridiron.

6. There was an outburst of applause as the violinist walked to the center of the stage and bowed, and then as he lifted his violin, the pianist struck a chord and a hush fell over the audience as they waited breathlessly for the first magic notes.

7. The batter struck the ball with a resounding thud and headed for first base where he paused instead of going on to second as he should have done because he had hit the ball deep into right field and the men in the outfield had played too close.

8. We are not permitted to speak unnecessarily in the library because it disturbs those who have gone there to read or to study and if we feel that there is something we must say, our voices must be kept low and not raised above a whisper but sometimes children forget this rule and have to be reminded of it by the librarian.

3. Vary the sentence structure in each of the following sentences by changing the word order:

1. The moon gleamed like a giant pearl high above the town.

2. The boys, shouting the songs of their alma mater, ran happily to their places in the stadium.

3. A group of roughly dressed men strode into the light of the campfire.

4. Our ancestors came here to build their homes many years ago.

5. They held the fort against the savages for seven days and seven nights.

6. Within three days you will be expected to give us your final answer.

7. In the cradle the tired and patient mother gently placed the sleeping baby.

8. From its perch on the top of the high picket fence a tiny wren sang merrily.

9. To help the ambitious boy I would willingly make any reasonable sacrifice.

10. Along the side of the winding trail grew dainty wild flowers.

3. Polishing Paragraphs

We polish paragraphs by improving the sentences that make up our paragraphs. To do this we apply all the methods we have learned in polishing sentences to the paragraph as a whole. We use vivid words and phrases in our sentences and we see that they have a pleasing variety. Some of our sentences will be long; others will be short. They will also vary in word order or structure.

Note how one pupil used the principles studied in this chapter to improve her paragraph:

FIRST DRAFT:
A GARDEN IN SPRING

The Brownings have always had many visitors to their suburban home. These guests are always attracted to the Brownings' charming garden. This garden lies to the rear of their house. This lovely spot is enclosed by a privet hedge which shields it from the look of passers-by. A flagstone path stretches from the back porch of the house to the center of the lawn and here in late spring and during the summer shining goldfish dart to and fro in a pool surrounded by a green carpet which is bordered by flowers. Daffodils nod wisely, full of important secrets the birds have told them. Iris stand tall

IMPROVED PARAGRAPH:
BEAUTY BECKONS

Visitors to the Brownings' suburban home are always attracted to the charming garden which lies to the rear of the house. This lovely spot is enclosed by a privet hedge which shields it from the gaze of passers-by. A flagstone path stretches from the back porch of the house to a crystal pool in the center of the garden. Here in late spring and during the summer shining goldfish dart to and fro. Surrounding the pool is a soft, green, velvet carpet bordered by a frieze of gaily colored flowers. Jaunty daffodils nod wisely, full of important secrets the birds have whispered into their petaled telephones. Delicate iris stand tall upon

upon their stems as if they would like to fly away. Pink, white, and purple hyacinths fill the whole garden with their fragrance. An old apple tree gives several families of robins a home in one corner of the garden, and this tree spreads out its branches as if to take the whole world into its embrace. Over the whole garden is an air of tranquil peace and quiet content, making it a place where one can go to escape the troublesome cares of a busy world.

their stems like lavender butterflies poised for flight. Pink, white, and purple hyacinths perfume the whole garden with their fragrance. In one corner a gnarled old apple tree serves as an apartment house for several families of robins. It spreads out protecting arms as if to take the entire world into its spacious embrace. Throughout the enclosure there reigns an air of tranquil peace and quiet content which makes this garden a welcome refuge from the troublesome cares of a busy world.

Which paragraph is more interesting to read, the first draft or the improved paragraph? Study these two versions carefully to see just what this pupil did. The first three sentences have been combined. In the fourth sentence the word *gaze* has been substituted for *look*. The

long fifth sentence has been divided into three sentences, and the order has been changed so that the reader knows the goldfish are in the pool and not in the center of the lawn. The picture words *crystal, velvet,* and *gaily colored* have also been added. Notice the many picture words that are used in the improved paragraph. The petals of the daffodils are compared to telephones, the iris to butter-flies, and the apple tree to an apartment house. Do the words *spreads out protecting arms* convey the same idea as *spreads out its branches?* Did the change in word order also improve this sentence about the apple tree? Point out any other changes that were made in the paragraph. Do not overlook the titles.

CLASS ASSIGNMENT

1. Read the following paragraphs carefully and then answer the questions that follow:

AFTER THE RAIN

Have you ever watched a street immediately after a storm? A few minutes before it is silent and deserted. Suddenly it is reoccupied by all who have been forced to take shelter. First come a few stray cats who have been hiding somewhere and who walk out into the open keeping out of the puddles and sniffing the air in a suspicious manner. A loud yell announces the arrival of a dozen children who have been kept indoors. They

REVIVAL AFTER THE STORM

Have you ever watched a street come to life immediately after a storm? Silent and deserted a few minutes before, it is suddenly reoccupied by all who have been forced to take hurried shelter. First come a few stray cats. Where they have been during the downpour nobody seems to know, but they now parade disdainfully into the open, skirting puddles and sniffing the air in a suspicious manner. An ear-splitting scream announces the arrival of a dozen children, who make their way to the nearest puddles. Here they splash contentedly until warning threats from various upstairs windows force them to dry land. By this time a few housewives have ventured out on a postponed shopping tour and they look suspiciously at the sky and argue with themselves about taking umbrellas. Finally the birds fly cautiously down and drink from their private pools of water, all the while keeping a wary eye cocked for cats. The street gradually assumes its usual busy appearance and you would not know that the storm had interfered with its familiar routine.

race out of their homes like prisoners released from temporary confinement. They tumble into the nearest puddles, where they splash contentedly until warning threats from various upstairs windows force them to dry land. By this time a few housewives have ventured out on a postponed shopping tour. They squint suspiciously at the sky and argue with themselves about taking umbrellas. Finally the birds swoop cautiously down and drink thirstily from their private rain-water reservoirs, all the while keeping a wary eye cocked for their feline enemies. Gradually the street assumes its usual busy appearance, as if no storm had ever interfered with its familiar routine.

1. What picture words have been substituted for *walk, keeping out, loud yell, make their way to, look, fly, pools of water, cats?*

2. Point out any sentences that have been combined.

3. Two long, stringy sentences have been divided. Can you find these sentences?

4. Name any picture words or phrases that have been added.

5. Has the word order been changed in any sentence?

6. Have any other connectives been substituted for *and* in the improved paragraph?

7. Are there any similes or metaphors in the improved paragraph?

8. Which paragraph has the more interesting title?

2. Point out the changes that have been made in the improved paragraph that follows on page 116:

FIRST DRAFT:
A GOOD LEADER

Every boy and girl wishes to become a leader. Many people think that leaders are born and not made. I think that each one of us can become an influence for good in the lives of others. A study of the things necessary to become a leader shows that anyone who wants to be a leader must, first of all, have an ideal he himself tries to imitate and we have this perfect ideal in Christ. Next, a leader must think for himself and not let others think for him. Here again the principles of our holy faith will guide us. The ability to win the confidence of others is another quality of leadership. To do this it is necessary to have self-confidence, but this can be obtained only through an unshaken confidence in God, so let us then work for these qualities in order that we may become leaders for Christ.

IMPROVED PARAGRAPH:
BE A LEADER!

How I wish I could be a leader! This is the longing of every boy and girl. Despite the belief of many people that leaders are born and not made, I believe each one of us can become an influence for good in the lives of others. A study of the qualifications necessary for leadership discloses that anyone who wishes to lead others must, first of all, have an ideal that he himself strives to imitate. We have this perfect exemplar in Jesus Christ. Secondly, a leader must think for himself and not be swayed by the opinions of others. Here again we will be guided by the principles of our holy faith, our North Star on the journey through life. Another characteristic of leadership is the ability to win the confidence of others. The secret of this is self-assurance, obtained through an unshaken trust in God. Let us cultivate these qualities, then, so that each one of us may become a magnet attracting others to Christ.

3. Improve the following paragraph. Make a perfect copy of the improved paragraph, following the directions on page 117.

Oil gushed from the earth at Titusville in 1859. Oil has grown in importance since that time. It is important, not only to Americans, but to all mankind. It lights lamps and this gives longer hours for work and amusements and devices have been run by it, therefore manual work has been decreased. It has carried steamships to the far corners of the globe. This helps trade. Gasoline obtained from oil is used by trucks and automobiles and by airplanes. Petroleum is very important to industry in America.

4. Write a paragraph on any subject that appeals to your class. Do not forget to polish the first draft.

Putting the Paragraph on Paper

After we have polished the paragraph to our satisfaction, only one thing remains to be done. We must make a perfect copy to be submitted to the teacher or to be placed in our composition books. If your school does not have special rules for written work, you may follow these rules in writing your compositions:

1. Leave a margin of at least an inch at the left of the paper and a margin of one-half inch at the right.

2. Place the title in the center of the first line.

3. Leave one line between the title and the first line of the paragraph.

4. Indent the first word of the paragraph about an inch from the left-hand margin.

5. Be careful of your handwriting. Always make it plain and neat.

6. Observe all the rules for spelling, punctuation, and capitalization.

7. When the paragraph is completed, leave one line blank and write your name on the right-hand side of the next line.

8. Write the date on the same line as your name, on the left-hand side.

4. Writing for the Class Newspaper

Students have another excellent opportunity to work together in producing a class newspaper, for the best paper is one to which all the pupils of the class contribute. In a newspaper they can discuss their classroom problems, arouse interest in school and parish events, and report on important national and local affairs. The classroom can be turned into a miniature newspaper office, and various groups may be asked to contribute some of the following types of articles.

News Stories

A news story is a straightforward account of some event that has taken place. In this account, however, the most important facts are stated first. We do not lead up to the climax step by step as in a composition. The opening paragraph, and sometimes the first sentence, tells *what* happened, *who* was concerned in it, *when* it happened, *how* it happened, and *why* it happened. Newspaper writers call such a paragraph or sentence the *lead*. A news story should be so written that the reader can find out the answers to all these questions merely by reading the lead. In the remainder of the article further details are given. Personal opinions have no place in a news story.

Editorials

In an editorial a writer has an opportunity of expressing his views or opinions on a variety of topics. His opinions, however, should be backed up by several good arguments based on facts. Editorials are written in the first person plural, the editorial *we*. They should never be narrow or

EIGHTH-GRADERS FROLIC
AT JACK-O'-LANTERN PARTY

A highly successful Halloween
party was given in the auditorium
by the eighth grade on Monday evening, October 31.

Jack-o'-lanterns, oak leaves,
and huge cornstalks gave the hall
a festive air and showed evidence
of genuine hard work on the part
of the committee in charge of the
decorations.

Each of the forty-two boys
and girls present was dressed as
some character from literature.
The identity of some cleverly
dressed pupils remained a complete
mystery until the signal to unmask
was given. The prize for the best
costume was awarded to John Brown,
who as Will Scarlett looked as if
he had just stepped from the green
depths of Sherwood Forest.

A delicious and appetizing
lunch was served by the refresh-
ment committee.

PRIEST PRAISES MISSION WORK

An enthusiastic audience
gathered in the school hall last
Tuesday to hear a talk given by
Reverend Paul Gordon, assistant
diocesan director of the Society
for the Propagation of the Faith.
The title of his speech was
"Missions at Home and Abroad."

Father Gordon spoke earnestly of the work being done by the
missionaries from the United
States, both in our own land and
in foreign fields. He also empha-
sized the necessity of strong support by the Catholics of America
if these missions are to be maintained.

Although Trinity has always
ranked high on the list of mission
supporters, Father Gordon's talk
should spur us on to even greater
efforts to help those who are
spreading Christ's kingdom to the
ends of the earth.

SCHOOL OFFICIALLY OPENS
NEW LIBRARY ON ALL SOULS' DAY

Long lines of prospective
readers from every grade in the
school gathered outside the new
library on Wednesday afternoon,
November 2, to watch our pastor,
Father Mark Hoy, as he officially
opened the new school library.

After Father Hoy unlocked
the library door he presented the
keys to our principal, Sister
Peter. Then he spoke to the assembled teachers and students. He
reminded them that the new library
can be both useful and interesting
for all. The well-stocked bookcases should provide students with
material helpful to them in their
school work, as well as with interesting reading for their leisure hours.

This long-cherished project
has been made possible by the gen-
erosity of Father Hoy who had the
old committee room equipped as a
library. Father also made the initial donation toward the purchase
of new books. Other benefactors
are Dr. John Graham and Mrs. Guy
Harrell.

Boys and girls will find in
the new library books to suit
every taste. There are picture
books and fairy tales for the
younger children; hobby books,
biography, and works of fiction
for the older ones. Of special interest to the students of the
upper grades is the reference section which may be used on any
afternoon except Friday.

GIRL SCOUTS SOLICIT TOYS

Donations of new or used
toys, to be distributed with Christmas baskets to the needy of the
parish, will be gratefully accepted
by the Girl Scouts.

Please send all donations to
the school auditorium, Monday to
Friday inclusive, between four and
five o'clock.

The CLARION

A student newspaper published
three times yearly in Toledo,
Ohio at TRINITY SCHOOL.

News Editor..........John Bow

Features.............Mary Dee

Business Manager
    .....Francis Walters

Assistant Manager
    ....Margaret More

ABOUT OUR ALUMNI

Elizabeth Young has been
elected president of her class at
Loretto Academy for the second
year. Congratulations, Elizabeth!

At the recent open house held
at Little Flower High School, Mary
Crunkleton gave an inspiring talk
on the literary value of Cardinal
Newman's works.

Distinguished Spanish tourists
visited De Paul Academy last week.
Our former classmate, Ricardo Juan
Ortega, welcomed them to America
and to the campus in their native
tongue.

Among the winners of certificates for superior work in Latin
at Campion High School were eleven
former pupils at Trinity.

AUTUMN

The artist Autumn dons his smock
  And sets to work with mirth,
And on his tripod universe
  He pins his canvas--earth.

He splashes boldly at a tree
  Which heretofore was green.
With his brilliant red and umbers
  He creates a forest queen.

* * *

HELP THE CAUSE

Although the library shelves
are well stocked, there is room for
more books. Any boy or girl wishing
to donate a volume is requested to
bring it to the library and give it
to the girl in charge.

EDITORIALS . . . .

THANKS BE TO GOD

While it may be true that our
thoughts have not as yet turned to
"turkey and trimmings," ideas about
Thanksgiving can never be premature.
Our daily lives should be a constant hymn of gratitude, for where
can we turn and not see things for
which to be grateful? From the moment we open our sleep-laden eyes
to behold another day, God in His
goodness showers upon us blessings
without number. How often do we take
time to say "Thank You"?

Let us determine to turn this
month in which the civil feast of
Thanksgiving occurs into a time of
ardent thanksgiving to our Lord.
Many of us echo the prayer of our
budding poetess, Jean Reilly, who
penned these lines:

For the flowers that bloom and
    the waters that flow,

For the beautiful moon and
    the stars that glow,

For my faith, my home, in
    this "land of the free,"

Father in heaven, I thank Thee!

* * *

STUDENTS HAIL PASTOR'S GIFT

All Trinity students are well
acquainted with the fact that our
pastor, Father Hoy, has renovated
the gymnasium. Everything that
could possibly be desired by way
of athletic equipment has been installed.

We should like to take this
opportunity to thank Father Hoy
for this improvement in our school.
It is but another evidence of the
generous and fatherly interest he
maintains in his parishioners.

The new equipment is in perfect condition. If each student
takes proper care of everything he
uses when in the gym, the equipment will serve us for a long time.
The cost of the renovation was a
huge one. Let us do our share to
see that not one cent will have to
be expended for repairs caused by
careless or thoughtless students.

unpleasantly critical; an editorial writer must strive to be fair and honest at all times.

Announcements and Notices

Announcements of future events, meetings, and notices giving the results of games or contests add interest to the paper. They usually consist of a single short paragraph.

Other Features

In addition to news stories, editorials, and notices, each issue of a school newspaper should include other features. Human-interest stories, interviews with well-known persons, reviews of motion pictures and books, descriptions of works of art, hints on etiquette, science notes, and a poetry corner will enliven a newspaper and make it appealing to a greater number of people.

Headlines

Headlines attract attention. They save the time of the reader by furnishing him with a few brief statements to explain the nature of the article. The headline should be short and "catchy"; it is usually the last part of the item to be written. Every news story, editorial, and feature article requires a headline. Some notices may also take headlines, although they are not necessary.

CLASS ASSIGNMENT

1. Write a news story based on any one of the following leads:

1. The Cape and Sword Players are holding daily rehearsals in preparation for their annual dramatic offering, which will be presented in the school auditorium, Saturday evening, November 16, at 8:30 p.m. The play, a three-act comedy, is entitled "Dorothy's Dilemma."

2. Scoring fourteen of the total twenty points, René Rubio led Saint Ambrose to an overwhelming victory over La Salle Academy last night in the stadium, thereby giving his team the right to meet Holy Savior for the city football title next Friday.

3. Through the kindness of a friend, who wishes to remain anonymous, Saint Ignatius School was presented with a new motion-picture machine on Friday, October 23.

2. Write a news story reporting some event that took place in your school or your city.

3. Write an editorial to be used in a newspaper. Any of the following topics or some topic in which you are personally interested may be used:

School spirit   Devotion to Our Lady of Fatima
Obedience to authority   Courtesy in the classroom
Honesty in the classroom   Aid for the missions

4. Plan and produce at least one issue of an eighth-grade newspaper. Select the members of the editorial staff, appoint reporters to bring in the news, and nominate those who are to type the paper.

5. Choral Speaking

The following tuning-up exercises are an important preparation for choral speaking.

TUNING-UP EXERCISES

Breathing:
Inhale, hold breath ten counts, exhale with *ou,* keeping mouth very round as in *o.*

Enunciation:
Pronounce *ringing, singing* in medium, high, and low pitch.

Nonsense jingle spoken in unison:
> Ding, dong, dell,
> Pussy's in the well,
> Ping, pong, pout,
> Who'll draw her out?

Flanders Fields

The poem we will read for choral speaking, "In Flanders Fields," was written during the First World War (1914-1918). Flanders is a district in Belgium where a number of battles were fought. A military cemetery is now located there. The author of the poem was an officer in the Canadian army.

In the first stanza the poet pictures the graveyard that was once a battlefield. The dead speak. They challenge the living to keep faith with all those brave soldiers who gave their lives that the world might in the future be safe for democracy.

Can you imagine what kind of voice the dead would have? Try a slow, uninflected tone (neither up nor down), very low in pitch. First read the poem together out loud, keeping mind and heart alive to the changes of thought and feeling in the simple lines. Then divide the class into three groups and follow the directions given.

IN FLANDERS FIELDS

By John D. McCrae

First Group,
Medium
Voices

In Flanders \ Fields the poppies blow //
Between the crosses, \ row on row, //
  That mark our place; \ and in the sky /

Second Group,
Light Voices

The larks, // still bravely singing, \ fly //
Scarce heard \ amid the guns below. //

Third Group,
Dark Voices

We are the dead. // Short days ago
We lived, / felt dawn, \ saw sunset glow, //
  Loved \ and were loved, // and now we lie
  In Flanders Fields. //

Unison

Take up / our quarrel with the foe; //
To you \ from failing hands we throw
  The torch; // be yours \ to hold it high. //
  If ye break faith with us / who die //
We shall not sleep, \ though poppies grow //
  In Flanders Fields. //

6. Chapter Challenge

1. Cardinal .... was a great English writer who rewrote phrases many times before he obtained the effect he desired.

2. We communicate our thoughts to others through our written or spoken ....

3. Our brain receives sensations of sound, sight, taste, odor, and touch through the five ....

4. We polish .... by using vivid, expressive terms for commonplace and dull ....

5. Synonyms are words that ....
....

6. Sentences may be polished in four ways: (1) By
.... colorful pictures and comparisons; (2) by
combining ...., ... sentences; (3)
by .... long, rambling sentences; (4) by changing the ....

7. A figure of speech that compares two unlike things
by using the word *like* or *as* is called a ....

8. An implied comparison is known as a ....

9. When we make a final copy of a composition we
leave a wider margin on the .... than on the
....

10. The title should be placed in the .... of
the .... line.

11. The first word of every paragraph should be
....

12. The opening paragraph of a news story is called
the ....

13. A newspaper writer may express his own views and
opinions in an ....

14. Headlines are used to ....

15. The colorful phrases *scarce heard amid the guns
below, sunset glow, failing hands,* and *throw the torch* are
found in ....

CHAPTER FIVE Writing Letters

*In which we write many types of social
and business letters*

Letters are conversations by mail. The writer is the speaker and the recipient is the listener. The reader has an opportunity to speak and express his views when he answers the letter. It is very important that we learn to converse by mail while in school, for letters may be the only form of writing that we practice when we are older. We want to know how to write letters that are interesting, what to say when we extend an invitation or accept one, how to express our sympathy in time of sorrow and death, and different ways of saying "Thank you." We also wish to learn how to write business letters.

1. Social Letters

Social letters are letters that we write to friends and relatives. Such a letter has five parts as shown in the model letter on page 128.

The body of the letter contains the message. It is here that we carry on our conversation with our correspondent. When we write to a friend we discuss or report events which we know interest him, just as we would do if we were talking with him. There will probably be several paragraphs in the body of the letter, for we must follow the rules of good paragraph writing and limit each paragraph to a single topic.

MODEL: A FRIENDLY LETTER

6312 South Oakley Avenue
Chicago 37, Illinois
April 5, 19__

Dear David,

Have you found so many new friends in Buffalo that you have forgotten your former companions? No, we know you better than that, but we are eagerly awaiting a letter telling us about your new home.

Our biggest news right now is the announcement that a Scout troop has been formed. Five patrols have already been organized and additional members are applying every day. Father Daly has agreed to give us the auditorium for our Friday meetings and has donated a large part of our equipment. Mr. Kelly, our scoutmaster, has planned an overnight hike for this month and has made reservations for two weeks at Treasure Island next July.

Do you remember the field behind the church? Father McHugh has decided to turn it into a ball field. Every boy in the eighth grade now carries a spade, a pick, or an ax to school, for Father has adopted John Smith's policy and says, "If you don't work on this field, you don't play on it."

We're going to miss our excellent first baseman when the baseball season starts, David. Leo Horan says he will try to fill your place, but he knows that it will be a stiff assignment.

Please write and tell us about your new school. We'll be glad to hear from you.

Your old pal,

Ralph Lees

Note that the *heading* includes the address of the writer and the date. It is usually written on three lines and in block form as in the model letter. We may omit the address if we are writing to a person who knows it very well, but we never omit the date.

The heading is written slightly to the right of the center of the paper, about an inch from the top. If the letter is extremely short, the heading may be lowered. Every word begins with a capital letter and no abbreviations are used. There are two commas: one separates the city and zone number from the state and the other separates the day of the month from the year.

The *salutation* is the greeting at the beginning of the letter. It is written at the left-hand margin of the paper, below the heading and is followed by a comma. The first word and the name of the person to whom we are writing begin with capital letters, but such words as *dear* and *dearest* are not capitalized unless they are the first words. The type of salutation depends upon the relationship between the writer of the letter and the person to whom it is written.

In the *body* of the letter we deliver our message. This may take the form of a friendly conversation, an invitation, a request for information, an expression of gratitude, or a combination of a number of these forms. Whenever we introduce a new subject, we must begin a new paragraph. The first word of every paragraph is indented.

The *complimentary close* ends the letter; it is our word of farewell. The words used for a complimentary close depend upon the degree of intimacy between the writer and the recipient of the letter. The first word of the closing is written directly under the first word of the heading. Only the first word is capitalized. The complimentary close is followed by a comma.

The *signature* is the name of the person who is writing the letter. When we are writing to relatives or close friends, we use only our first name. If the person to whom we are writing does not know us well, we sign our full name. The signature is begun under the first word of the complimentary close and should line up with it.

The illustrations in this chapter trace the history of letter writing, from the time of the Egyptians to the distribution of mail in a modern post office.

Appearance of Letters

Since our letter represents us and we are frequently judged by it, we should be careful of its appearance as well as of the contents. Our letter makes a good impression if we select a good quality of white stationery, use black

or blue ink, and write clearly and neatly. If the paper is in folded sheets, the folded edge should be at the left of the letter. The margin at the left should also be slightly wider than the margin at the right of the paper.

When we have finished writing we fold the lower half over the upper half and place it in the envelope with the crease at the bottom. If we should happen to use a rather large single sheet of paper, sometimes called typewriter paper, the lower half should be folded over the upper half until it almost reaches the top. Then the double thickness of paper is folded in thirds, the right side first and the left side over the right. Put the letter into the envelope with the folded edge down.

Addressing the Envelope

The envelope should contain the full name and address of the person to whom the letter is being sent. We usually begin writing the name just above the center of the envelope and slightly to the left of center. This is the first line on the envelope. On the second line we write the street address, on the third line the city and the zone number, if any, and on the fourth line the name of the state. Some persons write the name of the city, the zone number, and the state on the same line, but postal authorities prefer a separate line for the state. It is customary to write our own address, the return address, in the upper left-hand corner.

CLASS ASSIGNMENT

1. Write each of the following addresses and dates in the proper form for the heading of a letter:

1. Portsmouth, New Hampshire, 31 Saratoga Way, September 12, 19....

2. June 27, 19...., 6333 Herbert Street, Detroit 10, Michigan

3. Shamrock Hotel, May 3, 19...., Houston 3, Texas

4. 252 East Twelfth Street, February 10, 19...., St. Paul 1, Minnesota

5. May 22, 19...., Winston-Salem, North Carolina, 44 Mozart Street

6. 2219 Forest Avenue, October 26, 19...., Cleveland 23, Ohio

2. Write a salutation for a letter addressed to each of the following persons:

1. Your father	6. Your parish priest
2. A classmate	7. An aunt
3. Your teacher	8. Your grandparents
4. Your cousin	9. Mrs. Dormer
5. A dear friend	10. Your sister

3. Write the following sentences in the form of a letter. Supply the missing parts, use capital letters as they are needed, and paragraph the letter properly:

your delightful letter and the picture you enclosed were a real joy to me. how happy you all look in your new surroundings! we can hardly believe that paul has grown so tall and that little susan is walking now. last week my mother decided that my present wardrobe was inadequate because i have added several inches to my height since you moved. a shopping expedition has made me the proud possessor of a forest-green gabardine suit, two lovely dresses, and the kind of purse that i have wanted for a long time. of course there had to be several skirts and blouses too. you would like one of my skirts, maryanne. it is a gay plaid with glass buttons on the side. i found a plaid ribbon to match and before i started this letter my sister rose helped me make a few hair bows. your proposed trip to mexico sounds very exciting. i do hope your dad can arrange it. keep a diary, maryanne, for i shall want to know everything you see and do.

4. Match the following salutations and complimentary closings. Rewrite, capitalizing and punctuating each one correctly:

SALUTATION   COMPLIMENTARY CLOSE

1. reverend and dear father schmidt   your loving son
2. dear aunt lucy   respectfully yours
3. mother dear   affectionately yours
4. dear sister cecilia   your devoted friend
5. my dear jane   your pupil

5. Write the following names and addresses as they should be written on envelopes. Use your own return address:

1. Miss Helen Love, 2820 West Fourth Street, Phoenix 10, Arizona
2. Mr. John Conners, 4823 Webster Street, Omaha 3, Nebraska
3. Mrs. Thomas Campbell, 4218 North Hermitage Avenue, Chicago 28, Illinois
4. Miss Sheila Kane, 903 East Woodin Road, Dallas 16, Texas
5. Dr. Henry Nash, 2510 Elsinor Avenue, Baltimore 33, Maryland

6. Write a letter to your mother telling her about your experiences at camp.

Invitations

Letters of invitation may be formal or informal. Those to a close friend are informal. They should make the recipient feel that he is being invited because he is really wanted. Invitations must give complete information about the date, the time, the place, and the nature of the party or the gathering.

Model: A Letter of Invitation

1714 Ritner Street
Ogden, Utah
April 28, 19....

Dear Elizabeth,

Are you in the mood for a few days in the mountains? Mother said that I may invite four girls to our cottage at Wildwood for the week end of May fifth and I want you to be one of them.

I've started to plan the fun we'll have riding the trails and bathing in the lake. Of course the skating rink will be on our list for Saturday night.

Daddy is driving up on Friday evening and there will be ample room in the car for all of us. If you can join us, we shall call for you about seven o'clock.

Your friend,
Joan

When we receive such an invitation we are, of course, very eager to accept it. We should reply without delay and show our appreciation. In a letter of acceptance we repeat the occasion, the date, the time, and the place.

Model: A Letter of Acceptance

5601 Moulton Street
Ogden, Utah
April 30, 19....

Dear Joan,

What fun it will be to go to the mountains for a week end! Of course I accept your invitation.

Have no fears about Friday evening, May fifth, at seven o'clock. I'll be waiting, bag packed, at the front door. My only worry is that Friday won't come soon enough.

I am looking forward to a very enjoyable week end.

Gratefully yours,
Elizabeth

If we are not able to accept an invitation, we must send our regrets. It is always courteous to mention our reasons for declining the invitation.

> 401 Lindley Avenue
> Ogden, Utah
> April 30, 19....

Dear Joan,

How sad I am, for much to my regret I shall not be able to spend the week end of May fifth with you at Wildwood.

My parents have accepted an invitation to a dinner party on Saturday evening and I must take care of the twins. Mother and Daddy had made all their plans before I received your invitation and had assumed that I would be here to take care of Ruth and Mary. It is so seldom they are able to go out that I do not want to disappoint them.

Thank your father for his offer to drive me to your cottage.

> Your loving friend,
> Judith

A letter inviting a prominent man or woman to speak at an assembly program would be more formal than the model letter of invitation on page 134. All letters, however, should be cordial and courteous, and should make the person feel that his presence is really desired. Invitations always contain complete information; they mention the date, the time, the place, and the occasion.

"Thank-You" Letters

The well-bred person always says "Thank you" for any gift or favor. The letter need not be long, but it should be friendly and sincere and express our pleasure and appreciation. We must learn to be prompt in expressing our gratitude to those who have been kind to us.

MODEL: A "THANK-YOU" LETTER

> 4620 Concord Lane
> Geneva, Wisconsin
> November 5, 19....

Dear Mrs. Doyle,

Nothing you could do for my father would have pleased him more than to have enrolled him in the Purgatorial Society. The spiritual benefits he will receive are innumerable, and it is a great comfort to my dear mother to have him so thoughtfully remembered by those who knew him.

Dad counted you and Mr. Doyle among his dearest friends. You have given proof of your friendship again. We are all grateful to you for your kind thought.

> Sincerely yours,
> Mary Ellen Ryan

The letter of appreciation that a person writes after enjoying a visit is sometimes called a "bread-and-butter" letter. It should be written as soon as we return home.

MODEL: A "BREAD-AND-BUTTER" LETTER

816 Walnut Street
Hartford 6, Connecticut
March 12, 19....

Dear Mrs. Cray,

How can I ever thank you sufficiently for such a pleasant day as yesterday? Mother claims I even talked about it in my sleep last night!

The trip to Radio City was a delightful experience, and the visit to Mother Cabrini's shrine was most impressive. Indeed, the entire day, from the moment we set foot in New York until we boarded the train for Hartford, was a real joy.

I want you to know that I am very grateful to you for inviting me to share this memorable experience with Jeanne. I am sure we shall never forget our first visit to New York.

Affectionately yours,
Patricia Dacey

CLASS ASSIGNMENT

1. Criticize the following letter of invitation. Is it cordial and sincere? Does it contain all the necessary information? Are all the parts of the letter correctly arranged?

> 1615 Main Street
> Des Moines 2, Iowa
> November 12, 19....

Dear Ronald,

Thanksgiving holidays are only two weeks away. It will add greatly to my fun to have you spend your vacation with me. Will you do that?

I promise you a perfect week end. We'll cheer Campion to victory over Smedley in their annual game. We'll go skating on the lake if the weather remains cold. We may even have time to explore that old cave down by the creek. Doesn't that sound like an exciting program?

Come on Wednesday, November twenty-fourth, if that is possible. Dad will gladly drive down to the station to meet you if you let me know at what time you expect to arrive. Please do not disappoint me.

> Your pal,
>
> Vincent Runti

2. Write a reply to the invitation in the first assignment. The class may be divided into two groups, one of which will write a letter of acceptance and the other group a letter of regret.

3. Copy the following in letter form. Paragraph it properly and use the correct punctuation and capitalization:

807 woodland avenue lincoln 7 nebraska october 15 19.... dear mr mylotte thank you very much for recommending me for membership in the swimming club i know i dont deserve all the complimentary remarks you made about me but i shall do my very best to measure up to them mr wilson the instructor told me about your calling him and i want you to know that i am grateful for your interest respectfully yours harold boles

4. Write a letter to your aunt and uncle, thanking them for a week end in the country.

5. Thank a friend for a book he gave you and tell him how much you enjoyed reading it.

6. In your city there are undoubtedly many persons who could give interesting talks on various subjects. Pretend that you are the chairman of the program committee of the Catholic Action Club. Write a letter inviting some noted person to address your group. Do not forget to tell him or her the date, the time, and the place where the meeting will be held. You must also mention the subject that you wish to have discussed.

7. Write a letter to a relative (your grandfather, your aunt, or a cousin) in which you thank him for a present you received.

Other Social Letters

Courtesy requires us to sympathize with a sorrowing friend and to congratulate those who have earned some special honor. A letter of condolence should be brief, kind, and simple.

MODEL: A LETTER OF SYMPATHY

> 305 Sixth Avenue
> Buffalo 16, New York
> January 4, 19....

Dear Kathleen,

It is difficult for me to express in words the sorrow I felt on learning of the death of your mother. You have lost your dearest treasure and I have been deprived of a very kind and loving friend. How pleasant she always made my visits to your home!

Father Morley will offer a Mass next Saturday for the repose of her soul, and I shall pray both for her and for you.

May our Blessed Lady comfort you in your loss and be a true Mother to you.

> Your devoted friend,
> Helene

MODEL: A LETTER OF CONGRATULATION

1615 Fulton Street
Peoria 19, Illinois
June 5, 19....

Dear Paul,

Congratulations on the honor you received at graduation! I knew you would continue to lead your class.

May your high-school days be as successful as the years spent in Saint Peter School. With your love for knowledge and books, I am sure that you will make very good use of your talents at Saint Joseph High School.

Your chum,
Austin Hart

A letter is sometimes written to introduce one of our friends to another friend who has similar interests. Such a letter should include the reason for the introduction and also make clear why we expect our friends to enjoy each other's company.

MODEL: A LETTER OF INTRODUCTION

8515 Florissant Road
St. Louis 42, Missouri
October 11, 19....

Dear Albert,

Next week a friend of mine, Ralph Daly, is moving to Chicago. He will attend Saint Gregory School and I would like him to feel that he has a friend there waiting for him.

He was quarterback on our football team and plays a good game of basketball. Besides that, he has a stamp collection that I know will interest you.

Please give him a welcome, Albert, for my sake. When you know Ralph better you'll like him for himself.

Your old pal,
George Weber

CLASS ASSIGNMENT

1. Write a letter of condolence to a classmate whose father has died.

2. Read the following letter of congratulation and then answer the letter:

750 Cathedral Street
Elkton, Maryland
June 2, 19....

Dear Clare,

Is there room for one more voice in the chorus of congratulations? I was overjoyed when Mother told me you had called announcing the good news. Imagine winning a full four-year scholarship! I know now why you asked me for the extra prayers last month.

Perhaps when you are given the folder from the academy you will let us see where you expect to receive your high-school education. I can hardly wait to find out all about Villa Maria. I shall indeed be proud to claim one of its students as my cousin.

Affectionately,
Eileen

3. Show your good sportsmanship by writing a letter of congratulation to the captain of a rival team that won a victory over your team.

4. Write a letter to your cousin in Savannah, Georgia, introducing a friend who is moving to that city.

2. Business Letters

Business letters should be brief, courteous, and clear. The form of a business letter is very similar to that of a social letter. It does, however, contain one part that is not found in a social letter. This part is the inside address.

MODEL: A BUSINESS LETTER

Heading	Saint Francis Xavier School
	2324 Green Street
	Philadelphia 39, Pennsylvania
	September 10, 19....
Inside address	Keystone Automobile Association
	220 South Broad Street
	Philadelphia 2, Pennsylvania
Salutation	Gentlemen:

Body

It is the wish of our pastor, Reverend Joseph T. Lyons, that a safety squad be organized in Saint Francis Xavier School during the coming semester.

Will you kindly send a representative to the eighth-grade classroom to give us the necessary directions for this step and to aid us in establishing the patrol? Please let us know the date on which we may expect your agent.

We thank you for your cooperation and prompt attention to this matter.

Complimentary close	Very truly yours,
Signature	John Billow

A business letter contains six parts:

1. THE HEADING. This is the same as the heading of a social letter.

2. THE INSIDE ADDRESS. This is the one part of a business letter that is not found in a social letter. It consists of the complete name and address of the person or the firm to whom the letter is written. The inside address is written at the left-hand margin of the page above the salutation. The style should be the same as that of the heading, which is usually in block form.

> 607 Lincoln Drive
> Dubuque, Iowa
> January 20, 19....

Loyola University Press
3441 North Ashland Avenue
Chicago 13, Illinois

3. THE SALUTATION. The salutation, or greeting, is more formal than in a social letter. It is usually followed by a colon.

Dear Sir:	Dear Ladies:	Dear Mr. Kane:
Gentlemen:	Dear Madam:	Dear Mrs. Moynihan:

4. THE BODY. The body of the letter contains the message. The message must be courteous, clear, accurate, and brief. Since a letter is our representative before a business firm, we should endeavor to be courteous in our manner and to be clear and accurate in our statements. The importance of brevity in a business letter cannot be overemphasized. The reader should be able to pick out of our letter all the needed information as quickly as possible.

5. THE COMPLIMENTARY CLOSE. The complimentary close is also more formal in a business letter. It consists of

a short phrase indicating respect for the person addressed in the letter and is followed by a comma.

Yours truly,   Yours respectfully,   Yours sincerely,
Very truly yours,   Respectfully yours,   Yours very truly,

6. THE SIGNATURE. The signature of a business letter contains the full name of the writer.

        John Collins   Mary Mayer

3. Kinds of Business Letters

There are many types of business letters. They differ very much from one another in content and purpose. For the present we shall study only those types which students in school have occasion to write.

Letters Placing Orders

Accuracy and clearness are essential to letters in which we order merchandise. We must state the exact quantity, quality, size, and color of the goods, and we should tell how the package is to be shipped and how payment is to be made.

MODEL: A LETTER PLACING AN ORDER

Saint Lucy School
332 Summer Street
Boston 11, Massachusetts
September 7, 19....

Franciscan Guild Studio
Thirty-second Street and Seventh Avenue
New York 3, New York

Gentlemen:

Enclosed you will find a postal money order for $8.25. Please send by parcel post the following books:

"Running Waters," by Covelle Newcomb............$3.25
"Champlain," by Louise Hall Tharp.......................... 2.50
"American Saint," by Mabel Farnum....................... 2.50
$8.25

As we plan to enlarge our school library in the near future, please include a copy of your latest book catalogue.

Respectfully yours,
Cecilia Mullen

The following simple rules will remind us of the essential features that should be included in all business letters containing orders for goods:

1. Describe each article accurately. State size, color, brand, quality, and so forth.

2. Order by catalogue number if possible.

3. State the exact quantity desired.

4. State the price, if known.

5. Give explicit shipping directions, as parcel post, express, freight.

6. Mention method of payment. It may be by money order, check, or collect on delivery (C.O.D.).

CLASS ASSIGNMENT

1. Criticize the following letter. Does it have all the requirements of a good business letter?

> 1027 Superior Avenue
> Cleveland 14, Ohio
> November 22, 19....

E. M. Lohmann Company
413 Sibley Street
St. Paul 1, Minnesota
Gentlemen:

Please send by express the ivory-and-gold statue of Our Lady of Grace listed in your catalogue as S-214. I enclose a check for eight dollars ($8.00), the amount specified in your price list.

> Yours very truly,
> Adelaide Jefferys

2. Complete the following order, supplying all necessary details:

Maryknoll, New York

Dear Father Chin:

Please send me a year's subscription to the *Field Afar*.

> Robert Gill

3. Write a letter to Montgomery Ward and Company, 618 West Chicago Avenue, Chicago 10, Illinois, ordering any three of the following articles:

    1 tennis racket, No. 6H 1229, $3.59
    1 tennis cap, No. 6H 1259, size 7, $.50
    3 tennis balls, No. 6H 1231, $.40 each
    1 baseball, No. 6H 1607, $.89
    1 baseball bat, No. 6H 01740, $1.56
    1 catcher's mitt, No. 6H 1643, $4.48

Add shipping directions and method of payment. Use your own address and signature.

4. Write a letter subscribing to a well-known Catholic magazine.

Letters of Application

Frequently employers demand a letter of application as a means of deciding upon the ability of a prospective employee. In such a letter we may apply for a specific position, or the letter may be one applying for employment of any kind. A letter of application should be brief, clear, and courteous.

MODEL: A LETTER OF APPLICATION

> 561 Boston Avenue
> Bridgeport 14, Connecticut
> May 4, 19....

Mr. David Merenda
1430 Elmtree Road
Bridgeport 16, Connecticut
Dear Mr. Merenda:

In today's *Morning Herald* you advertise for an office boy. I should like to be considered an applicant for this position.

I am fourteen years old and am in the eighth grade of Loyola School. Our school closes on June 7 and reopens on September 5.

For information about my character I refer you to Reverend Benjamin Kiernan, 650 Peace Street. Since September I have delivered circulars for Ward and Nelson Company.

I shall be glad to call at any time for a personal interview. My telephone number is Main 1903.

> Very truly yours,
>
> George Misnack

Learn the following six rules concerning letters of application. They will help you to write a letter that makes a good impression on any business firm.

1. Mention the position for which you are applying.

2. State briefly your qualifications for the position, particularly your age and education.

3. Mention your experience, if any, in the type of work being offered.

4. Include the names of persons who will vouch for your character and fitness for the work.

5. Arrange for a personal interview.

6. Give your telephone number.

CLASS ASSIGNMENT

1. Study this letter of application and then answer the questions that follow:

> 250 Lake Avenue
> Milwaukee 20, Wisconsin
> November 6, 19....

Mrs. James Meehan
684 Flower Street
Milwaukee 8, Wisconsin

Dear Mrs. Meehan:

Yesterday I learned from Mrs. Sheeran that you wish to secure a young girl to stay with your little daughter on Saturday evenings. I should like to apply for the position.

I am thirteen years old and a pupil in the eighth grade at Sacred Heart School. I have had some experience in this kind of work, as I cared for a number of children in our neighborhood during the past half year.

Besides Mrs. Sheeran, I refer you to Sister Vincenza, principal of Sacred Heart School.

If you are interested in my application, I shall be glad to call at your home at any time convenient to you. My telephone number is Juniper 2-8771.

> Yours respectfully,
> Margaret Cook

1. Does this letter give the prospective employer definite information about the writer?

2. Is the letter clear, correct, and courteous?

3. Have all the necessary items for a letter of application been included?

4. Do you think that Mrs. Meehan would like to interview Margaret? Give reasons for your answers.

2. Write in correct form the following letter. The punctuation and capitalization must be added. Use your own name and address, and the present date:

miss terese platzer librarian of childrens department goshen public library goshen indiana dear miss platzer please consider me an applicant for the position of assistant librarian advertised in todays *sentinel* i am fourteen years old and am in the eighth grade of saint stanislaus school i have held a library card for five years and i possess two certificates issued by the vacation club for references i have permission to name the principal of our school sister rosarita and my teacher sister regina anne very truly yours

3. Write a letter of application in answer to one of the following advertisements:

1. BAGGAGE BOY. Large railroad company desires young boy to help in baggage room. Must be strong and dependable. Write American Storage Co., 412 N. Wells St.

2. BOY to work after school in machine shop. Should have elementary knowledge of automobile parts. State age. H. Neeham, 1728 Main St.

3. YOUNG GIRL to accompany family to seashore as mother's helper; two children. Mrs. Walter Murphy, 130 N. Carol Blvd.

4. GIRL to help fold circulars after school and on Saturday. Apply Mayfair Printing Co., 1056 W. Van Buren St.

Reporting Errors

Most of our orders are filled promptly and accurately. At some time, however, we may have to write a letter reporting some error or delay. Such a letter should be courteous, and we should explain in detail the type of error made and what action we wish the business firm to take.

Model: A Letter Reporting an Error

Holy Name School
137 Locust Avenue
Spokane 2, Washington
October 11, 19....

Enley Sport Shop
932 North Tacoma Street
Tacoma 9, Washington

Dear Sir:

On October 2 I ordered one dozen blue-and-white football jerseys. The blue-and-gold ones which arrived today are not satisfactory substitutes, since our school colors are blue and white.

I am returning these jerseys collect. Kindly send the colors ordered as soon as possible. Our opening game is on October 19.

Very truly yours,
William Leahy

Letters of Inquiry and Request

A letter may be written when we desire some information or request some favor. In a letter of this type we explain our difficulty or our request as accurately as possible. We usually include a stamped, self-addressed envelope for the reply.

MODEL: A LETTER OF REQUEST

Resurrection School
Dayton 7, Ohio
January 3, 19....

Mr. Michael Boyd
George A. Pflaum Company
124 East Third Street
Dayton 2, Ohio
Dear Sir:

Our history class is now studying the work of the Catholic press. In connection with this subject we should like very much to see a Catholic publication in the making. May we visit your publishing house some afternoon during the next two weeks?

There are thirty-eight pupils in our class. We know that your staff could give us much valuable information and show us many interesting steps in printing. If you can grant our request, please notify us what day will be most convenient for you.

Respectfully yours,
Dorothy Rothusin
(Secretary)

CLASS ASSIGNMENT

1. Paragraph the following letter correctly and insert all capitals and punctuation. Supply the heading, inside address, salutation, complimentary close, and signature:

i regret to state that the television set which you recently installed in our home has not been giving satisfaction it has been almost impossible for us to tune in clearly on two local stations i have no doubt that the defect is due to one of those minor imperfections or mistakes which even the best firms cannot always avoid kindly send a repair man to make the necessary adjustments you may prefer to notify the manufacturer that the television is not giving satisfaction and have him replace it.

2. A bicycle which you ordered from one of your local stores was damaged and one of the cotton web straps was missing when it was delivered. Write a letter to the firm reporting these defects.

3. You are planning to spend your vacation at Camp Leo, 2679 Yale Station, New Haven 10, Connecticut. Write to Reverend Edwin Grimes, making a reservation for the two weeks beginning August 1. Ask for the rates and a list of required supplies.

4. The bill which you received from a local merchant includes $1.19 for a photograph album that you returned. Write a letter asking him to correct the bill.

5. One month ago you ordered from the Bruce Publishing Company, 208 Montgomery Building, Milwaukee 1, Wisconsin, *The Glowing Lily,* by Eugenia Markowa. Write a letter inquiring why you did not receive the book.

6. Write to your local librarian, asking her to address your class sometime during Book Week.

7. Write to Station KDKA, Grant Building, Pittsburgh 2, Pennsylvania, requesting permission to visit the studio.

Letters by Telegraph

On occasions that require special speed we send telegrams. These messages travel by wire and are delivered to the recipient within a short space of time. The telegraph company makes a specific charge for ten words and an extra charge for each additional word. For this reason telegrams are usually brief.

Occasions that may require telegrams are a sudden change of plans, notice to distant members of sickness in the family, cancellation or change of an order sent by mail. It is also customary to send telegrams of congratulation upon such occasions as birthdays, weddings, graduations, and the like.

The telegraph company also sends day letters and night letters. These travel at a slower rate of speed, but the charge is lower.

MODEL: A TELEGRAM

LOS ANGELES CALIF OCTOBER 30 19....

MRS MARY MILES

PRATT LANE APARTMENTS CHICAGO ILL

MOTHER LEFT HOSPITAL TODAY STOP WILL RETURN ON CHIEF NOVEMBER EIGHTH—

MARJORIE

CLASS ASSIGNMENT

Reduce each of the following statements to a ten-word telegraph message:

1. I am sorry that a previous engagement prevents my addressing the coming meeting of the Cue and Curtain Club.

2. Our lease expires in two days. We would be grateful if you could secure an apartment for us somewhere in your vicinity.

3. I have secured an excellent bargain in a used station wagon. Would you be interested in it?

4. We had a slight accident with the car. Our start will be delayed. Probably we'll arrive early on Tuesday evening.

5. I missed my train connections at New York. I'm coming by bus. I shall arrive at Union Terminal at five o'clock on Thursday evening.

6. Mother is very ill. She was taken to the hospital today. Come home immediately.

4. Choral Speaking

The poems we learn for choral speaking and the progress made by our group frequently offer interesting topics for letter writing.

TUNING-UP EXERCISES

Breathing:

Inhale, hold breath for ten counts, exhale with *ah.* Do this five times, each time in a different pitch.

Tone:

Practice saying *m* in medium, high, low pitch. Repeat it in singing tone.

Pronounce with accent on *m* and *n* and *ing:*

moaning   groaning

Practice *toning, loaning* in the same manner. These two exercises will give resonance, hence carrying power to the voice.

Enunciation:

Repeat the following words with the long simple sound *aw:* law, saw, awe, jaw, crawl, fawn, naught.

Nonsense jingle spoken in unison:

See saw, Marjory Daw
On the lawn in the dawn.

CROSSING THE BAR

By Alfred Lord Tennyson

Medium Voices

Sunset \ and evening star, //
   And one clear call for me! //
And may there be no moaning of the bar, //
   When I \ put out to sea, //

Heavy Voices

But such \ a tide as moving seems asleep, //
   Too full for sound \ and foam, //
When that which drew from out the boundless deep //
   Turns \ again home. //

Light Voices

Twilight \ and evening bell, //
   And after that the dark! //
And may there be no sadness of farewell, //
   When I embark; //

Unison

For though from out our bourne of Time and Place //
   The flood / may bear me far, //
I hope to see my Pilot / face to face //
   When I \ have crossed the bar. //

STUDY OF THE POEM

This is a lyric poem. It is like a song in which the poet tells how he feels about death.

Death is a voyage on which the poet sets out. At the entrance to many harbors there is a sandbar which the vessel must pass before it sails out into the open sea. Across the sandbar of the harbor of life the vessel of our soul must pass, piloted by God Himself, when it sets sail for the unknown sea of eternity. At the end of the voyage, however, the poet is sure he will see his pilot, Christ, face to face. Hence he does not wish anyone to mourn for him, nor even to say good-by.

Preparing for Choral Speaking

1. Read the poem over very carefully.

2. Note the descriptions of nature, the sunset, the evening star, the full tide, the twilight. Sunset on earth is the end of day—like life's sunset. The clear call is the summons of death; the twilight and the dark are the closing in of death. In the end trust in God, who is the hope of every soul, expresses itself in the desire to see God when the journey is ended.

3. Look up the meanings of any unfamiliar words in the dictionary.

4. After three readings the class may read the poem in unison aloud.

5. The tone should be soft and low in pitch. Why? The time should be slow. Why?

6. As the class progresses, let the medium voices take Stanza 1, the heavy voices Stanza 2, and the light voices Stanza 3, the last stanza being said in unison. The concluding two lines should be richer and fuller in tone, with rising pitch and quicker time.

TREES

By Joyce Kilmer

Unison

I think ╱ that I shall never see
A poem ╲ lovely as a tree. ╱╱

Medium Voices

A tree whose hungry mouth ╱ is prest
Against the earth's ╱ sweet ╱ flowing breast; ╱╱

Light Voices

A tree that looks at God ╱╱ all day, ╱╱
And lifts her leafy arms to pray; ╱╱

Unison

A tree that may in Summer ╲ wear
A nest of robins ╲ in her hair; ╱╱

Heavy Voices

Upon whose bosom snow ╲ has lain; ╱╱
Who intimately lives with rain. ╱╱

Unison

Poems ╲ are made by fools like me, ╱╱
But only God ╱╱ can make ╱ a tree. ╱╱

STUDY OF THE POEM

Analyze the different thoughts in the couplets, or two rhyming lines. Three seasons of the year are clearly represented in the poem. Quote the lines which describe these different seasons. What picture does the whole poem bring to your mind?

Because of its unity of thought, the poem is really for unison speaking. The different couplets (two lines), however, give different pictures of the tree, and may be read by groups. The first, fourth, and last couplets should be read by the entire choir.

5. Chapter Challenge

1. .... letters are letters that we write to friends and relatives.

2. The heading of a letter is usually written on .... lines. It includes the .... and the ....

3. The two commas in the heading of a letter separate the .... from the .... and the .... from the ....

4. We never use .... in the heading of a letter.

5. The salutation or .... is written at the .... margin of the paper. The .... and the .... begin with capital letters.

6. The body of a social letter usually contains several ....

7. The first word of the .... should line up with the first word of the heading, and the .... is written under the first word of the ....

8. Our letter makes a good impression if we use a good quality of ...., ... or .... ink, and write .... and ....

9. The envelope contains the .... and the
.... of the person to whom the letter is being
sent and our ....

10. Invitations should contain complete information
about the ...., the ...., the ....,
and the ....

11. A "bread-and-butter" letter is one that a person
writes ....

12. That part of a business letter that is not found in a
social letter is called the ....

13. In a letter of application we should: (1) Mention
the position for which we .... (2) State our
.... as to age and education briefly. (3) Mention any .... we may have had. (4) Include the
names of persons who will vouch for our ....
and .... for the work. (5) Arrange for an
.... (6) Give our ....
....

14. We may send .... in place of letters on
occasions when special speed is required.

CHAPTER SIX Living Life
through Books

*In which we learn to evaluate books
and to take our part in forums*

To live life through books we must learn to enjoy books, especially those written by Catholic authors. Holy Mother Church is the mother of learning. She has safeguarded the best in knowledge and culture and transmitted it to her children as a precious heritage. Shall we not, then, learn to read books intelligently, since they will teach us to live life so fully?

1. Sharing Books with Others

After we have read an interesting book we like to talk about the characters in the book or the incidents that stirred our imaginations. If we talk to those older than ourselves, they help us to form judgments about characters and events. It always gives us pleasure to recommend good books to our companions or our younger brothers and sisters and persuade them to read worth-while and wholesome stories.

Advertising Books

The book reviews that we read in magazines and newspapers often arouse our interest in a particular book or books. We might say that a review advertises a book, for it tells what impression the book has made on one reader and lets us know the type of story that we will find in the book. Book advertisements promote the sale and the reading of books.

We, too, can advertise books. They need not be new books, but they should be books that we have found interesting. Our advertisement should let our classmates know the impression the book has made on us. It should not reveal the entire story, but should give just enough information about the plot and the characters to enable others to decide whether they would like to read such a book.

Model: A Book Advertisement

Kenny never wanted anything so much as he wanted Flicka. She finally became his, even though the attempt nearly cost them both their lives. How he "gentled" the beautiful filly and won her lifelong friendship makes a tale that no animal lover will want to miss. Read the unforgettable story of a boy and his horse in *My Friend Flicka,* by Mary O'Hara.

CLASS ASSIGNMENT

1. Read the following advertisement and answer the questions that follow:

Lad was a handsome mahogany-and-white collie, a thoroughbred in body and spirit. True to his instincts and training, he would spring instantly to the aid of the defenseless, more than once endangering his own life to save others. Although justly feared by any intruder on the premises of his master, he was always gracious to guests and even submitted patiently to their attentions. If you like dogs, you'll like Lad. Albert Payson Terhune tells about his many adventures in *Lad, a Dog*.

1. Does this advertisement give you an idea of what the book is about?

2. Does it reveal the plot of the story?

3. Does it "sell" the book to you?

2. Read the following book review. What type of book would you expect *White House Gang* to be?

The "White House gang" was the terror of every Washington official. Led by Quentin, President Roosevelt's son, the gang managed to make life exciting for themselves and for everyone they encountered. Needless to say, they were brought to justice more than once. The presiding officer at the court was none other than Theodore Roosevelt. Kindly and understanding, he dealt with the boys in a manner that won their everlasting admiration. Earle Looker reveals many daring adventures in *White House Gang,* for he himself was once a very active member of the gang.

3. Write an advertisement for some outstanding book written by a Catholic author. The following list may prove helpful: *Mangled Hands,* by Neil Boyton; *Start of the Trail,* by Louise Dickinson Rich; *Cortez, the Conqueror,* by Covelle Newcomb; *Pius XII, Rock of Peace,* by Lottie Helen Lenn and Mary A. Reardon; *The Bells of Heaven,* by Christopher Bick; *Princess Poverty,* by Sara Maynard; *Bernadette, Maid of Lourdes,* by Frances P. Keyes; *Heaven on Thursday,* by M. K. Richardson.

Book Reports

A good way to remember the books we have read is to write a report on each. There is no definite instruction for writing a book report. The following suggestions may prove helpful:

1. Read the book carefully, keeping a notebook close at hand to jot down what you will want to remember.

2. Pay particular attention to the characters, the setting, and the author's style. Record your impressions while they are fresh in your mind.

3. In your report include: the title of the book; the author; the type; the principal characters; a brief summary of the main events of the story; your personal reaction.

MODEL: A BOOK REPORT

TITLE: *The Knight of the Bow*

AUTHOR: James L. Meagher

TYPE: Adventure

CHARACTERS: Edmund of Dorchester; Rauol, his friend; Henry Baker, his servant; Estelle, Rauol's sister

SUMMARY: This is the story of young Edmund of Dorchester, who helps us relive the thrilling adventures of knights in armor. Imitating the Christlike teachings of his mother, Edmund first wins our admiration by his goodness to his villeins. As the story unfolds, it is packed with one daring feat after another: a skillful maneuvering of a boat in the whirling waters of the flooding Thames, an escape from murder, a rescue of a king from a would-be assassin, and an encounter with a renegade knight. The excitement reaches its peak as Edmund succeeds in carrying a secret message to Rome.

MY REACTION: Edmund's dauntless courage, his sense of justice, his straightforwardness and honesty, and above all his ambition to please and serve God filled me with desire to imitate his virtues.

CLASS ASSIGNMENT

1. Read the following book report and discuss it in your class-room:

TITLE: *Calico Bush*

AUTHOR: Rachel Field

TYPE: Fiction

CHARACTERS: Marguerite Ladoux, the Sargent family

SUMMARY: An English family accompanied by Maggie, their "bound-out girl," were traveling westward to make a new home for themselves in Indian territory. The quick thinking and fearless action of the little servant maid more than once saved the group from disaster. Indeed, the family became so dependent on her resourcefulness that Marguerite, faced with the opportunity of returning to her own country, decided to remain with these people whom she had grown to love.

MY REACTION: The author's portrayal of life on the frontier made me wish that I had lived in pioneer times and faced the dangers of Indian skirmishes in a frontier settlement. It also made me realize that a girl may make herself useful in any age and that she will meet many situations which require as much courage as was shown by the little heroine of bygone days.

2. Interest your classmates in people of other countries by making a book report on one of the following: *Singing Tree,* by Kate Seredy; *City Set on a Hill,* by James Van der Veldt; *Happy Times in Norway,* by Sigrid Undset; *Trumpeter of Krakow,* by Eric Kelly; *Adventures of Don Quixote de la Mancha,* by Cervantes; *Cottage at Bantry Bay,* by Hilda Van Stockum; *Wings over Central America,* by Pachita Crespi; *Empty Tower,* by Jean Bothwell; *At the Palace Gates,* by Helen Rand Parish; *When a Cobbler Ruled the King,* by Augusta H. Seaman; *Masha, a Little Russian Girl,* by Sonia Mazer; *King Richard's Squire,* by Regina Kelly; *Girl Who Ruled a Kingdom,* by Charlotte Kellogg; *Lost Baron,* by Allen French; *Jacques the Goatherd,* by Maribelle Cormack and William P. Alexander; *Lake of Gold,* by John Buchan; *Hope Hacienda,* by Charlotte Baker.

3. Divide the class into groups. Let each group prepare a report on one of the following types of books: fiction, biography, travel, adventure, science.

Book Characters

In almost every story we read, one or two characters stand out more prominently than any of the others. When we know and like a friend very much we want others to meet him. Our book friends should be no exception. We like to have our classmates become acquainted with these friends and share their adventures as we have done.

MODEL: TWO BOOK CHARACTERS

(Ichabod Crane and Brom Bones from "The Legend of Sleepy Hollow")

Among the villagers of Sleepy Hollow there was hardly a young man whom Katrina Van Tassel could not number among her admirers. One by one they drifted away, however, leaving in the field of battle only Ichabod Crane, the gawky schoolmaster, and Brom Bones, the burly prankster of the village.

Ichabod was a ladies' man; he petted their children, rocked their cradles, and carried the latest gossip to their tea parties. He loved Katrina almost as much as he loved her father's wealth, and nothing stirred his affection for her so much as the sight of her mother's well-stocked pantry shelves. Although he was practical enough where his future welfare was concerned, Ichabod was a firm believer in the neighborhood tales of witchcraft.

Brom Bones, on the other hand, was a favorite among the young men of the town. His daring, adventurous spirit was admired in the village. He was a man of good humor and great strength, an excellent horseman, and the settler of all the disputes. If the Van Tassel possessions interested him, he gave no evidence of it. Perhaps it was this very show of indifference that gave him the victory over his rival, for it was Brom Bones who won the hand of Katrina Van Tassel.

CLASS ASSIGNMENT

1. Plan and write a character sketch of one of the following types of persons that you have met in your reading:

1. A peculiar character
2. An adventurous character
3. An unusual character
4. A mysterious character
5. A mischievous character
6. An amusing character
7. Your favorite character
8. The most outstanding character
9. An exciting character
10. A ridiculous character

2. Describe two contrasting characters from one of the books you have read recently. Tell why you consider the characters interesting.

Relating Incidents

Do we remember stories because of the people we have met in them or because some particular incident appealed to us? We may wish to tell our classmates of this incident and relive it with them. We should try to imitate the author in relating the incident, making it so vivid that we "sell" the book to our audience.

MODEL: THE BLACK SPOT

(An incident from *Treasure Island,* by Robert Louis Stevenson)

Treasure Island is a story of buried treasure, pirates, and adventure told by Jim Hawkins, a young boy living in England in the eighteenth century. This is his story of the black spot:

The blind man, who had so rudely gripped my arm when I offered to give him the directions he desired, now commanded that I take him to the captain. He clung to me, twitching my arm to show the punishment he would inflict upon me if I refused to obey his command.

We approached the parlor where the captain sat. In a trembling voice I announced that a visitor was with me. The poor captain quickly raised his eyes, which became filled with horror when he saw my blind companion. Was it a ghost or something evil that

stood before him? Deftly the sightless one passed something into the captain's hand, and then with incredible sureness of step he left the room.

The captain glanced sharply at the palm of his hand and quickly read the two words inscribed there. He sprang to his feet, swayed, and with a peculiar sound fell to the floor. The black spot had struck; he was dead.

CLASS ASSIGNMENT

1. Have you ever read *Treasure Island?* If so, describe another incident from this exciting novel.

2. Relate an interesting incident from any one of the following books: *Rose in Bloom,* by Louisa M. Alcott; *Covered Wagon,* by Emerson Hough; *Ramona,* by Helen Hunt Jackson; *Ships That Made U.S. History,* by Helen Mitchell and W. N. Wilson; *Royal Road,* by Charlie May Simon; *Chestry Oak,* by Kate Seredy; *Gold Prospector,* by William Marshall Rush; *Catcher from Double-A,* by Duane Decker; *Red Eagle, Buffalo Bill's Adopted Son,* by Mabel O'Moran; *Fire Patrol,* by Dickson Reynolds; *North Winds Blow Free,* by Elizabeth Howard; *Buckey O'Neill of Arizona,* by Jeanette Eaton; *Angelique,* by Gertrude Crown-

field; *Hidden Treasure of Glaston,* by Eleanore Myers Jewett; *South Pole Husky,* by Charles S. Strong; *Meg's Fortune,* by Gladys Malvern.

The Dictionary

One of the most valuable books that we own, and one which we treasure throughout our lifetime, is the dictionary. In this book we find not only the meaning of a word, but also its derivation and pronunciation. We likewise learn the parts of speech of words, the plural forms of nouns, the principal parts of verbs, and in many cases synonyms and antonyms. The English dictionary is a very valuable reference book.

CLASS ASSIGNMENT

1. Look up the following words in the dictionary. Tell the part of speech of each word, pronounce it, and give a synonym:

hostility	alter	force	salary
idle	repentance	vary	dismal
habit	stain	genial	contemplate
occupation	prophesy	digest	transparent

2. Without changing the meaning of the sentence, substitute another word or group of words for each of the italicized words in the following sentences:

1. Firemen *display* unusual heroism in time of danger.

2. The flower *display* attracted visitors from every section of the city.

3. The saints are noted for their absolute *trust* in God.

4. Mr. Sullivan, the president of a famous oil *trust,* addressed the student body yesterday.

5. In this cove we will be *secure* from the storm.

6. The enemy will *secure* troops for a surprise attack.

7. The aged monarch looked sadly upon the disloyal *subject.*

8. What is the *subject* of your discussion?

9. The Ten Commandments teach us the *right* way to live.
10. The man's *right* to the fortune was disputed.
11. Will you be kind enough to *post* these letters?
12. Thomas painted the *post* a vivid green.

3. The following words have more than one meaning and more than one pronunciation. Use each word in two sentences and tell how it is pronounced in each:

ferment	object	imprint	extract
compress	convict	console	insert
rebel	progress	attribute	transport

4. Find the language or languages from which each of the following words is borrowed:

papoose	biography	junior	vanilla
mattress	macaroni	cipher	tea
brunette	calisthenics	cotton	amen
balcony	cretonne	yacht	kindergarten
canyon	mosquito	piano	sonnet

5. What is the origin of each of these words?

curfew	volcano	calico	tally
tantalize	boycott	ampere	mentor
macadam	saxophone	bedlam	puritanical

2. Open Forums

What is a forum? In ancient Rome the Forum was the place of public assembly, and in it the people gathered to discuss their common affairs.

The Forums of America

In our own day, and particularly in the United States, the word *forum* or *open forum* has come to mean a meeting at which people express their opinions on some subject of interest to all and endeavor to arrive at the solution of a problem. How can we best preserve democracy in Amer-

ica? What should be our relations with other countries
of the world? In what ways should the government help
the people, and what should it refrain from doing? How
should our schools be conducted? These are but a few of
the problems that confront us.

If our nation is to use its wonderful resources as it
should, such problems ought not to be left to a few legis-
lators in Washington. All the people should understand
them, be interested in them, and have ideas concerning
them. Forums are being held constantly everywhere, and
our leaders encourage them. Before many years we shall
either take part in open forums or become citizens who are
unable or afraid to express ourselves and who permit other
persons, perhaps those who are not good and intelligent,
to shape public opinion.

The open-forum method of discussion has many advantages. Perhaps the most important is training in leadership, in parliamentary procedure, and in the formation of opinion. The subject for discussion at a forum should be timely. It should be a subject that has to do with one of the problems of our everyday life.

Book Forums

The book forum is an open discussion of books or of one particular book. In preparing for a book forum we should read the book carefully and then analyze it to discover why we like or dislike it.

The book to be discussed in an open forum should be assigned at least one week in advance of the meeting, so that all the students may be well informed. The chairman may appoint several pupils to make the principal speeches and assign a particular topic to each pupil.

On the appointed day the following procedures are usually adopted:

1. The chairman calls the meeting to order and announces the topic for discussion. He then calls upon one particular pupil or upon all the pupils to express their opinions concerning the book.

2. Each speaker rises, addresses the chair, and waits to be recognized; that is, given the floor.

3. After several speakers have expressed their opinions the chairman calls for a general discussion. Those present may ask questions of the chairman or the speakers. The questions are answered from the floor. Individuals in the audience may also express their own opinions or give additional information.

4. In matters where there may be differences of opinion on the part of the students, questions may be asked of the teacher or the sponsor of the program.

5. The forum is closed by the chairman when the time allotted for the forum has ended, or the discussion may be closed by a motion from the floor.

Preparing a Discussion

If the chairman has asked us to discuss some particular aspect of a novel, a poem, or a play, we should plan our speech carefully. We may ask ourselves such questions as "Why do I like or dislike this book?" "Which characters do I admire in this book?"

The speech that we make in the book forum should have three parts:

BEGINNING: An interesting introduction that mentions the title of the story, the poem, or the play, and the name of the author.

MIDDLE: A reason or reasons why we like or dislike the plot, the characters, or the theme of the book.

ENDING: A good, forceful conclusion.

MODEL: WHY I LIKE "ALL-STARS OF CHRIST"

American boys and girls are thoroughly familiar with all-star football and baseball teams. In a collection of absorbing biographies Robert G. North, S.J., offers for our enjoyment and inspiration his "team" of fifteen spiritual heroes. The title of the book is *All-Stars of Christ*.

This book is the perfect answer to those who seek variety in their reading. Time and distance are no obstacle to the author. He leads us at an exciting pace back and forth across the pages of history. Whether he is telling the story of Saint Sebastian in the third century or of Charlie Kenny in the twentieth, there is never a dull moment. At an unbelievable rate of speed we race across the world. A mere flip of the page transports us from the burning sands of Africa's deserts to the Notre Dame football stadium at South Bend, Indiana. Courage, adventure, and holiness stride hand in hand through each chapter.

No two stories are alike, and yet all fifteen are fundamentally the same. The time, the place, the characters, the circumstances differ, but one familiar theme runs throughout the book. From cover to cover each fascinating sketch tells the story of a boy who loved Christ and proved that love by leading an honest, clean, generous life; in other words, by being an "all-star of Christ."

The chairman calls on the other speakers in turn. In their talks they may state their reasons for liking or disliking some of the biographies in *All-Stars of Christ*. The discussion is then thrown open to the entire group. The chairman usually has a few leading questions to ask.

MODEL: GENERAL DISCUSSION IN A BOOK FORUM

CHAIRMAN. Which of the stories in *All-Stars of Christ* did you like best, George?

GEORGE. I liked the account of Herman, the helpless cripple of Reichenau. In spite of his great physical handicap, he maintained a cheerful disposition, never expressing the slightest self-pity.

NORMAN. Joseph Eckert showed that same happy resignation to God's will. He was obliged to leave the seminary to enter the army. He longed for the peaceful life he had shared with his fellow religious, yet up to the time of his death he accepted the situation as coming from the hand of God.

ANTHONY. Maybe I'm prejudiced because of his first name, but my favorite was Anthony Molle-Lazo. He gave his life while defending a convent in Spain. Anthony's courage was certainly inspiring to me.

CHAIRMAN. What about the girls' reactions to this book? Does a collection of boys' lives appeal to you, Regina?

REGINA. Yes, indeed. I was reluctant to read the book at first, but once I started it, I was captivated. Perhaps it's because I found the first story, that of Saint Sebastian, so interesting.

THERESA. I liked best the chapter that related the life of Joe Sullivan. Being an ardent Notre Dame fan, I enjoyed reading about this outstanding Catholic football hero. His plan was to mix sports with sanctity, a practice that any ordinary boy or girl could adopt.

CHAIRMAN. Yes, Theresa, and that can truly be said of all the stories. These boys led lives that can be imitated as well as admired. I am sorry to report that the time allotted for this discussion has ended. Let us close with a prayer that we may become "all-stars" of Christ.

CLASS ASSIGNMENT

1. The following is an opening speech in a book forum. The topic introduced by the chairman was "Why I Like *The Adventures of Tom Sawyer*." Appoint one pupil to act as the chairman

and other pupils to report on some of the adventures found in this book:

The joy and worry of Aunt Polly's life was her adventurous young nephew, Tom Sawyer, the son of her deceased brother. The small village of St. Petersburg could tell many exciting tales of this barefoot mischief. The hero of Mark Twain's book, *The Adventures of Tom Sawyer,* often bribed his way out of work he dreaded by bets and promises; his favorite pet was a pinchbug, which was often loosed during Sunday school. Tom's favorite pastime was playing pirate with Huckleberry Finn, a motherless waif who usually slept under the stars.

The Adventures of Tom Sawyer makes lively reading. The characters of Tom and Huckleberry are permanent pictures in the gallery of American stories. Lovable and real, the two capture the reader's heart, for though they are the plague of Aunt Polly's life, they represent the "eternal boy."

2. Conduct a book forum in your classroom. Any of the following topics could be discussed:

1. The story of Clara Barton is the inspiration of many nurses.

2. Boys and girls should be familiar with stories of children of other lands.

3. Most of us never grow too old for fairy tales.

4. *The Trumpeter of Krakow* symbolizes the courage of the Polish nation.

5. Lou Gehrig's story appeals to every American boy.

3. Creative Dramatics

Creative dramatics is a group activity in which students, using their own words, dramatize a story that has been read. By its very nature creative dramatics implies a creative act; that is, we must understand and interpret the story and supply the words and the actions that we think would be those of the characters in the story. In creative dramatics we do not write any words nor adopt stiff, formal manners. The actors may use any words they choose provided they follow the thought of the characters and keep the plot of the story unchanged.

Let us see how we may dramatize "The Man without a Country," by Edward Everett Hale.

Preparation

We would first read the story carefully, trying to visualize the events in terms of action. Drama always represents struggle, the characters being in a conflict of some kind, either mental or physical. In "The Man without a Country" the principal character, Philip Nolan, is under suspicion of treason. Having been found guilty, he is sentenced to life imprisonment on one ship after another, and the wish that he expressed at his trial is carried out.

Which parts of the story would make good scenes because they are filled with action? Let us take the first part of the story, the court-martial of Lieutenant Nolan. The text tells us the scene is the office of the judge (Colonel Morgan) at Fort Adams.

In a trial scene the principal characters are the judge, the defendant, and minor characters such as guards, witnesses, and the sergeant at arms. If the trial is a military one, the captain and other officers would probably be present also.

We can select the following characters, therefore, in the order of their appearance:

The judge, seated at a table or desk as the scene opens
The jury, usually twelve persons, seated at the right of the judge
The sergeant at arms, the errand boy of the judge
The guards
Philip Nolan, the defendant

Action and Dialogue

Having decided upon the setting and the characters, we must consider the actions which make up a court-martial, and at the same time we must begin to think in terms of dialogue. The following suggestions will help to prepare the necessary actions and dialogue for "The Man without a Country."

1. The judge calls for the prisoner. Whom does he send? The sergeant at arms. "Sergeant, call the prisoner." The sergeant answers, "Yes, Your Honor" as he salutes his superior officer and wheels off to the right.

2. The prisoner is brought into the court by the captain of the guards and is questioned by the judge. "What is your name, sir?" Nolan answers, "Philip Nolan, Your Honor, of the Legion of the West."

3. What is the next step or action in any trial? The accusation. How does the author word the accusation? Put it into your own words. How would Nolan answer? "Yes, Your Honor." Consult the text again. The author says that the judge gave the reason for Burr's using Nolan. Nolan would naturally defend Burr. The judge would rightly call him to order. How? By one word, "Silence!" or a similar expression.

4. The judge gives Nolan a chance to defend himself. Does Nolan offer any excuse? What is his answer? Here use the exact words of the author, not only because they bring the scene to a climax, or the highest point of interest, but because these words have become classic: "Damn the United States! I hope I may never see nor hear of her again!" The officers present rise in defense of their country's honor; the judge is white with anger. What is the

next move? The case is given to the jury. The men return almost immediately with the verdict.

5. What is the next action? Since the trial is over, the court is adjourned by the words of the judge, "The court is adjourned without day" (that is, without a special day set for future meeting).

The scene is now ready to be *walked through* by the group, or in other words, to be put into action. A table or a desk and chairs are the only properties needed.

Begin to act at once. The class may choose those who are to take the parts of the different characters. The words will come readily enough if the actors absorb the story and live the characters. The teacher may make suggestions where needed. The members of the class not taking part in the dramatization may judge the production:

Did it cover the story?

Was the dialogue or conversation natural?

How could the action have been made still more vivid and impressive?

CLASS ASSIGNMENT

1. Dramatize in your classroom the court scene from "The Man without a Country."

2. Dramatize the first scene from the poem "Evangeline." The setting is the great kitchen in the house of Evangeline in Grand Pré, early one evening in November. The characters are Evangeline, her father, the notary, Gabriel Lejeunesse, and his father Basil. Evangeline and her father talk of her coming marriage with Gabriel. The notary, René Leblanc, comes to draw up the contract of marriage. Shortly after, Gabriel and his father arrive and the ceremony of betrothal takes place. The two old men then play their game of chess in the firelight, leaving Gabriel and his future

bride to talk over their happiness. Soon nine solemn strokes from the belfry announce the hour of curfew, the signal for all good Acadians to be in bed. Gabriel and his father depart, leaving Evangeline and Benedict alone. The illustration may suggest groupings for the betrothal scene.

3. Dramatize a scene from the life of Saint Francis Xavier, Saint Thomas of Canterbury, or any other hero of our Church.

4. Writing an Original Dramatization

We may sometimes like to prepare dramatizations in a more finished manner and to keep permanent records of them. One class worked out three scenes from "The Singing Leaves," by James Russell Lowell. Scene 1 took place in the throne room of the king. Scene 2 was the mart, three days later; Scene 3, the castle gate at sunset.

The original poem written by James Russell Lowell may be found at the end of the chapter on page 184. Read this carefully before studying the dramatization.

MODEL: DRAMATIZATION OF "THE SINGING LEAVES"

SCENE 1

PLACE: The throne room of the king

TIME: Early one sunny morning in spring

CHARACTERS: The king, Walter the Page, a servant,[1] Elizabeth, Marie, Anne

(The king is seated on his throne as the curtains part and the play begins. Walter the Page is standing beside him. A servant is at the left, waiting the king's pleasure.)

KING. Bid my daughters come to me.

SERVANT. Yes, my Lord. *(Servant exits.)*

KING. Do you wish to come with me to Vanity Fair, Walter?

WALTER. I shall be honored, Your Majesty. *(The servant enters. He goes to the throne, escorting the daughters. When the three princesses are standing before the throne, the servant bows and withdraws to the side of the throne.)*

KING. My daughters, come near. Today I go to Vanity Fair.

DAUGHTERS. Oh Father! Father! Father! *(They clasp their hands in delight.)*

KING. Elizabeth, what gift shall I bring you on my return?

ELIZABETH *(bowing)*. My Father, I should like smooth pearls, gold rings, and beautiful diamonds that will sparkle on my fingers.

KING. You desire worth-while gifts, my daughter. You shall have your jewels. *(Turning to the second daughter)* Marie, what shall I bring you from Vanity Fair?

MARIE. I should like silks that stand alone, and a gold comb to shine in my black hair.

KING *(smiling)*. You, too, wish well, my daughter. *(Turning to the youngest daughter)* And now, Anne, it is your turn.

ANNE. My Father, last night as I lay awake, I heard a bird singing in my bower eaves. I thought it sang: "Ask for the Singing Leaves!" Therefore, dear Father, will you bring me the Singing Leaves?

---

[1] The servant is a new character added by the pupils for convenience.

KING *(red with anger)*. My daughter, how foolish! You are like a peasant girl binding wheat into sheaves, rather than the equal of your fine sisters. *(Suddenly he sees the girl's resemblance to her dear mother.)* Alas, I can refuse you nothing! You remind me so much of my dear dead wife—your mother. *(He pauses to gain calm.)* You shall have your Singing Leaves. Now, let me see: pearls, diamonds, gold rings for Elizabeth; stiff silks and a gold comb for Marie; and the Singing Leaves for Anne. *(He turns to Walter the Page.)* See that I do not forget, page. *(He rises.)* My daughters must have their gifts. I am ready to depart now, my dears. You shall have your gifts on my return. *(The king goes to the door with Walter the Page.)*

DAUGHTERS *(following)*. Good-by, dear Father, good-by!

Evaluating the Dramatization

After the play has been written, we will wish to select pupils in our classroom to play the characters. Perhaps two or three groups of actors will be chosen to portray each scene. Do not forget that cooperation and teamwork are necessary for a successful dramatization.

The following test will help determine whether the pupils have profited by the dramatization:

1. Did the class really understand the story or the poem on which the play was based?

2. Was the script well written? Did the characters tell the story in their own words?

3. Were there good and helpful class discussions on the staging of the play?

4. Did the pupils selected to play the characters in the story live their parts?

5. Was the class honest and fair in criticizing its own work, and were the proper steps taken to insure better work in the future?

CLASS ASSIGNMENT

1. Write the dramatizations of the second and the third scenes from "The Singing Leaves." The second scene may be laid in the market or in the forest.

2. Present the drama at a club meeting or an assembly program. The scenes may be played in the classroom without either scenery or costumes. Elaborately done as to settings and costumes, the drama makes excellent entertainment.

3. Read the rules and suggestions for ballad acting on pages 189-90. After the poem has been memorized by the verse-speaking choir, present the ballad as suggested.

5. Choral Speaking

Let us now extend our work in creative dramatics to include ballad acting. The tuning-up exercises will improve our enunciation and enrich our tone of voice.

TUNING-UP EXERCISES

Breathing:

Inhale, hold your breath for ten counts, exhale with sound of *t*.

Enunciation:

Strive for a clean *t*. Place the tip of the tongue back of the teeth. Use this phrase for practice for placing the voice in front of the mouth:

Tat-tat-tattoo

tat-tat-tattoo

Say this rhyme with special attention to crisp final *t*'s:

NIGHT BLESSING

Good night!
Sleep tight;
Wake up bright
In the morning light
To do what's right
With all your might.

Say these sentences with the lips only. Have certain members guess what is said:

The moo cow moos.
Spink, spank, spink.
Greedy gray gossoons.
Ding, dong, dell.
Brown donkeys yawn "He, haw!"
Sea shells shone on the seashore.

Ballad Acting

A ballad is a poem like the stories which minstrels used to sing to the king and his court at table to the accompaniment of the harp. One of the most famous ballads is "The Singing Leaves," by James Russell Lowell. This is an old-world story written in verse form.

Each stanza of a ballad consists of four lines, the second and fourth lines rhyming. In the old ballads one always finds special numbers used. In "The Singing Leaves" there are three daughters, the king rides for three days and three nights, and the Princess Anne brings her husband three earldoms.

THE SINGING LEAVES

By James Russell Lowell

I

King	"What fairings will ye that I bring?" //
Right	Said the King \ to his daughters three; //
King	"For I to Vanity Fair \ am bound, //
	Now say \ what shall they be?" //
Left	Then up and spake the eldest daughter,
	The lady tall and grand: //
Eldest	"Oh, bring me pearls \ and diamonds / great, //
Daughter	And gold rings \ for my hand." //

Right	Thereafter spake the second daughter, That was both white \ and red: //

Second
  Daughter
	"For me \ bring silks \ that will stand alone, //
	   And a gold comb \ for my head." //

Left	Then came the turn of the least daughter,
	   That was whiter than thistle-down, //
	And among the gold of her blithesome hair //
	   Dim \ shone the golden crown. //

Anne	"There came a bird this morning, //
	   And sang \ 'neath my bower eaves, //
	Till I dreamed, \ as his music \ made me,
	   'Ask thou for the Singing Leaves!' " //

Right	Then the brow \ of the King swelled crimson With a flush of angry scorn: //
King	"Well \ have ye spoken, my two eldest, And chosen \ as ye were born; //
King	"But she, \ like a thing of peasant \ race, That is happy binding the sheaves." //
Left	Then he saw her dear mother in her face, // And said, "Thou shalt have thy leaves." //

II

Right He mounted \ and rode / three days \ and nights, //
Till he came to Vanity Fair, //
And 'twas easy \ to buy the gems \ and the silk, //
But no Singing Leaves \ were there. //

Left Then deep in the greenwood \ rode he,
And asked of every tree, //
King "Oh, if you have ever a Singing Leaf, //
I pray you give \ it to me!" //

Right But the trees all kept their counsel, //
And never a word \ said they, //
Only there sighed from the pine-tops
A music of seas \ far away. //

Left Only the pattering aspen \
Made a sound of growing rain, //
That fell ever faster \ and faster, //
Then faltered to silence \ again. //

King "Oh, where shall I find a little foot-page
That would win both hose \ and shoon, //
And will bring to me the Singing Leaves //
If they grow under the moon?" //

Right Then lightly turned him Walter the Page, //
By the stirrup as he ran: //
Walter "Now pledge \ me the truesome word
Of a king \ and gentleman, //

Walter "That you will give the first, \ first / thing
You meet at your castle-gate, //
And the Princess shall get the Singing Leaves, //
Or mine \ be a traitor's \ fate." //

Left The King's head dropped upon his breast
A moment, \ as it might be; //

King   " 'Twill be my dog," \

Right   he thought, and said, //

King   "My faith I plight to thee." //

Left   Then Walter took from next his heart
            A packet small and thin, //

Walter   "Now give you this \ to the Princess Anne, //
            The Singing Leaves \ are therein." //

III

Right   As the King rode in at his castle-gate, //
            A maiden to meet him ran, //

Anne   And "Welcome, father!" //

Right   she laughed and cried
            Together, \ the Princess Anne. //

King   "Lo, here \ the Singing Leaves," //

Left   quoth he, //

King   "And woe, \ but they cost me dear!" //

Left   She took the packet, \ and the smile,
            Deepened down \ beneath the tear. //

Right   It deepened down till it reached her heart, //
            And then gushed up / again, //
     And lighted her tears \ as the sudden sun
            Transfigures the summer rain. //

Left   And the first Leaf, when it was opened
            Sang: //

Solo   "I am Walter the Page, //
     And the songs I sing 'neath thy window
            Are my only heritage." //

Right   And the second / Leaf sang: //

Solo   "But in the land
            That is neither on land \ nor sea, //
     My lute \ and I / are lords of more
            Than thrice \ this kingdom's fee." //

Right	And the third Leaf \ sang, //
Solo	"Be mine! Be mine!"
Left	And ever it sang, //
Solo	"Be mine!"
Left	Then sweeter it sang and ever sweeter,
	And said: "I am thine, / thine, \ thine!" //
Right	At the first \ Leaf she grew pale enough, //
	At the second \ she turned aside, //
	At the third, \ 'twas as if a lily \ flushed
	With a rose's \ red heart's tide. //
Anne	"Good counsel \ gave the bird," said she, //
	"I have my hope \ thrice \ o'er, //
	For they sing to my very heart," //
Left	she said,
Anne	"And it sings to them \ evermore." //
Both Sides	She \ brought to him her beauty \ and truth, //
	But and broad earldoms \ three, //
	And he \ made her queen of the broader lands //
	He held of his lute \ in fee. //

STUDY OF THE POEM

Read the poem over carefully. Why did the eldest daughter ask the king for pearls and diamonds and gold rings? Was her sister like her when she asked for silks that "stand alone"? Why did the Princess Anne want only the "Singing Leaves"? Did the king remain angry with the Princess Anne for long? Why?

How did the king obtain the gems and the silk? Explain the sentence "The trees all kept their counsel." Did Walter the Page expect a reward for giving the Singing Leaves? Did the leaves sing to the Princess Anne? What was the princess' marriage portion? What was the wealth of Walter the Page?

The Lesson

The lesson in the story of "The Singing Leaves" is this: Material things, gems and silk and gold, do not satisfy hearts that are made for higher things. The Singing Leaves represent the love of Walter the Page for the Princess Anne. Love is the force back of all good. God is love. Out of love He created the world and every person in the world. He wants us to love Him during our brief life on earth, and eternally in heaven. Love is greater than any material gift whatsoever, no matter how splendid or costly that gift may be. It comes straight from God Himself and has no other purpose than man's happiness here on earth and hereafter in heaven.

Steps in Ballad Acting

1. Have the group read the poem together, the single parts being taken by individual speakers.

2. Assign different parts of the narrative or story to be said by the right chorus and the left chorus.

3. Set the scenes and act the ballad. The individual speakers are the principal actors, the members of the chorus serving as narrators and accompanists. The different scenes may be managed with a traverse curtain; that is, a curtain traveling on a pulley across the middle of the stage. You may also use a chorus curtain; that is, a curtain formed by members of the chorus.

Scene 1. A room in the palace *(in front of the curtain)*.

Scene 2. The mart or market *(behind the curtain at right)*.

Scene 3. The forest *(behind the curtain at extreme left, actors walking left at the words, "Then deep in the greenwood")*.

Scene 4. The gate *(again in front of the curtain, the princess coming from the left and the king and Walter from the right)*.

Ballad acting is not the same as play acting. The success of many plays depends largely on ornate settings and striking costumes. In ballad acting, however, there is no elaborate staging nor lighting. There is simply the action and the grouping, with a chorus filling in the thoughts back of the words and serving as an accompaniment. Ballad acting employs physical expression (action, movement) to reinforce verbal expression (the words). The verses of a ballad and the story they tell are important. Everything else serves as a background. The author of the ballad wastes no time in description or explanation. The story is told rapidly, in a simple and direct manner. The choral performance should be undertaken in the same fashion. Simplicity of presentation is necessary if the spirit of the ballad is to be preserved.

6. Chapter Challenge

1. .... often arouse our interest in a particular book or books.

2. In a book advertisement we give only enough information about the .... and .... to enable others to decide whether they would like to read the book.

3. A book report should include: (1) the .... of the book; (2) the ....; (3) the ....; (4) the principal ....; (5) a brief .... of the story; (6) your personal ....

4. If we wish to know from what language a word comes or what its origin is, we consult the ....

5. The .... was the place of public assembly in ancient Rome.

6. A meeting at which people express their opinions on some subject of interest is often called a ....

7. In .... discussions we obtain training in ...., in .... procedure, and in the formation of ....

8. Many pupils may discuss a book in a ....

9. In creative dramatics the actors may use any words they choose provided they follow the thought of the .... and keep the .... of the story unchanged.

10. The principal character in "The Man without a Country" is ....

11. .... wrote "The Singing Leaves."

12. A poem similar to the stories which minstrels used to sing to the king and his court at table to the accompaniment of the harp is called a ....

CHAPTER SEVEN

Workshop
for Future Citizens

*In which we learn how to take part in
panel discussions and debates*

As good Catholic citizens we wish to be able to express
our opinions intelligently and to influence others. Our
classroom is a workshop in which we practice many of the
forms of speaking that we shall use in future years.

1. Panel Discussions

Panel is a term in law referring to an official list of persons summoned for jury duty or a group of persons appointed for some service, as an advisory panel. In a panel
discussion a given number of appointed speakers discuss a
question from different viewpoints or present several as-
pects of some problem. After these speeches have been
given there is an open forum, during which the chairman
does everything possible to obtain expressions of opinion
from the audience. Thus both speakers and audience participate in panel discussions.

Choosing the Participants

A chairman is elected by the class or appointed by the
teacher. He should be an interested student, one who is
capable of handling a group and who knows the rules of
parliamentary procedure. He prepares himself for the
panel by studying the subject carefully to see what phases

or topics it presents. The chairman, moreover, should cultivate a good delivery and a clear voice, pitched to reach the farthest person in the audience. His tone should be friendly so that he encourages others to voice their opinions. Above all, he should be unfailingly courteous.

From four to eight is the usual number of speakers for a panel discussion. They, too, are chosen by the method usually followed in the class. The speakers should be given their topics well in advance of the day set for the presentation of the panel. Each speaker studies the entire subject and gathers material on the topic he is to discuss. He must also be prepared to answer any questions.

Procedure

The chairman opens the discussion by a brief address explaining the subject in general. He then introduces each speaker in turn, stating the phase of the subject which he is to discuss. For the panel discussion the speakers are arranged in a semicircle or around a table, with the chairman in the center of the group. In a classroom the chairman might sit at the desk in the front of the room, the speakers on either side. The chairman remains seated during the discussions of the individual speakers.

MODEL: A PANEL DISCUSSION ON PAN-AMERICANISM

CHAIRMAN *(standing)*. The subject for discussion this afternoon is pan-Americanism. By this we mean cooperation among the republics of North and South America in political and economic matters. The subject has been divided into the following topics:

1. Origin of the term pan-Americanism
2. Leaders in the promotion of pan-Americanism
3. Countries included in the Pan-American Union
4. What Americans can do to promote the good-neighbor policy

5. The part of the Catholic Church in pan-Americanism
6. Accomplishments of the last Inter-American Conference

Philip Connors will begin our discussion with a talk on the origin of pan-Americanism. Philip Connors.

PHILIP *(rising and bowing to the chairman)*. Thank you, Mr. Chairman. It may surprise many of you to know that as early as 1826 the great South American patriot, Simón Bolívar, called a conference of American republics to meet in Panama.

(Philip continues his speech on the origin of the term pan-Americanism and is followed by other speakers in turn. The chairman thanks each speaker and makes some appropriate comment.)

CHAIRMAN. Thank you, Blanche Thompson, for telling us about the countries represented in the Pan-American Union. We shall now hear from Dennis Maher, who will tell us what we can do to promote the good-neighbor policy.

DENNIS *(rising)*. Daily improvements in sea and air transportation and the tremendous growth of international trade have served to emphasize the fact that America is not an island outpost of civilization. Indeed, America lies at the heart of the modern world and hence Americans cannot escape the consequences of their location or their responsibilities toward one another.

Real friendship and cooperation with our Latin-American neighbors is not only desirable but essential for the welfare of all. We in the United States must remember that America was discovered and colonized by Spain. Her territory once extended from California to the southern tip of South America. The United States was only a thin strip of territory on the Atlantic coast. Then our nation began to grow. Many former Latin-American colonies became part of the United States.

We in the United States can truly boast of our heritage. We must not blind ourselves, however, to the fact that another's heritage may be equally glorious. The culture of the people to the south is of Spanish and Portuguese origin. It is not at all like that with which we are familiar. We must learn to understand and appreciate the traditions and ideals of these southern neighbors.

Differences in customs and beliefs have always bred suspicion and distrust. A firm and permanent friendship with our Latin-American neighbors must be built upon respect and appreciation. A knowledge of the language cannot be too strongly recommended as a means to better understanding.

In addition to this, we must be absolutely fair in our commercial relationships with these people. In past times they have felt that they were being exploited by the United States. Our leaders have worked hard to overcome this attitude, which has now been replaced by the good-neighbor policy. The United States has made many trade agreements with the Latin-American republics. Tariffs have been lowered and loans have been made to develop natural resources. Following these practices, we shall show the world that all the twenty-one republics of the Americas are enthusiastic believers in the American way of life.

Enlivening the Discussion

Should the chairman feel that interest in the discussion is flagging, he may remind the audience of a statement made by a given speaker which may be challenged later in the open forum; or he himself may be the best example of unflagging interest by his posture, his manner, and his facial expression.

When all the speakers have delivered their main speeches, the chairman again takes up the role of leader. He gives each member of the panel an opportunity to ask questions or to explain some point in his speech which may not have been understood.

CHAIRMAN. Catherine, do you care to ask any questions?

CATHERINE. Mr. Chairman, I should like to ask Dennis Maher to explain how the culture of our southern neighbors differs from ours.

(The speaker answers the question if he can, or expresses regret if he is unable to answer. Catherine thanks him courteously for his explanation.)

It is well to remember that the purpose of a panel discussion is not to solve a problem, but to give a better understanding of different phases of a subject.

The open forum at the end admits the audience to the discussion. As in club procedure, the speaker from the floor must first address the chairman, as "Mr. Chairman, Mary Ellen Dormer." No pupil is permitted to speak from the floor a second time until every member of the class has had a chance to speak. A summary of the discussion is given by the chairman at the end of the panel.

CLASS ASSIGNMENT

1. Select any one of the following subjects and hold a panel discussion in your class:

1. The pioneers in America braved many dangers and hardships to extend civilization westward. The topics that may be developed by the members of the panel are: (1) Difficulties of transportation, (2) Hardships of clearing land and building homes, (3) Prob-

lems of farming on unfamiliar soil, (4) Struggles with hostile Indians, (5) Deficiencies in frontier governments, (6) Difficulties in providing schools for the education of children.

2. Our health can be vastly improved through systematic hygienic living. Possible topics for this subject are: (1) Proper food furnishes brain and nerves with pure blood. (2) Fresh air keeps up active circulation. (3) Sunshine and rest invigorate and stimulate the body. (4) Sleep enables the nervous system to regain its strength. (5) Recreation quiets the brain and the nerves. (6) Exercise improves the appetite and stimulates digestion.

3. The history of aviation can be traced back into the remote past. (1) Attempts of Pythagoras and ancient Greeks, (2) Attempts during Nero's Roman holidays, (3) Ideas on flying depicted in Leonardo da Vinci's sketchbook, (4) Gliding experiments during the sixteenth and seventeenth centuries, (5) Langley's attempt with a small monoplane in 1896, (6) Orville and Wilbur Wright's successful flight in 1903.

4. Man's progress in the field of medicine is largely due to the efforts of patient, persistent men. (1) Dr. Edward Jenner discovered vaccination for smallpox. (2) Louis Pasteur made outstanding researches and discoveries in the field of bacteriology. (3) Sir Joseph Lister introduced antiseptics into surgery. (4) Dr. Edward Trudeau taught the proper method of preventing tuberculosis. (5) Major Walter Reed fought the scourge of yellow fever on the island of Cuba. (6) Colonel Gorgas' strenuous labors made Panama a healthful place in which to live.

5. Our conservation policy has greatly aided the preservation of our natural resources. (1) Important natural resources, (2) Need for conservation in the United States, (3) Leaders in the conservation movement, (4) The forest ranger, (5) Great conservation projects—Boulder Dam, Roosevelt Dam, (6) The farmer's part in the conservation movement.

2. Make a list of the different topics that might be treated in panel discussions of the following subjects:

1. Educational opportunities of today
2. Improvement of radio programs

3. Courtesy in everyday life
4. Transportation today and yesterday
5. Seven Lady days
6. Our trade with European countries
7. Edison's great contributions to science
8. Vocations for boys and girls

2. Formal Debates

The value of debating in the classroom cannot be over-estimated. It satisfies the love of argument which is innate in every human being, to a greater or a less degree. It develops sportsmanship. It vitalizes the ordinary class-room routine by arousing interest and stimulating and clarifying thought. Most important of all, it prepares students for life, giving them the power to convince and win others to their opinions.

The Debaters

In every debate there are two teams of two or three members each. One team, the *affirmative*, upholds the truth of the proposition to be debated. The other team, the *negative*, seeks to disprove the proposition. A chairman opens the debate by announcing the subject of the debate. The proposition is always stated clearly and concisely in the form of a sentence. It must be a proposition that is debatable, a question on which there may be differences of opinion. The chairman introduces each speaker in turn. He may also serve as timekeeper.

The members of each team study the proposition and decide upon the reasons that they will use to defend or disprove the proposition. An outline is very helpful when preparing for a debate.

Model: A Debate Outline

PROPOSITION: Examinations should be discontinued in the elementary schools.

AFFIRMATIVE

1. A teacher knows her class well enough to give grades without examinations.

2. Examinations are not a true indication of a pupil's ability because they place pupils under a strain.

3. Neither the teacher nor her pupils derive any lasting benefit from examinations.

NEGATIVE

1. *Examinations provide the teacher with a concrete basis for determining the grades she gives her pupils.*

2. *Examinations give pupils who are timid about expressing themselves in class an opportunity to prove their knowledge of the subject matter.*

3. *High marks on examinations are a source of great satisfaction to those pupils who have worked diligently throughout the school year.*

Conducting the Debate

The pupils who are to take part in the debate, the chairman and those making up the affirmative and negative teams, take their places in the front of the classroom or on the stage. The affirmative team sits on one side of the chairman and the negative team on the other. The chairman rises, bows to the audience, and states the question.

Model: A Classroom Debate

CHAIRMAN. The question for debate this afternoon is "Resolved: Examinations should be discontinued in the elementary schools." The first speaker on the affirmative, Miss Rose Mayer, will begin the discussion.

(Miss Mayer rises when her name is called. The chairman says "Miss Mayer." Rose then begins her argument.)

Rose. Mr. Chairman, honorable judges, worthy opponents, students of the eighth grade: We of the affirmative believe that examinations should be discontinued in elementary schools. We will endeavor to prove our statement by the following points:

1. A teacher knows her class well enough to give grades without examinations.

2. Examinations are not a true indication of a pupil's ability because they place pupils under a strain.

3. Neither the teacher nor her pupils derive any lasting benefit from examinations.

It is my task to explain the first of these assertions: A teacher knows her class well enough to give grades without examinations.

In most schools pupils are under the care of a teacher for almost an entire year before the final examinations are scheduled. During that period she has had time to observe closely the work of the individual child. Daily recitations enable her to judge the amount of time and the attention that each pupil gives to preparing assignments. Weekly or biweekly tests assure the teacher of the student's ability to retain what he has learned. These observations form a far more reliable basis for judging a pupil's work than examinations taken only once or twice a year. For this reason I feel that examinations in elementary schools should be discontinued. I thank you.

The chairman then introduces the first speaker on the negative, who proceeds to develop his argument. He is followed by the second speaker for the affirmative side, who in turn is followed by the second speaker for the negative, and so on.

The Rebuttal

After the speeches each team is given time to prepare a rebuttal. The rebuttal is the answer to the arguments of the opposing team. One member of each team may deliver the rebuttal speech. In the rebuttal the order of the speakers is usually reversed—the negative side is presented first. The rebuttals present no new arguments, as their purpose is to refute the arguments presented.

In a debate we never refer to any of those participating by their own names. The speaker will say in the rebuttal, "My worthy opponent, the first speaker on the negative" or "My colleague, the second speaker on the affirmative." The following forms of address are used in a debate:

Mr. Chairman, for the presiding officer
My colleagues, for persons on the same team
My opponents, for persons on the opposite team
The first speaker on the affirmative, for the one who spoke first on the affirmative side.

At the end of the debate the winning side and the best debater will be selected by appointed judges or by vote of the class.

Courtesy to a Visiting Team

We may invite a team from another section of the eighth grade to take part in a debate. The chairman introduces the debate by welcoming the visiting team.

MODEL: INTRODUCTION OF A VISITING TEAM

CHAIRMAN. Before presenting the question for debate this afternoon, I wish to welcome the visiting team from Room 12. We trust that you will feel perfectly at home during your short stay in Room 11, and that this occasion may be only one of many pleasant associations. It is my pleasure to present John Brown of Room 12.

JOHN. I wish to thank the chairman for his cordial welcome. We are glad to be here, and we trust that this first debate will be the beginning of many friendly arguments.

CLASS ASSIGNMENT

1. Select one of the following propositions as the subject of a classroom debate:

1. The presidency should be limited to one term.
2. Written homework should be abolished.
3. Detention for tardy pupils should be established in our school.
4. Washington was a greater president than Lincoln.
5. Our government should own and operate radio stations.
6. Arithmetic is a more useful study than English.
7. Pupils with failures should be barred from athletic teams.
8. Our girls should be obliged to wear school uniforms.
9. Departmental work should be introduced into the eighth grade.
10. A farmer's life is harder than a doctor's life.

2. State two arguments supporting and two denying each of the following resolutions:

1. Boys have more hobbies than girls.
2. Children should be compelled to attend school until they are eighteen years of age.
3. More attention should be given to school athletics.
4. The ability to speak effectively is more important than the ability to write effectively.
5. Country life has more advantages than city life.

3. A Radio Workshop

Radio and television have become very important means of communication. Programs of all kinds may be received in our homes with the turn of a dial. The news of the election of a pope is carried in an instant by radio to the farthest parts of the earth, and millions all over the world may listen to the words of the holy father himself as he addresses all the members of the flock entrusted to him by Christ. The inauguration of a president of the United States, once witnessed by only a small percentage of our country's population, may now be seen by television viewers hundreds of miles away.

We can obtain much knowledge and enjoyment from the proper use of our radio and television receivers. We must learn, however, to evaluate the programs which are presented, being guided always by the good judgment of our elders and the high standards that have been set for us by our training in Catholic schools. We must learn to distinguish good and useful programs from those which are harmful or worthless.

Classroom Broadcasting

Radio and television programs can be made into entertaining and instructive class projects. Let us form a radio club and conduct our own broadcasts. We shall appoint a chairman to take charge of the broadcast. Acting as director, he may choose a member of the class with a very good speaking voice as the announcer.

There are many different types of programs to offer, but for this occasion we shall choose one which will inspire us with greater love for our Blessed Lady. We shall dramatize the first apparition of our Blessed Lady to the children of Fatima.

After reading the account of the first apparition we are prepared to write a radio script depicting this scene.

MODEL RADIO SCRIPT: THE FIRST APPARITION OF OUR LADY OF FATIMA

ANNOUNCER. We are in Fatima, a little out-of-the-way town in Portugal. It is the year 1917. Three peasant children, Lucia, Jacinta, and Francisco, are tending sheep in the green pasture outside the town. Reciting the rosary is the custom of all the pious people of Portugal and these youngsters claim no exception. Unschooled, uncultured, unaware of the place they are to have in God's providence, the little ones are saluting Christ's dear Mother. Their young voices are skipping over a few words, as they depend upon Mary to understand their haste to return to the playhouse they are building as they watch the sheep. Lucia, the eldest, speaks first.

LUCIA. Hurry, Francisco, with the Hail Marys. I see three beautiful stones that will be just right for the house we are building.

FRANCISCO. One is too big; we'll never be able to lift it. Besides, a storm is coming. See the flashes of lightning over there?

JACINTA. I'm afraid of lightning, Lucia. Let's go home. The sheep are afraid too. Look how they are scattering.

LUCIA. Yes, I suppose we had better try to gather the sheep. It doesn't feel like a storm, though. If it weren't for the lightning . . . Look! above the holm oak!

ANNOUNCER. A young lady of dazzling beauty appears before their timid eyes. She seems to be not many years older than Lucia. Her face, indescribably beautiful, seems sad. Her hands are reverently joined and a rosary of bright pearls hangs from them. Her snowy white dress, fastened at the neck by a golden cord, reaches to her feet. The lady speaks to the frightened children. Her tone is mild, encouraging.

LADY. Do not be afraid, children. I shall not hurt you.

LUCIA. Where do you come from?

LADY. I come from heaven.

LUCIA. Why did you leave heaven to come here?

LADY. I have special work for you children. I want you to come here the thirteenth day of each month at this time. In October I will tell you what I want you to do. Be faithful to my rosary. I will bless you if you are.

LUCIA. Will you tell us your—why she is gone. Francisco, she is not there!

FRANCISCO. Wasn't she beautiful, Lucia! I couldn't speak, I was so happy just to look at her, Jacinta. Look, Lucia, look at Jacinta. She is not moving.

LUCIA. Do not bother her, Francisco. Your little sister is still thinking about the beautiful lady.

FRANCISCO. What shall we do, Lucia?

LUCIA. Come, Jacinta. We'll gather the sheep and hurry home.

JACINTA. Do you think she will really come again, Lucia? I do so want to see her again.

LUCIA. If you say your rosary, Jacinta, as she said, I'm sure the lovely lady will come again next month.

(The children's voices fade away as they hurry home.)

CLASS ASSIGNMENT

1. Using the script given on the preceding pages, present "The First Apparition of Our Lady of Fatima" as a radio or television program in your classroom.

2. Prepare a serial broadcast dramatizing events from your history lessons. A quizmaster might be appointed. It is his duty to formulate questions on each program. He begins the next broadcast by asking questions about the previous program. A secretary may tabulate the results.

3. Select pupils from the class to form a verse choir. This choir may present on radio programs one or several of the poems required for study in your grade.

4. Using the model as a guide, write a radio script based on some incident in the life of your favorite saint.

5. Appoint a pupil to act as news commentator. It will be his duty to gather news of current events and items of interest about pupils in the school. The news may be broadcast once a week, or oftener if desired.

4. Choral Speaking

Through choral speaking you will prepare yourself for taking part in discussions of various kinds, for the exercises in breathing and enunciation will help your tone of voice and your enunciation.

TUNING-UP EXERCISES

Breathing:

Repeat the breathing exercises on pages 29, 63, 89, 123, 154, and 183.

Inhale, hold breath for ten counts, exhale with *wh, wh.*

Enunciation:

Exercises in use of long *e:*

> bee bee bee   wee wee wee
> deep keep leap steep

Nonsense rhyme spoken in unison:

Rock-a-bye, baby, thy cradle is green;
Father's a nobleman, Mother's a queen;
Sister's a lady, and wears a gold ring;
And Brother's a drummer, and drums for the King.

The poem we will now memorize is called a sonnet. A sonnet is a fourteen-line poem. The letters a, b, c, d, e, and f show how the lines rhyme. Each line of the poem contains five feet; and each foot usually has two syllables, with the stress on the second syllable.

THE VIRGIN

By William Wordsworth

First Group (Medium Voices)	Rhyme scheme
Mother! Whose virgin bosom was uncrost	a
With the least shade of thought to sin / allied; //	b
Woman! / above all \ women / glorified, //	b
Our tainted nature's / solitary boast; //	a

Second Group (Light Voices)

Purer than foam \ on central \ ocean tost; //	a
Brighter / than eastern skies / at daybreak strewn	c
With fancied roses, \ than the unblemished moon /	c

Third Group (Heavy Voices)

Before her wane \ begins on heaven's blue coast; //	a octave
Thy image falls to earth. //	

Unison

Yet some, \ I ween, //	d
Not unforgiven, \ the suppliant knee might bend, //	e
As to a visible \ power, in which did blend	e
All that was mixed and reconciled in thee //	f
Of mother's \ love / with maiden \ purity, //	f
Of high / with low, \ celestial \ with terrene. //	d sestet

Preparing to Read the Poem

The purity of our Blessed Mother shines through every line of the whole poem. Read the lines at first silently. Are there any words that need explanation?

Read the poem aloud in unison. Does it lend itself well to unison reading? Yes, but it could also be read by different groups taking the different lines describing the purity of our Lady as indicated.

"The Virgin" was written by William Wordsworth, an English poet, who was not a Catholic. It is a beautiful tribute to the purity of our Blessed Mother. Most non-Catholics do not believe in loving God's Mother so much, yet they love their own mothers. Her picture is their dearest possession. As Catholics love their own mother and kneel at her knee to tell her all they want, so do they love the Mother of God still more and kneel to ask her intercession with her Son in all their needs of soul and body.

THE MAGNIFICAT

(Luke 1:46-55)

Medium   My soul doth magnify the Lord. //

Light   And my spirit \ hath rejoiced in God my Savior. //

Medium   Because He hath regarded the humility \ of His handmaid; //

Unison   For behold / from henceforth all generations \ shall call me blessed. //

Medium   Because He that is mighty \ hath done great things to me; //

Unison   And holy \ is His name. //

Light   And His mercy \ is from generation unto generations, / to them that fear Him. //

Medium   He hath showed might \ in His arm; // He hath scattered the proud \ in the conceit of their heart. //

Unison   He hath put down the mighty \ from their seat, //
         and hath exalted the humble. //

Light   He hath filled the hungry \ with good things; // and
         the rich \ He hath sent empty away. //

Medium   He hath received Israel His servant, \ being mindful
         of His mercy. //

Light   As He spoke to our fathers, \ to Abraham / and to
         his seed \ forever. //

Unison   Glory be to the Father, / and to the Son, / and to
         the Holy Ghost, //

         As it was in the beginning, / is now, / and ever shall
         be / world without end. // Amen. //

STUDY OF THE POEM

This is our Lady's song of praise to God for the great
and inestimable privilege He bestowed on her in the Incar-
nation. Picture the Mother of God meeting her aged cousin
Elizabeth when she traveled over the green hills to share

her great joy and to comfort Elizabeth. Recall the words with which Elizabeth greeted the Blessed Virgin: "Blessed art thou among women and blessed is the fruit of thy womb! And how have I deserved that the mother of my Lord should come to me?"

The verses should be read quickly, in a high pitch, for this is a song of joy. Thus you will learn to render praise to God in the very words of Mary Immaculate.

5. Chapter Challenge

1. In a .... discussion a given number of appointed speakers discuss a question from different .... or present several .... of some problem of interest to the class.

2. In the .... following the discussion, the chairman does everything possible to obtain expressions of opinion from the audience.

3. The chairman prepares himself for the .... by studying the subject carefully; he should cultivate a good .... and a .... voice.

4. From .... to .... is the usual number of speakers in a .... discussion.

5. Pan-Americanism refers to the cooperation of the republics of .... and .... in political and .... matters.

6. In every debate there are .... teams of .... or ....members each.

7. The .... upholds the truth of the proposition debated; the .... seeks to disprove it.

8. An .... is very helpful in preparing for a debate.

9. The .... is the answer to the arguments of the opposing team.

10. In a debate a speaker refers to a person on his own team as his .... and to someone on the opposite side of the argument as his ....

11. We should learn to .... radio programs and to select only .... programs.

12. The model radio script in this chapter tells of ....

13. .... wrote "The Virgin," a tribute to ....

14. A sonnet has .... lines.

PART TWO

GRAMMAR

CHAPTER ONE Nouns

A noun is a name word.

KINDS OF NOUNS

1. *Proper Nouns and Common Nouns*

There are two main classes of nouns, *proper nouns* and *common nouns*.

A proper noun names a particular person, place, or thing.

A common noun names any one of a class of persons, places, or things.

Maryland was the first *colony* in *America* to enjoy religious *freedom*.

EXERCISE I

Place all the proper nouns in the following sentences in one column and all the common nouns in another column:

1. Altar boys have a patron and model in Saint John Berchmans.
2. Many shoes are manufactured in Massachusetts.
3. Florence Nightingale was a nurse in the Crimean War.
4. "The Transfiguration" was painted by Raphael.
5. Judas betrayed Christ for thirty pieces of silver.
6. The pope is the successor of Saint Peter.
7. Charles A. Lindbergh made the first nonstop flight from New York to Paris.
8. Formosa is an island off the coast of China.
9. Many churches are dedicated to the archangel Michael.
10. Can you name the six New England states?
11. My parents were married in Saint Alice Church.
12. Pope Pius XII was a church diplomat and statesman for several years.
13. Canada exports farm and forest products.

14. The attorney general is the legal adviser to the president.
15. Louis Pasteur was a noted French scientist.

2. *Collective Nouns*

A collective noun denotes a group of persons, animals, or things considered as one.

A vast *audience* heard the school *orchestra* play last evening.

EXERCISE 2

Make a list of all the collective nouns found in the following sentences:

1. The Senate acts as the jury at trials of impeachment.
2. Christ preached to the multitude from the boat.
3. Our class prays for the holy souls during November.
4. The family is the first community to which a man belongs.
5. The picture shows a drove of horses in a large field.
6. A troop of strange gypsies camped near the regiment.
7. A covey of birds flew over the French fleet.
8. The city of Jerusalem was captured by the army of Titus.
9. The congregation responded to the appeal of the missionary.
10. Our club has made plans for a Halloween party.
11. The Holy Name Society will meet this evening.
12. A company of soldiers jogged along the snow-packed road.

3. *Abstract Nouns*

An abstract noun expresses a quality, a condition, or an action apart from any object or thing.

Justice should be tempered with *mercy*.

EXERCISE 3

List all the abstract nouns found in the following sentences:

1. Rip Van Winkle's wife talked continually about his idleness.
2. Literature has a lasting influence on character.
3. Courtesy is a mark of a well-bred person.

4. Sins against faith, hope, and charity violate the First Commandment.
5. Cheerfulness and self-control are important habits to cultivate.
6. Slavery was a remote cause of the Civil War.
7. Haste is often waste.
8. Saint Joseph is the patron of labor.
9. Honesty is the best policy.
10. Knowledge is power.
11. Cleanliness is next to godliness.
12. The general's reputation saved him from suspicion.
13. The man won our confidence by his sincerity.
14. Obedience, loyalty, and patriotism are fostered in every Catholic school.
15. Health is not valued until sickness comes.

MODIFICATIONS OF NOUNS

1. *Person*

Person is that quality of a noun through which the speaker, the one spoken to, or the one spoken about is indicated.

The first person denotes the speaker.

We, the *citizens*, petitioned the mayor.

The second person denotes the one spoken to.

Children, obey your parents.

The third person denotes the one spoken about.

Saint Patrick converted *Ireland*.

EXERCISE 4

Give the person of each noun printed in italics in the following sentences:

1. I, your *pastor*, exhort you to pray for the holy souls.
2. *Paterson, New Jersey*, is the greatest silk manufacturing center of the world.
3. "*Children*, endeavor to receive *Holy Communion* frequently," said the teacher.
4. We, the *pedestrians*, demand proper safety protection.
5. Sweetest *Jesus*, come spiritually into my heart.
6. Proper *rest* is necessary for the *health* of the nervous system.
7. O *Walter!* Don't hurry so.
8. You are late, my *child*.
9. The *racers* broke all records.
10. *Boys*, he will lead you to *victory*.
11. The *news* was exciting.
12. The *world* owes a great debt to the Catholic Church.
13. It is your duty, *citizens*, to vote.
14. *William Harvey* made important discoveries about the circulation of the blood.
15. *Son*, behold thy Mother.

2. *Number*

Number is that quality of a noun which denotes whether it refers to one person or thing (singular number) or more than one (plural number).

One of the three *branches* of our government is the executive *branch*.

METHODS OF FORMING THE PLURAL

There are sixteen well-known rules for forming the plural of various types of nouns. If you wish to use the plural of some noun that does not seem to be included in the rules, consult the dictionary. A choice of plural forms is given for some words; for example, the plural of *scarf* may be *scarfs* or *scarves*.

1. Most nouns form the plural by adding *s* to the singular.

Singular, miracle; *plural,* miracles

2. For the sake of euphony, nouns ending in *s, x, z, ch,* and *sh* form the plural by adding *es* to the singular.

Singular, Mass; *plural,* Masses

3. Nouns ending in *y* preceded by a consonant form the plural by changing the *y* to *i* and adding *es.*

Singular, victory; *plural,* victories

NOTE. Nouns ending in *y* preceded by a vowel form the plural by adding *s* to the singular.

Singular, valley; *plural,* valleys

4. The following nouns form the plural by changing the *f* or *fe* to *ves:* calf, elf, half, knife, leaf, life, loaf, self, sheaf, shelf, thief, wife, wolf.

5. Nouns ending in *o:*

a. All nouns ending in *o* preceded by a vowel form the plural by adding *s* to the singular.

Singular, igloo; *plural,* igloos

b. Nouns ending in *o* preceded by a consonant generally form the plural by adding *es* to the singular.

Singular, Negro; *plural,* Negroes

c. Some nouns ending in *o* preceded by a consonant form the plural by adding *s* to the singular.

Singular, silo; *plural,* silos

d. Some nouns ending in *o* preceded by a consonant may form the plural by adding *s* or *es* to the singular.

Singular, buffalo; *plural,* buffaloes or buffalos

6. A few nouns form the plural by a change within the singular.

Singular, man; *plural*, men

7. A few nouns form the plural by the addition of the Old English ending *en*.

Singular, ox; *plural*, oxen

8. A few nouns retain the same form in the plural as in the singular.

SINGULAR	PLURAL	SINGULAR	PLURAL
series	series	corps	corps
species	species	salmon	salmon
sheep	sheep	cod	cod
deer	deer	trout	trout
swine	swine	Portuguese	Portuguese

9. When a name is preceded by a title, either the name or the title may be pluralized.

SINGULAR	PLURAL
Miss Meehan	The Misses Meehan or The Miss Meehans
Mr. Snyder	The Messrs. Snyder or The Mr. Snyders
Dr. Heard	The Doctors Heard or The Dr. Heards

NOTE. The title *Mrs.* is an exception to this rule, as it cannot be pluralized.

Singular, Mrs. Fisher; *plural*, The Mrs. Fishers

10. Some nouns taken from foreign languages retain their foreign plurals.

SINGULAR	PLURAL	SINGULAR	PLURAL
radius	radii	crisis	crises
alumna	alumnae	oasis	oases
alumnus	alumni	larva	larvae
basis	bases	thesis	theses
analysis	analyses	stratum	strata
synopsis	synopses	vertebra	vertebrae
datum	data	bacterium	bacteria

11. Some nouns taken from foreign languages have both a foreign and an English plural. The English form is preferred.

SINGULAR	ENGLISH PLURAL	FOREIGN PLURAL
formula	formulas	formulae
memorandum	memorandums	memoranda
curriculum	curriculums	curricula
appendix	appendixes	appendices
index	indexes	indices
tableau	tableaus	tableaux

12. Some nouns are used only in the plural.

ashes	goods	scissors
banns	pliers	trousers
clothes	pincers	tweezers

13. Some nouns are plural in form, but singular in meaning and use.

civics	physics	aeronautics
mathematics	measles	news

14. Compound nouns usually form the plural by adding *s* to the most important word or words.

SINGULAR	PLURAL
governor general	governors general
sergeant at arms	sergeants at arms
manservant	menservants[1]

15. Compound nouns ending in *ful* form the plural by adding *s* to the last syllable.

Singular, handful; *plural,* handfuls

NOTE. If more than one hand, pail, or glass is filled, two words are used; as two hands full, three glasses full.

16. Numbers, letters, and symbols form the plural by adding *'s*.
Singular, 7; *plural,* 7's. *Singular,* e; *plural,* e's. *Singular,* $+$; *plural,* $+$'s

EXERCISE 5

Write the plural of each of the following nouns:

Lady, suffix, trespass, sash, dispatch, heresy, jockey, tiff, ratio, kimono, mumps, shelf, alumna, appendix, gash, sketch, sacristy,

---

[1] Both of the words are pluralized.

bed, desk, floor, pulley, trophy, infant, Miss Brown, Master Wilson, Mrs. Tracey, child, politics, turkey, starch, Chinese, salmon, dishful, pansy, newsboy, studio, chimney, 8, John

EXERCISE 6

Arrange the following nouns in two columns. In the first column put the singular nouns; in the second, the plural nouns:

Beef, spoonfuls, allies, piano, alley, gentlemen, wives, sheriffs, trolleys, queries, fox, iris, switch, porches, galoshes, Campbells, sandwich, alms, memento, tomatoes, cameos, valleys, jellies, The Misses Butler, Eleanors, trios, buoy, industries, oasis, mice, tradesmen, trout, pocketful, 4, passers-by, ?, mother-in-law, d, Knights Templars, pliers, Donalds, salesman, peach, altos, brief case

3. *Gender*

Gender is that quality of a noun by which sex is distinguished. There are three genders: masculine, feminine, and neuter.

The masculine gender denotes the male sex.

man, boy

The feminine gender denotes the female sex.

woman, girl

The neuter gender denotes objects that have no sex.

house, football

MASCULINE   FEMININE   NEUTER

A noun that may be taken as either masculine or feminine is considered masculine gender.

children, teacher

HOW GENDER IS DISTINGUISHED

Gender may be distinguished in three ways:

1. By using a different word.

Masculine, monk; *feminine,* nun

2. By using a different ending.

Masculine, prince; *feminine,* princess

3. By changing part of the word.

Masculine, grandnephew; *feminine,* grandniece

EXERCISE 7

Classify the following nouns with regard to gender:

Widower, lamp, poetess, invalid, Negress, kitchen, laundryman, boy, relative, scout, Marie, friend, foreigner, juror, ladder, lad, bridesmaid, stepbrother, costume, prophet, book, library, house, ledger, cousin, directress, girl, goddess, groomsman, laundress, widow, count, prince, waiter, trombone, shepherdess, deacon, heir, uncle, duke, Paul, lass, postmistress, salesman, proprietress, hero, stepmother, benefactor, Francis, Geraldine, poet, Bernardine, Joseph, sister, nephew, dairymaid, grandfather, groom, spinster

4. *Case*

Case is that quality of a noun which shows its relation to some other word or words in the sentence. There are three cases: nominative, possessive, and objective.

Before a noun can be classified according to case, its use or syntax must be determined.

NOMINATIVE CASE

The uses of the nominative case that have been studied in previous years are as follows:

Subject. A noun used as the subject of a finite verb is in the nominative case.

Mary was presented in the Temple in Jerusalem.
Through the Panama Canal sail *ships* of many nations.
The most important *crop* of the United States is corn.

Predicate Nominative. A noun used as a predicate nominative or subjective complement is in the nominative case.

A noun that follows a copulative or linking verb is in the nominative case if it refers to the same person or thing as its subject.

The blood of the martyrs is the *seed* of the Church.
Saint Charles Borromeo became a *cardinal* at an early age.
The child was named *John*.

Apposition. A noun in apposition is in the same case as the noun it explains.

A noun that explains a subject or a predicate nominative is in the nominative case.

Saint Paul, the *Apostle* of the Gentiles, was born in Tarsus.
Lincoln, the *Emancipator*, was shot by John Wilkes Booth.
John's favorite hero is Father Pro, the Mexican *martyr*.

Address. A noun used in direct address is in the nominative case.

Father, forgive them, for they do not know what they are doing.
Saint Christopher, *boys*, is the patron of travelers.
Obey your teachers, *children*.

Exclamation. A noun used independently to express a strong emotion is in the nominative case.

Action! The play needs action.
Happy little *girl!* She is a child of Mary.
Oh, the poor *man!* We are so sorry for him.

NOMINATIVE ABSOLUTE

A noun before a participle in an independent phrase is in the nominative case absolute.

A participle, a word that does the twofold work of a verb and an adjective, is sometimes used with a noun or a pronoun in an independent adverbial phrase to express the time, the condition, the cause, or the circumstances of the action expressed by the main verb in the sentence. The noun or the pronoun used in this absolute construction is in the nominative case.

Mary being our model, we pattern our lives on hers.
Winter coming on, the people moved to the South.
Morning *prayers* having been said, we commenced our day.

EXERCISE 8

Select the nouns in the nominative case and give the syntax of each:

1. Donald, always say your morning and night prayers.
2. The first steamboat was called the *Clermont.*
3. John, my son, you are entering upon a new life.
4. Marshal Foch became commander in chief of the Allied forces.
5. The king having returned from the fair, Princess Anne met him at the gate.
6. Miss Smith, the librarian, came in quietly.
7. The river! It has overflowed its banks.
8. Jerome remained captain of the team for the season.
9. Thomas, come and help me.
10. President Wilson attended the Paris Peace Conference.
11. I do not think, sir, that this will answer.
12. Water power is sometimes called white coal.
13. Lincoln having been assassinated, Johnson succeeded him.
14. London is the largest city in Europe.
15. My pen! Where have I laid it?
16. Agnes has been a good friend of mine for many years.
17. Cardinal Dougherty blessed the children.
18. My brother is a doctor.
19. Father Marquette was an early missionary.
20. Basil, the blacksmith, was the father of Gabriel.
21. The name Mississippi was given to the river by the Indians.
22. Nitrogen and oxygen are the chief gases in the air.

23. Your parents are your best friends, children.
24. Bethlehem, the birthplace of Christ, is sacred to all Christians.
25. Into the fort stumbled the exhausted messenger.

POSSESSIVE CASE

A noun which expresses possession, ownership, or connection is in the possessive case.

The Civil War, which divided the United States into two hostile camps, took place during *Lincoln's* administration.

The sign of the possessive case is the apostrophe and *s*.

METHODS OF FORMING THE POSSESSIVE CASE OF NOUNS

1. To form the possessive singular, add *'s* to the singular form of the noun.

> Joseph, Joseph's; captain, captain's

NOTE. The apostrophe and *s* is *not* used with nouns relating to inanimate things.

> Steeple of the church (*not* church's steeple)

The apostrophe and *s* is used with the names of certain inanimate objects which have become idiomatic from common usage.

> earth's surface; sun's ray

2. To form the possessive plural of nouns ending in *s,* add the apostrophe only.

> boys, boys'; baby, babies'

NOTE. If the plural form of the noun does not end in *s,* add *'s.*

> children, children's; policemen, policemen's

3. Proper names ending in *s* usually form the possessive case by adding *'s* after words of one syllable and the apostrophe only after words of more than one syllable.

> Mr. Burns, Mr. Burns's; Dickens, Dickens'

EXCEPTION. If the proper name is followed by a word beginning with *s,* the apostrophe only is used.

> James' sweater; Mars' sword

4. In compound nouns the *'s* is added to the end of the word.

NOUN	SINGULAR POSSESSIVE	PLURAL POSSESSIVE
father-in-law	father-in-law's	fathers-in-law's

EXERCISE 9

Write the possessive singular form and the possessive plural form of each of the following nouns:

brother-in-law	student	professor	mouse
woman	man	gentleman	horse
sergeant at arms	lady	sister	ox
manservant	child	Thomas	deer
attorney general	Jane	king	goose
stepsister	boy	princess	bird
Mr. Dolan	Scout	pupil	animal
maid of honor	girl	father	lion

EXERCISE 10

Copy the following sentences, filling in each blank with the possessive form of the noun at the left. In some sentences you will use the singular number and in other sentences the plural:

settler
1. The early .... homes were very crude.

man
2. The blind .... neighbors were amazed at the miracle.

Shakespeare
3. In high school you may read .... *Merchant of Venice.*

Saint Peter
4. Three thousand people were converted by .... first sermon.

child
5. Grandmother gave my little sister a book of .... poems.

brother-in-law
6. Jean works in her .... store.

boy
7. The .... camp is located on the river bank.

Dickens
8. On television we saw a dramatization of one of .... works.

God	9. Despair is a loss of hope in .... mercy.
bird	10. High in the tree Kevin found a .... nest.
Francis	11. Have you seen .... pencil?
major general	12. Has Mr. Sullivan reported at the .... office?
deer	13. The .... horns are shed and renewed annually.
Washington	14. In February we celebrate .... birthday.
leader, soldier	15. The .... courage, together with the .... confidence, brought victory.
baby	16. Book ends are often made from .... shoes.

SEPARATE AND JOINT POSSESSION OR OWNERSHIP

If two or more nouns are used together to indicate separate ownership—that is, to show that each person possesses something independently of the other—the 's is used after each noun.

Irving's and Scott's literary works are well worth reading.

Webster's and Hayne's speeches have been studied by many pupils.

If two or more nouns are used together to indicate joint ownership—that is, to show that one thing is possessed by the group jointly—the 's is used after the last noun only.

The secretary and the treasurer's office is on the third floor.

Kelly and King's store has been remodeled.

JOINT OWNERSHIP   SEPARATE OWNERSHIP

EXERCISE 11

Indicate possession in the following sentences:

1. Janice and Herbert compositions were interesting.
2. David, Horace, and Desmond den is very cozy.
3. We study Longfellow and Holmes poems.
4. Riley and Barrow store is noted for splendid window displays.
5. Da Vinci and Raphael paintings are well known.
6. Campbell and Breslin market sells imported cheese.
7. Hayes and Kenworthy factory is very busy.
8. I have read many of Kilmer and Maynard poems.
9. Louise and Anne mother is charming.
10. Did you see Jean and Helen new homes?
11. My father met us at Moore and Wisher Conservatory.
12. We received the doctor and the nurse reports.
13. Marian and Ruth poster won first prize.
14. John and Luke dogs are the same breed.
15. The children played both Bach and Mozart compositions.
16. We patronize Black and French store.
17. Daniel and Edward boat is painted red.
18. There was a fire at Bailey and Lowe shop last night.

OBJECTIVE CASE

The uses of the objective case are as follows:

Direct Object. A noun used as the direct object of a verb is in the objective case.

A priest may celebrate three *Masses* on All Souls' Day.
Francis Thompson wrote beautiful *poems.*
Christ instituted seven *sacraments.*

Indirect Object. A noun used as the indirect object of a verb is in the objective case.

God gave *Moses* the Ten Commandments.
Send your *brother* some candy.
They gave the *bride* beautiful flowers.

NOTE. The preposition *to* or *for* can usually be inserted before the indirect object without changing the meaning of the sentence.

Object of a Preposition. A noun used as the object of a preposition is in the objective case.

We should pray for the *souls* in *purgatory*.
Washington performed his duties with great *courage*.
The South objected to a protective *tariff*.

Apposition. A noun in apposition is in the same case as the noun it explains.

A noun that explains a direct object, an indirect object, or an object of a preposition is in the objective case.

We honor Mary, our *Queen*.
We gave Rose, our sick *friend*, a basket of flowers.
The representative spoke of America, our *country*.

Adverbial Objective. A noun used as an adverbial objective is in the objective case.

We should pray for the holy souls every *day*.
John can jump five *feet*.
This *morning* the ground was covered with frost.

NOTE. An *adverbial objective* is a noun used as an adverb. Adverbial objectives may tell *when, where, how long,* or *how far*.

Retained Object. A noun used as a retained object is in the objective case.

Margaret was given a miraculous *medal*.
Francis was left a large *estate* by his uncle.
Why was James refused *admittance?*

NOTE. A *retained object* is the object of an active verb which is "retained" when the verb is changed to the passive voice. Note that the noun *medal,* the direct object of the verb *gave,* is the retained object of *was given*.

He gave Margaret a miraculous medal. *(Active voice)*
Margaret was given a miraculous medal. *(Passive voice)*

Objective Complement. A noun used as an objective complement is in the objective case.

Saint Anne and Saint Joachim named their child *Mary*.
My father appointed Joseph *guardian*.
The girls chose Rose *chairman*.

NOTE. In the first sentence the noun *Mary* is used to complete the meaning of the verb *named* and refers to the same person as the direct object, *child*.

Some of the more common verbs which may take objective complements are *appoint, call, choose, elect, make, name.*

Cognate Object. A noun used as a cognate object is in the objective case.

He dreamed a *dream* of future greatness.

The nation prayed a *prayer* for peace.

Frances sang a *song* of joy.

NOTE. A cognate object is a noun that repeats the meaning of and closely resembles the verb of which it is the object.

EXERCISE 12

Select the nouns in the objective case and give the syntax of each noun:

1. Constantine granted the Christians freedom of worship.
2. We must wait two hours.
3. Mr. Smith was given a substantial increase in salary.
4. The professor explained the problem to the class.
5. The girls danced the dance of the fairies.
6. Christ remained in the tomb forty hours.
7. The teacher told the children a story.
8. He gave George, my brother, a football.
9. The name of Lucy, virgin and martyr, is mentioned in every Mass.
10. We should pray to the saints, the chosen friends of God.
11. Thomas was left a large estate by his father.
12. When did that boy receive his diploma?
13. My father consulted Mr. Parker, our agent.
14. The season of Christmas brings children great joy.
15. The Kennedys lived twenty years in this parish.
16. Christ fasted forty days.
17. The boys chose Stanislaus captain.
18. The senator spoke three hours in Congress.

19. We met his uncle, a member of the Royal Canadian Mounted Police.
20. I sent Mary a long letter.
21. The club elected Robert Bresch president.
22. Christ's earthly life lasted thirty-three years.
23. The child was paid the reward.
24. Benedict enjoyed *Black Treasure*.
25. The boys considered Timothy a discoverer.
26. Pope Pius XI lived an active life.
27. The man sold his boat this morning.
28. The president can veto an act of Congress.
29. We visited Norway, the land of the midnight sun.
30. The coach taught the boys a new play.
31. Baptism makes us children of God.
32. Margaret smiled a smile of happiness.
33. Will you send my sister Jane the message?
34. This book cost three dollars.
35. Did you show Patrick your new watch?

EXERCISE 13

Read this selection very carefully and then answer the questions that follow:

[1] In the Louvre in Paris hangs a painting by the celebrated American artist James McNeill Whistler. [2] "An Arrangement in Gray and Black" is the imposing title of this portrait, but to the millions who know and love it the likeness is known as "The Artist's Mother." [3] The picture, when it first appeared, was given very little attention and it brought the artist scant recognition. [4] Many years later, however, it was the opinion of more than one committee of critics that this picture alone would have made Whistler a leader among painters. [5] For connoisseurs of art the beauty of this painting lies in the harmony achieved by perfect spacing and the many tones of gray produced by skillful blending. [6] Its appeal to the heart of the ordinary man rests in the noble traits of motherhood which Whistler has captured and enshrined forever on canvas.

1. Name the proper nouns in the first sentence.
2. Select a collective noun in the fourth sentence.
3. What kind of noun is *motherhood* in the sixth sentence?
4. Write the singular form of the noun *connoisseurs* in the fifth sentence.
5. In what person are all the nouns in this selection?
6. Select a masculine and a neuter noun in the third sentence.
7. What is the subject of the first sentence?
8. What is the case of *Artist's* in the second sentence?
9. The noun *title* in the second sentence is in what case? Why?
10. Name the direct and the indirect objects in the third sentence.
11. Find an adverbial objective in the paragraph.
12. Name the nouns in the fifth sentence that are objects of prepositions.
13. Find an appositive in the paragraph. In what case is it?
14. Why is the noun *attention* in the third sentence in the objective case?
15. Name an objective complement in the fourth sentence.

CHAPTER TWO

Pronouns

A pronoun is a word used in place of a noun.

When Columbus discovered the West Indies, *he* found cotton growing in that region.

The word to which a pronoun refers is called its antecedent. In this sentence the antecedent of the pronoun *he* is *Columbus*.

PERSONAL PRONOUNS

A personal pronoun is a pronoun that denotes by its form the speaker, the person spoken to, or the person or the thing spoken of.

You and *I* believe in the one true God.

It belongs to *him* or *her*.

The pronouns of the first person (the speaker) are *I, mine, me, we, ours, us*. The pronouns of the second person (the person spoken to) are *you* and *yours*. The pronouns of the third person (the person or the thing spoken of) are *he, she, it, his, hers, its, him, her, they, theirs, them*.

Pronouns change form to denote case and number. The nominative case is used when the pronoun is the subject of a sentence or a predicate nominative. The possessive case is used to denote possession. The objective case is used for a direct object, an indirect object, or the object of a preposition.

The personal pronouns are declined in the following way. In the third person singular there are distinct forms for masculine, feminine, and neuter genders.

DECLENSION OF THE PERSONAL PRONOUNS

CASE	SINGULAR	PLURAL
	First Person	
Nominative	I	we
Possessive	my,[1] mine	our,[1] ours
Objective	me	us
	Second Person	
Nominative	you	you
Possessive	your,[1] yours	your,[1] yours
Objective	you	you
	Third Person	
Nominative	he, she, it	they
Possessive	his, her,[1] hers, its	their,[1] theirs
Objective	him, her, it	them

EXERCISE 14

Name the personal pronouns in the following sentences and give the person, the number, the gender, and the case of each:

1. She called him as he entered the room.
2. Bring it with you to school.
3. I told her that she was mistaken.
4. He reminded you that it would happen.
5. They come when they are called.
6. She told them and us about the party.
7. We should pray often to the Holy Spirit.
8. They brought her with them.
9. He asked me about it.
10. You may go with them if you are ready.
11. He gave us three books.
12. She recognized me when she opened the door.

---

[1] The possessive adjectives *my, our,* and so forth, are included in this table for the sake of completeness.

COMPOUND PERSONAL PRONOUNS

Compound personal pronouns are pronouns made by adding *self* or *selves* to certain forms of the personal pronouns.

FORMS OF THE COMPOUND PERSONAL PRONOUNS

	SINGULAR	PLURAL
First Person	myself	ourselves
Second Person	yourself	yourselves
Third Person	himself, herself, itself	themselves

A compound personal pronoun may be used to give emphasis to a noun or as an object referring to the subject.

An intensive pronoun is used to emphasize a preceding noun or pronoun.

God *Himself* gave the Ten Commandments.

A reflexive pronoun is used as an object referring to and denoting the same person or thing as the subject.

We must prepare *ourselves* daily for our judgment.

EXERCISE 15

Underline the compound personal pronouns in the following exercise and tell whether they are intensive or reflexive:

1. We should deny ourselves frequently.
2. It was evident that the guide himself had lost his way.
3. Our Lord called Himself the Good Shepherd.
4. Grant himself submitted the terms to Lee.
5. God Himself gave us a free will to save our souls.
6. They can see themselves in the water.
7. The Bible itself is not the sole guide to salvation.
8. I hurt only myself by disobeying God.
9. Christ offered Himself for the sins of men.
10. Marie dressed herself in her best gown.
11. Some girls are always talking about themselves.
12. Mary seems herself[1] again.

---

[1] An intensive pronoun may be used alone as a predicate nominative as illustrated in this sentence.

13. Children, make yourselves comfortable.
14. Albert has purchased a new suit for himself.
15. The boys were proud of themselves.
16. We are made to the image of God Himself.
17. Spot stretched himself before the fireplace.
18. The baby hid himself under the table.

INTERROGATIVE PRONOUNS

An interrogative pronoun is a pronoun used in asking a question.

The interrogative pronouns are *who, which,* and *what.* They are used in both direct and indirect questions.

Who betrayed our Lord?
With *whom* was Saint Peter imprisoned?
Which of the saints is your favorite?
We asked Marie *what* she wanted.

Who is used in speaking of persons. *Which* is used in speaking of persons and things, and to denote one of a definite class. *What* is used in speaking of things, and in seeking information.

DECLENSION OF WHO[1]

	SINGULAR	PLURAL
Nominative	who	who
Possessive	whose	whose
Objective	whom	whom

EXERCISE 16

In the following sentences tell whether the interrogative pronouns refer to persons, to things, or seek information. Give the syntax of each:

1. What were the direct causes of the First World War?
2. To whom did General Lee surrender?
3. Whom did you meet at the door?
4. Whom did they select?

---

[1] The other interrogative pronouns are not generally inflected.

5. From what is rayon made?
6. Which of the Great Lakes is the largest?
7. The teacher asked which was the most important sense organ.
8. From what is kerosene obtained?
9. Who is the chief justice of the Supreme Court?
10. He asked me who lived in that house.
11. Who wrote *Uncle Tom's Cabin?*
12. By whom was the first transatlantic solo flight made?
13. By which of the political parties was Truman nominated?
14. What was the work of the seven deacons?
15. By whom was the South Pole discovered?
16. Who is the present head of the Catholic Church?
17. With whom did our Lord live?
18. Who was our Lord's favorite apostle?
19. What is the function of motor nerves?
20. They asked which was the fastest means of transportation.
21. By whom are the members of the Supreme Court appointed?

RELATIVE PRONOUNS

A relative pronoun is a pronoun that does the work of a conjunction by joining to its antecedent the subordinate clause of which it is a part.

Examine these two sentences:

Saul went to the house of Ananias, *who* cured him of his blindness.
Saul went to the house of Ananias, *and he* cured him of his blindness.

In the first sentence *who* takes the place of *and* and *he*. The antecedent, or the word in the main clause to which the pronoun *who* refers, is *Ananias*.

The relative pronouns are *who, which, what, that, but,* and *as. Who* refers to persons; *which* refers to animals or things; *that* refers to persons, animals, or things; *what* refers to things. The words *but* and *as* are considered relative pronouns only under certain conditions. Thus, *but* is considered a relative pronoun after a negative construction; *as* is considered a relative pronoun when used with *such* and *same*.

Blessed are they *who* suffer persecution for the sake of Christ.

The book *that* I read is very interesting.

God knows *what* is good for us.

None knew her *but* loved her.

The boys have the same assignment *as* the girls (have).

Since the relative pronoun *what* is equivalent to *that which* or the *thing which,* it is sometimes called a double relative.

God knows *what* we do.

In this sentence *what* is equivalent to *that which.* The pronoun *that* is the antecedent; *which* is the relative pronoun. The pronoun *but* has the meaning of *who does not* in this sentence:

There is no one *but* admires this great hero.

EXERCISE 17

Point out the relative pronouns in the following sentences and name the antecedent of each:

1. The Little Flower is a saint whom I admire greatly.
2. There are three sacraments which can be received only once.
3. New York, which is our largest city, is a great seaport.
4. The Delaware River, which separates Pennsylvania from New Jersey, flows into the Atlantic Ocean.
5. The Panama Canal, which was built by the United States, revolutionized ocean traffic.
6. He can command who has learned obedience.
7. My mother is welcome to such things as I have.
8. There is no child here but thinks as I do.
9. The *Clermont,* for which Fulton risked his fortune, was successful.
10. Saint John was the apostle to whom our Lord entrusted His Blessed Mother.
11. The catacombs were underground passages in which the early Christians buried their dead.
12. Duluth is located on Lake Superior, which is one of the Great Lakes.
13. He who hesitates is lost.

14. Our Lord promised a reward to all who follow Him.
15. We should do what we think is right.
16. Vitamin A, which is essential to good health, is found in leafy vegetables. *Principle*
17. The apostles were men to whom Christ entrusted the foundation of His Church.
18. The early Christians divided such things as they had.

AGREEMENT OF RELATIVE PRONOUNS

A relative pronoun agrees with its antecedent in person, number, and gender, but its case depends upon its use in the subordinate clause.

Saint Bernadette, to *whom* our Blessed Lady appeared, was a peasant girl of France.

In this sentence the relative pronoun is in the third person, singular number, feminine gender to agree with its antecedent, *Saint Bernadette*. It is in the objective case because it is the object of the preposition *to*.

EXERCISE 18

Name the relative pronouns in the following sentences. Explain the agreement of each pronoun with its antecedent and give its case and use in the sentence:

1. A martyr is a person who voluntarily suffers death for Christ.
2. Saint Paul, who did such great work for the Master, was not one of the Twelve.
3. Her blouse is made of nylon, which is a very durable synthetic material.
4. The Supreme Court, which is the highest judicial body in our country, passes judgment on the constitutionality of an act of Congress.
5. The nerves that carry messages to the brain are called sensory nerves.
6. The chalice is the vessel which holds the precious blood.
7. Judas betrayed the confidence that our Lord placed in him.

8. Saint Peter was the apostle to whom our Lord entrusted the keys of heaven.
9. Modern trade is promoted by such exhibits as we have just witnessed.
10. The boy who is serving Mass is my brother.

COMPOUND RELATIVE PRONOUNS

Compound relative pronouns are pronouns formed by adding *ever* or *soever* to *who, whom, which,* and *what*.

The compound relatives usually contain their own antecedents.

Whosoever (He who) does not carry his cross and follow Me, cannot be My disciple.

Whatever (That which) thou shalt bind on earth shall be bound also in heaven.

REMEMBER: The case of a relative pronoun depends upon its use in the subordinate clause.

EXERCISE 19

Give the syntax of the compound relative pronouns in the following sentences:
1. Give the prize to whoever receives the highest average.
2. The boys took whatever was necessary for the trip.
3. You may keep whichever you desire.
4. We rewarded whoever was most faithful.
5. Our Lord consoled whomever He met on the road.
6. My mother admires whatever is good and true.
7. Whoever is easily influenced will soon succumb to evil.
8. The medal will be awarded to whoever wins the contest.
9. Do whatever you can for your friend.
10. John will do whatever you request.
11. You may send the book to whoever asks for it first.
12. He spoke to whomever he met.
13. Mary, select whichever you prefer.
14. You may call whomever you wish.
15. Herod promised the dancer whatever she might ask.

ADJECTIVE PRONOUNS

An adjective pronoun is a pronoun that may also be used as an adjective.

This has been declared an article of faith.
This doctrine has been declared an article of faith.

Some of the types of adjective pronouns are: (1) demonstrative pronouns, (2) indefinite pronouns, (3) distributive pronouns, and (4) possessive pronouns.

1. *Demonstrative Pronouns*

A demonstrative pronoun is a pronoun that points out a definite person, place, or thing.

The demonstrative pronouns are *this, that, these,* and *those. This* and *these* denote objects that are near. *That* and *those* denote distant objects.

EXERCISE 20

Select the demonstratives in the following sentences. Tell whether they are adjectives or pronouns:

1. These oranges were grown in California.
2. This cotton is from the South.
3. Do you prefer these or those?
4. This diet is not balanced.
5. That is the best food you can eat.
6. This is a statue of the Infant of Prague.
7. These cities are located on the Fall Line.
8. These roads were old Indian paths.
9. That decision of the Supreme Court ended the discussion.
10. These football players are expert in their technique.
11. This is the loveliest sunset I ever saw.
12. What is that?
13. Those are giant skyscrapers.
14. Is this your eraser?
15. That house is very modern.
16. Those pupils are diligent.

17. Do you like these?
18. That girl has a charming personality.

2. *Indefinite Pronouns*

An indefinite pronoun is a pronoun that points out no particular person, place, or thing.

Many of the early Christians suffered martyrdom.
Some were persecuted, but *some* escaped.

In all, there are about thirty indefinite pronouns. The most commonly used are:

all	anyone	everyone	much	one	somebody
another	anything	everything	no one	same	someone
any	both	few	nobody	several	something
anybody	everybody	many	none	some	such

EXERCISE 21

Select all the indefinite pronouns and give the syntax of each:

1. Nobody knows the answer to the question.
2. Everybody did his best.
3. Much of our coffee is imported from Brazil.
4. You may have both.
5. Anyone who wishes may go to the game.
6. Many of our modern inventions are the work of Americans.
7. Have you questioned everybody?
8. I think someone should do this work.
9. Is Elizabeth waiting for somebody?
10. Before the Industrial Revolution much of the work was done in the home.
11. Sherman destroyed everything before him in his march to the sea.
12. The discovery of gold in California brought many to that region.
13. He chose several from each group.
14. All who were listening to Him were amazed at His understanding and His answers.

3. *Distributive Pronouns*

A distributive pronoun is a pronoun that refers to each person, place, or thing separately.

Each of the boys reported promptly.

The distributive pronouns are *each, either,* and *neither.*

EXERCISE 22

Select the distributives in the following sentences. Tell whether they are adjectives or pronouns:

1. Each of the first three commandments refers directly to God.
2. Mother will be pleased with either bag.
3. Neither country would assume the war debt.
4. Each expected the other to do the work.
5. Coal may be found in either of these regions.
6. Each did his duty.
7. Neither of the pupils has returned.
8. Do you prefer either of these clocks?
9. May I have a little of each?
10. Each habit is formed by repetition.

4. *Possessive Pronouns*

A possessive pronoun is a pronoun used to denote possession or ownership by the speaker, the person spoken to, or the person or the thing spoken of.

The possessive pronouns *mine, ours, yours, his, hers, its,* and *theirs* are sometimes called independent possessives because they may be used alone to take the place of nouns. *My, our, your, his, her, its,* and *their* modify nouns. The possessives that modify nouns are called possessive adjectives.

POSSESSIVE PRONOUNS	POSSESSIVE ADJECTIVES
Mine is blue.	*My* uniform is blue.
This is *yours.*	This is *your* pen.
Mr. Cook sold *his.*	Mr. Cook sold *his* car.
Sister has examined *theirs.*	Sister has examined *their* posters.

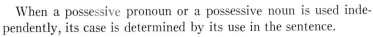

When a possessive pronoun or a possessive noun is used independently, its case is determined by its use in the sentence.

Leo's is here.	*His* is here.	*(Subject)*
She saw *Helen's*.	She saw *yours*.	*(Direct object)*
This is *Mother's*.	This is *mine*.	*(Predicate nominative)*

EXERCISE 23

Select the possessives in the following sentences and tell whether they are pronouns or adjectives:

1. Have you forgotten our address?
2. Take mine, but leave theirs.
3. This book is hers but that is his.
4. The Mississippi River has played a prominent role in the development of our country.
5. The poor bird has broken its wing.
6. Our faith is a precious heritage.
7. Saint Philip Neri received his education in a monastery.
8. We exchanged ours for theirs.
9. Joseph helps his grandparents on their farm.
10. Have you found yours and mine?

THE CORRECT USE OF PRONOUNS

1. *The Nominative Case*

SUBJECT OF A VERB

A pronoun used as the subject of a finite verb is in the nominative case.

Grace and (I, me) study together.

The correct form is: Grace and *I* study together.

EXERCISE 24

Select the correct form of the personal pronoun in each of the following. Give the reason for your choice:

1. William and (I, me) will pack the lunch.
2. The captain and (he, him) amused the children.

3. Anna and (she, her) opened the treasure chest.
4. Ruth and (I, me) were invited to the party.
5. George and (I, me) worked the same problem.
6. (They, them) and (we, us) live on the same street.
7. My brother and (I, me) rowed the boat.
8. (She, her) and Pauline dance well.
9. (He, him) and (I, me) carried the banners.
10. (She, her) and (I, me) rode in my father's car.

PREDICATE NOMINATIVE

A pronoun used as a predicate nominative or subjective complement is in the nominative case.

It is (he, him).

The correct form is: It is *he.*

EXERCISE 25

Select the correct form of the personal pronoun in each of the following sentences. Give the reason for your choice:

1. The winner of the prize was (she, her).
2. She said it was (they, them).
3. It may be (he, him).
4. It was (I, me) who knocked.
5. Was it (she, her)?
6. Could it be (we, us) they mean?
7. It might have been (they, them).
8. It was (he, him) who came.
9. Can it be (we, us)?
10. Did you know it was (I, me) who called?

EXERCISE 26 [Drill on the Nominative Case]

Rewrite, omitting the incorrect form:

1. Francis and (he, him) were here.
2. Michael and (I, me) are brothers.
3. James thought it was (she, her).
4. Therese and (she, her) will work the problem.

5. John and (I, me) are going to the game.
6. I knew it was (he, him) when I heard the step.
7. Mark and (he, him) moved the furniture.
8. Mother, Alice, and (I, me) intend to take a trip to Europe next summer.
9. Bernard and (he, him) decorated the stage.
10. Mary, Joan, and (I, me) planned a hike.
11. The children and (I, me) walked to town.
12. They believed it was (we, us).
13. My father and (they, them) work in the coal mines.
14. It was (she, her) who answered the letter.
15. Are these (they, them)?
16. Margaret and (she, her) are my best friends.
17. If anyone is chosen, it will be (he, him).
18. It was (we, us) whom they met at the studio.
19. Why are (they, them) late?
20. It was (he, him) who discovered the leak.

EXERCISE 27

Fill in each blank with the correct form of a personal pronoun. Give the reason for your choice:

1. .... am eager to see the World Series.
2. Is that you? Yes, it is ....
3. .... intends to make a pilgrimage to Lourdes.
4. Are Virginia and .... with you? ~~spoken~~
5. Helen and .... will help.
6. Jean and .... attended the opera.
7. .... visited his uncle last week.
8. Was it .... who made the touchdown in the game this afternoon?
9. Vincent and .... are making a stamp collection.
10. It was .... who found the lost child.
11. You know that the guilty person is ....
12. Was it .... who answered the telephone?
13. Here are Mary and ....
14. In the machine were Ruth, Susan, and ....

15. He and .... were delighted with the new ball.
16. You must admit it was ....
17. Will .... be ready on time?
18. My brother, as well as .... , is coming.
19. Either Albert or .... rang the bell.
20. It was .... who won the race.

2. *The Objective Case*

DIRECT OBJECT

A pronoun used as the direct object of a verb is in the objective case.

I met David and (he, him) at the station.

The correct form is: I met David and *him* at the station.

EXERCISE 28

Copy the following sentences, using the correct form of each pronoun. Give the reason for your choice:

1. Frederick took Mother and (I, me) for a ride.
2. The guard assisted Father and (he, him) in the search.
3. Did you invite your brother and (they, them)?
4. The salesman directed Daniel and (she, her) to the proper department.
5. Mother asked Adele and (I, me) for the paintings.
6. The gypsies passed Timothy and (I, me) on the road.
7. They thanked Jane and (he, him).
8. The old woman could not hear Clare or (I, me).
9. The teacher called Marion and (I, me).
10. Did you meet (she, her) when you were in Duluth?

INDIRECT OBJECT

A pronoun used as the indirect object of a verb is in the objective case.

Give Paul and (I, me) the papers.

The correct form is: Give Paul and *me* the papers.

EXERCISE 29

Copy the following sentences, using the correct form of each pronoun. Give the reason for your choice:

1. We brought Miss Carr and (they, them) some flowers.
2. Dorothy's father gave (we, us) a radio.
3. Daniel wrote Mother and (I, me) a long letter yesterday.
4. Celine knit (I, me) a sweater.
5. Marita brought Jane and (she, her) some fruit.
6. Will you please lend Paula and (I, me) your dictionary?
7. The guide showed Rosemary and (they, them) the art collection.
8. The boys offered (he, him) and (I, me) the pennants.
9. My brother lent Charles and (he, him) the car.
10. They owe Mr. Davis and (he, him) a large sum of money for that property.

OBJECT OF A PREPOSITION

A pronoun used as the object of a preposition is in the objective case.

I have not heard from Jean or (she, her).

The correct form is: I have not heard from Jean or *her*.

EXERCISE 30

Copy the following sentences, using the correct form of each pronoun. Give the reason for your choice:

1. This work is too difficult for (I, me).
2. We were coasting down the hill with him and (she, her).
3. Father stood behind (we, us).
4. These directions were suggested by (she, her).
5. Leo may stand between John and (she, her).
6. The coach is waiting for James and (he, him).
7. Alfred walked beside William and (he, him).
8. A strange animal was seen by (they, them).
9. Francis, sit between (he, him) and (I, me).
10. Everybody gave a donation but Mr. Mahan and (he, him).

EXERCISE 31 [Drill on the Objective Case]

Select the correct form of the personal pronoun:

1. The crowd separated Catherine from (we, us).
2. Is this mail for (he, him) or (I, me)?
3. Regina is going with (I, me).
4. The artist painted a picture of (she, her).
5. His brother bought (he, him) a beautiful pen.
6. Andrew told (I, me) an exciting story.
7. He asked Charles and (she, her) for a ticket.
8. The pitcher threw (I, me) the ball.
9. Uncle Thomas showed Father and (she, her) his souvenirs.
10. Father reproved Francis and (I, me) for our misbehavior.
11. Marie owes you and (I, me) some money.
12. The noise was behind Helen and (I, me).
13. Alice called (she, her) to the door.
14. Between you and (he, him) there should be no quarrels.
15. Nobody used that entrance but Gerald and (we, us).
16. Give Teresa and (I, me) the directions.
17. The librarian sent (she, her) a book.
18. Does he live near Mr. Craft or (he, him)?
19. The money was divided among Patrick and (they, them).
20. Take (we, us) with you.

EXERCISE 32

Fill in each blank with the proper form of a personal pronoun. Give the reason for your choice:

1. He went with .... to see the game.
2. The English prizes were won by Mary and ....
3. The teacher gave .... the book.
4. His father promised .... a car.
5. They visited .... over the week end.
6. They saw .... at the moving pictures.
7. The strange noise startled ....
8. The gentleman in the trolley car offered .... his seat.
9. Will you take .... to school?

10. Did you call .... on the telephone last evening?
11. Did you give Arthur and .... the package?
12. The storm carried .... out to sea.
13. Mother divided the cookies between .... and ....
14. Father called Paul and ....
15. I shall mail .... the letter.
16. You have rendered Mother and .... a great service.

3. *The Case Used after* Than *and* As

After the conjunctions *than* and *as* there is an omission of words. The pronoun following these conjunctions must be in the same case as the word with which it is compared.

Regina reads better than (she, her).

The correct form is: Regina reads better than *she* (reads).

We saw him before (she, her).

The correct form is: We saw him before (we saw) *her*.

or We saw him before *she* (saw him).

obj. p. 229

EXERCISE 33

Select the correct form of the pronoun:

1. Evelyn walks more gracefully than (she, her).
2. He prints better than (I, me).
3. Richard Evans drives more carefully than (he, him).
4. They trusted William more than (he, him).
5. Anne walks as fast as (she, her).
6. He was thought to be no better than (she, her).
7. David is not so studious as (he, him).
8. Mother bakes as well as (she, her).
9. She prepares her work better than (I, me).
10. He studies more diligently than (they, them).
11. Edmund is as tall as (she, her).
12. My sister is as lovable as (she, her).
13. I think Jane is more efficient than (he, him).
14. I wish I were as successful as (she, her).
15. I am determined to be as persevering as (they, them).

16. Our boys run faster than (they, them).
17. I hope to be as proficient as (he, him).
18. You can do it as well as (he, him).
19. They are not so fortunate as (we, us).
20. They like Ellen better than (she, her).
21. I arrived earlier than (she, her).
22. Catherine tries harder than (he, him).
23. They entertained him as well as (she, her).
24. I think George is more thoughtful than (he, him).
25. He called louder than (I, me).

EXERCISE 34 [General Exercise on Personal Pronouns]

Choose the correct pronoun in each of the following sentences. Give the reason for your choice:

1. We thought that it was (she, her).
2. May (we, us) three girls leave early?
3. The cat followed John and (I, me).
4. Did the teacher ask Andrew and (he, him) a question?
5. That tall girl is (she, her).
6. All were excused except Anne and (she, her).
7. (She, her) and (I, me) were invited to a party.
8. Who called? It was (I, me).
9. The woman saw (they, them) from the window.
10. Is it (he, him) you want?
11. All of (we, us) boys belong to the basketball team.
12. Everybody but you and (he, him) may be excused.
13. The argument was between (they, them) and (we, us).
14. Did you think it was (she, her) who found it?
15. Would you go if you were (I, me)?
16. Sister instructed (we, us) in the use of the missal.
17. He shared his candy with Peter and (I, me).
18. Her brother sent (she, her) a gay scarf from Mexico.
19. I have admission cards for you and (he, him).
20. (They, them) are the best baseball players here.
21. Who broke the cup? It was (I, me).
22. The baby looks like (she, her).

23. Mother baked (we, us) a delicious cake.
24. I recognized (she, her) from her picture.
25. Martha answered more quickly than (she, her).
26. (He, him) and (she, her) will arrive soon.
27. The manager asked (we, us) our names.
28. They went to the game without Patrick and (he, him).
29. Agnes told (we, us) her plans.
30. Sister praised Joseph and (he, him) for their work.
31. Mother divided the fruit between (he, him) and (I, me).
32. You have rendered my sister and (I, me) a great service.
33. We brought Eleanor and (she, her) with us.
34. Did you sit beside Arthur or (she, her)?
35. Can you run as fast as (he, him)?
36. That is (he, him) in the first row.
37. Are you looking for (he, him) or (I, me)?
38. She seems more friendly than (he, him).
39. Last evening Grandmother surprised my sister and (I, me).
40. I hope they elect you or (he, him).

4. *Drill on Interrogative Pronouns*

The interrogative pronoun *who* is used when the sentence requires a pronoun in the nominative case.

The interrogative pronoun *whom* is used when the sentence requires a pronoun in the objective case.

Who converted Ireland? *(Subject)*
By *whom* was Ireland converted? *(Object of preposition)*

EXERCISE 35

Fill in each blank with the correct form, *who* or *whom:*

1. .... is the first speaker?
2. By .... were you received?
3. .... do you think is at the door?
4. With .... did you come to school today?
5. .... accompanied you on your trip?
6. To .... are we indebted for the printing press?

7. .... delivered the radio address?
8. .... was elected captain of the football team?
9. To .... did you explain your absence?
10. By .... was the telephone invented?
11. By .... is baptism usually administered?
12. .... is your patron saint?
13. .... was the first American cardinal?
14. Mother wants to know .... washed the dishes.
15. .... do you think drank all the milk?
16. .... do you suppose she means?
17. .... does your cousin resemble?
18. Jean asked .... called to her from the boat.
19. .... are your friends?
20. .... should we adore?

5. *Drill on Relative Pronouns*

The relative pronoun *who* is used when the pronoun is the subject of a verb.

The relative pronoun *whom* is used when the pronoun is the object of a verb or of a preposition.

Saint Gabriel was the archangel *who* appeared to Mary.
Tobias was the young man *whom* the archangel Raphael guided.

EXERCISE 36

Select the correct form of the relative pronoun:

1. Mr. Joyce is a man in (who, whom) I have great confidence.
2. I will send a boy (who, whom) you can trust.
3. Miss Flynn is a nurse (who, whom) will give good service.
4. Mr. Hopson, from (who, whom) we bought our sweeper, is an honest salesman.
5. We have a friend visiting us (who, whom) will entertain you.
6. You may bring (whoever, whomever) you wish.
7. Was it Father to (who, whom) you spoke?
8. Here is the man for (who, whom) you have been waiting.
9. I do not know the gentleman with (who, whom) he is sitting.

10. (Whoever, whomever) writes the best essay will receive a prize.
11. My brother spoke to (whoever, whomever) he met.
12. He encouraged (whoever, whomever) made an effort.
13. Sell it to (whoever, whomever) offers the best price.
14. Are they the children (who, whom) are visiting you?
15. We study about General Lee, (who, whom) led the Confederate forces.
16. Give it to (whoever, whomever) opens the door.
17. He watched the men (who, whom) were building the bridge.
18. Theresa, (who, whom) has an unusually clear voice, will make the announcements.
19. I am not certain (who, whom) answered first.
20. Saint John was the only apostle (who, whom) died a natural death.

6. *Agreement with Distributive and Indefinite Pronouns*

Pronouns and possessive adjectives must agree with their antecedents in person, number, and gender.

The distributive pronouns *each, either, neither,* and the indefinite pronouns *one, anyone, no one, anybody, nobody, everyone, everybody, someone, somebody* are always singular. Pronouns and possessive adjectives referring to these pronouns as antecedents must be singular in number.

Such indefinite pronouns as *all, both, few, many, several,* and *some* are generally plural. Pronouns and possessive adjectives referring to these pronouns as antecedents must be plural.

Each did *his* best.
Both did *their* best.

The expressions *each other* and *one another* are called reciprocal pronouns by some grammarians. *Each other* is used in speaking of two persons or things. *One another* is used in speaking of more than two.

The two brothers resemble *each other*.
The men greeted *one another* pleasantly.

EXERCISE 37

Select the correct form of the pronoun in each sentence:

1. If somebody calls for Mr. Amberg, ask (him, them) to wait.
2. Each of the girls brought (her, their) sewing kit.
3. Everyone must wait (his, their) turn.
4. Each of the children thought (himself, themselves) entitled to a holiday.
5. Everybody should write (his, their) name in the register.
6. Three roads cross (each other, one another) at that intersection.
7. My mother told everybody to do as (he, they) pleased.
8. Some of the students received (his, their) cards yesterday.
9. Has everybody paid (his, their) dues?
10. Richard and Thomas recognized (each other, one another) immediately.
11. Has anybody finished (his, their) problems?
12. Neither of the sailors would admit that (he, they) was to blame.
13. Christ commanded His disciples to love (each other, one another).
14. If everybody does (his, their) best, we cannot lose.

15. Both forgot to bring (his, their) skates.
16. Many have already purchased (his, their) tickets.
17. If anyone wishes to start, (she, they) may do so now.
18. Both offered (his, their) cars for the trip.
19. If anybody has finished, (he, they) may go.
20. All the members of the team helped (each other, one another).

7. *Agreement of Compound Personal Pronouns*

A compound personal pronoun must agree with its antecedent in person, number, and gender.

Compound personal pronouns have two distinct uses, as intensive and as reflexive pronouns.

King Ethelbert *himself* received the missionaries. *(Intensive)*
We seldom see *ourselves* as others see us. *(Reflexive)*

EXERCISE 38

Supply the correct form of the compound personal pronoun in each of the following sentences and tell whether it is intensive or reflexive:

1. Thomas blamed .... for the misunderstanding.
2. He cut .... on a piece of glass.
3. We must answer for ....
4. They .... could do no better.
5. You have heard the verdict ....
6. I .... would never have thought of that suggestion.
7. The bird injured .... when it fell from the tree.
8. Children, you may distribute the materials ....
9. The voters disagreed among ....
10. The citizens brought that strict law upon ....
11. Our Blessed Lady called .... the Immaculate Conception.
12. Christ hid .... from the crowd.
13. We should love our neighbors as we love ....
14. Mother .... gave us these instructions.
15. Saint Therese sanctified .... in her little way.

EXERCISE 39 [Test on Pronouns]

Read this selection carefully and then answer the questions:

¹ Each of you, Catholic boys and girls, belongs to three distinct societies: the family, the state, and the Church. ² "What," you may ask, "is the obligation that membership in these societies imposes?" ³ The answer is this. ⁴ You must give a respectful obedience to those in authority, perform your duties conscientiously, and strive to live in charity with your fellow men. ⁵ In other words, you must develop in yourself whatever will make you a worth-while member of each group. ⁶ Such is the attitude of a good Christian. ⁷ It should also be yours.

1. Name a personal pronoun found in the first sentence.
2. In what person is the personal pronoun in the second sentence?
3. Name a personal pronoun in the seventh sentence that is neuter in gender.
4. In the fourth sentence select a personal pronoun that is used as the subject.
5. Find a compound personal pronoun in the fifth sentence.
6. Is the compound personal pronoun in the fifth sentence used intensively or reflexively?
7. Find an interrogative pronoun in the paragraph.
8. In what case is the interrogative pronoun? Why?
9. Find a relative pronoun in the second sentence and name its antecedent.
10. In what case is the relative pronoun in the second sentence? Why?
11. Give the syntax of the only compound relative pronoun in the paragraph.
12. What kind of pronoun is the first word in the paragraph?
13. Is the demonstrative in the second sentence a pronoun or an adjective?
14. Find a demonstrative pronoun that is singular in number.
15. What kind of pronoun does the sixth sentence contain?
16. Is the possessive in the seventh sentence a pronoun or an adjective?

CHAPTER THREE Adjectives

An adjective is a word that describes or limits a noun or a pronoun.

CLASSES OF ADJECTIVES

Adjectives may be divided into two general classes, *descriptive adjectives* and *limiting adjectives*.

1. *Descriptive Adjectives*

A descriptive adjective is an adjective that describes a noun or a pronoun.

A *long, narrow* lane led to the grotto.

There are two types of descriptive adjectives, *proper adjectives* and *common adjectives*.

A proper adjective is an adjective that is formed from a proper noun.

A common adjective is an adjective that expresses the ordinary qualities of a noun or a pronoun.

The *American* flag waved in the breeze.

He gazed at the *swift* waters.

NOTE. Many participles may be used as descriptive adjectives.

The *broken* rib caused pain.

The *smiling* child greeted us.

EXERCISE 40

Select the descriptive adjectives and tell whether they are common or proper:

1. Canada is famous for picturesque lakes and majestic mountains.
2. The Chinese people have developed remarkable skill in the textile industry.
3. Along the European coast are useful harbors.
4. Amateur photography is an absorbing hobby.
5. Fresh air and abundant sunshine are necessary for good health.
6. The great Cathedral of Notre Dame is an outstanding example of Gothic architecture.
7. Multicolored flags lined the sides of the long arcade.
8. Byzantine culture spread to Europe after the Crusades.
9. The Amazon jungles contain rubber trees.
10. Pope Benedict XV was a saintly man.
11. The kind old watchman has clear blue eyes.
12. In the art museum we saw paintings of French, Italian, Dutch, and Spanish artists.
13. The western tip of the Alaskan mainland almost touches Siberia.
14. In Cuba we visited a large sugar plantation owned by an American company.
15. Saint Vincent de Paul was a French peasant who became a zealous priest.

2. *Limiting Adjectives*

A limiting adjective is an adjective that either points out an object or denotes number.

The limiting adjectives may be subdivided into the following three classes: (1) articles, (2) numeral adjectives, and (3) pronominal adjectives.

The articles *the, an,* and *a* show whether the noun is used definitely or indefinitely.

The parade was very colorful. *(Definite)*
An artist must use his imagination. *(Indefinite)*

A numeral adjective is an adjective that denotes exact number.

The little boy paid *five* cents for his *second* ride.

A pronominal adjective is an adjective that may also be used as a pronoun.

Each girl was asked the question.

EXERCISE 41

In the following sentences select the articles, the numeral adjectives, and the pronominal adjectives:

1. Several airplanes flew over our school.
2. Do you know the names of the nine choirs of angels?
3. Some girls will take part in the play.
4. His book was lost.
5. Which school won the prize?
6. Each man cast his vote.
7. He sat in the second desk.
8. Neither statement is correct.
9. Our club has elected its officers.
10. At what time does your club meet?
11. Many lives were saved by the sailors.
12. My prayer was answered on the sixth day of the novena.
13. Few men ever reach such success.
14. Which question did you answer incorrectly?

15. A right angle contains ninety degrees.
16. On which days are the five sorrowful mysteries of the rosary said?
17. Mary and Jane live in the same apartment house.
18. The diameter of that circle is fourteen inches.
19. Whose book is this?
20. Have you met their parents?
21. Lent is seven weeks of preparation for Easter.
22. The United States has five important forest belts.
23. That bag is filled with money.
24. To which class do you belong?
25. Both children told the same story.

FURTHER STUDY OF PRONOMINAL ADJECTIVES

Pronominal adjectives are usually divided into the following five classes:

A demonstrative adjective is an adjective that points out a definite person, place, or thing *(this, that, these, those).*

A possessive adjective is an adjective that denotes ownership *(my, our, your, his, her, its, their, whose).*

A distributive adjective is an adjective that refers to each person, place, or thing separately *(each, every, either, neither).*

An indefinite adjective is an adjective that points out no particular person, place, or thing *(any, all, another, both, few, many, much, several, some, such,* **and so forth).**

An interrogative adjective is an adjective that is used in asking a question *(which, what).*

EXERCISE 42

Select the pronominal adjectives in the following sentences and tell to which class each belongs:

1. Some pupils have arrived early.
2. I never saw those boys before.
3. Every sin is an act of ingratitude to God.

4. Which course does he intend to follow?
5. Leather has many uses.
6. With what prayer do we praise the Blessed Trinity?
7. Animals do much work on our farms.
8. Has either letter been answered?
9. Every Catholic should carry his rosary.
10. Each state has its constitution.
11. A few books have been replaced.
12. Whose fault was it?
13. Each member of the panel gave a short talk on some phase of the topic.
14. Such work calls for strength.
15. That tree is an elm.
16. Some children have too much money.
17. Every industrious pupil studies his lessons.
18. Those berries are peculiar to this climate.
19. We should dedicate every thought to God.
20. All the men have their support.
21. Many pagans were converted by Saint Paul.
22. What college does your brother attend?
23. You may have another cookie.
24. Neither man is guilty.
25. That statue is my favorite.

POSITION OF ADJECTIVES

1. The usual position of the adjective is before the substantive. Such an adjective is called an attributive adjective.

The child has *bright blue* eyes.

2. A predicate adjective follows and completes a copulative verb.

The room was *large* and *comfortable*.

3. An adjective that follows the direct object and at the same time completes the thought expressed by a transitive verb is called an objective complement.

The announcement made him *angry*.

EXERCISE 43

Select the adjectives in the following sentences and give the syntax of each adjective:

1. Michael keeps his desk neat.
2. The faithful nurse became ill.
3. He painted the house red.
4. American skyscrapers have become famous throughout the world.
5. Her new hat is very attractive.
6. He appears indifferent.
7. The plans proved highly successful.
8. The captain seemed eager to start.
9. My mother ironed the collar smooth.
10. The boy looks ill.
11. We consider such conduct rude.
12. The rising temperature caused alarm.
13. The evening weather broadcast made the members of the track team happy.
14. The boys planned a scouting trip.
15. An armed vessel took the prisoner to New Orleans.
16. Mrs. McNamara met many interesting people on her trip around the world.
17. Paul grew restless during the lecture.
18. The rich young man refused Christ's invitation.

ATTRIBUTIVE ADJECTIVE	PREDICATE ADJECTIVE	OBJECTIVE COMPLEMENT

STANDS BEFORE A NOUN	FOLLOWS A COPULATIVE VERB	FOLLOWS THE DIRECT OBJECT

19. Joan burned the toast black.
20. He made the board even.
21. He purchased a summer cottage.
22. The stained-glass window was installed yesterday.

COMPARISON OF ADJECTIVES

Comparison is the change that adjectives undergo to express different degrees of quality, quantity, or value.

Most adjectives have three degrees of comparison: positive, comparative, and superlative.

This is a *large* apple. *(Positive degree)*
This is a *larger* apple than yours. *(Comparative degree)*
This is the *largest* apple in the basket. *(Superlative degree)*

The positive degree denotes quality.

The comparative degree denotes quality in a greater or a less degree.

The superlative degree denotes quality in the greatest or the least degree.

METHODS OF COMPARISON

1. Most adjectives of one syllable and some adjectives of two syllables (generally those ending in *ow, y,* and *e*) form the comparative degree by adding *er* to the positive, and the superlative degree by adding *est* to the positive.

POSITIVE	COMPARATIVE	SUPERLATIVE
noble	nobler	noblest
merry	merrier	merriest
narrow	narrower	narrowest

2. Adjectives of three or more syllables, and some of two syllables, form the comparative and the superlative degrees by prefixing *more* and *most* or *less* and *least* to the positive form of the adjective.

POSITIVE	COMPARATIVE	SUPERLATIVE
industrious	more industrious	most industrious
thoughtful	less thoughtful	least thoughtful

3. Certain adjectives are compared irregularly. Those used frequently are:

POSITIVE	COMPARATIVE	SUPERLATIVE
little	less	least
bad, ill, evil	worse	worst
good	better	best
many, much	more	most
late	later, latter	latest, last
far	farther	farthest
fore	former	foremost, first
old	older, elder	oldest, eldest
near	nearer	nearest, next
....	*further	furthest
....	*inner	innermost, inmost
....	*outer	outermost, outmost
....	*upper	uppermost, upmost

4. Some adjectives do not admit of comparison, as *dead, perpendicular, eternal, supreme,* and so forth.

EXERCISE 44

Make two columns. In one column list the adjectives that are capable of being compared and tell the degree of comparison of each. In the other, list the adjectives that cannot be compared:

1. Pennsylvania mines more coal than Ohio.
2. Music is a universal language.
3. The little girl held a small doll under her arm.
4. The population of New York is greater than that of Philadelphia.
5. She put on her most attractive dress.
6. Leo thought they were his worst enemies.
7. He is taller than his sister.
8. Much sugar is imported from Cuba.
9. Canals became less important with the coming of the railroads.
10. Mary is her eldest daughter.
11. The surest way to heaven is not always the easiest way.

---

* These adjectives have no positive form.

12. Montreal is the largest city in Canada.
13. An honest man is the noblest work of God.
14. That purse contains the most money.
15. Joan wrote a longer paragraph than Barbara.
16. The last room on the west side of the building is the sixth-grade classroom.

THE CORRECT USE OF ADJECTIVES

1. *Comparative and Superlative Degrees*

The comparative degree of the adjective is used when two are compared. The superlative degree is used when more than two are compared.

Which river is longer, the Missouri or the Mississippi?
The Mississippi is the longest river in our country.

EXERCISE 45

Select the correct degree of the adjective in each of the following sentences:

1. Which is (more useful, most useful), copper or silver?
2. The Pacific is the (larger, largest) ocean.
3. Baptism is the (more necessary, most necessary) sacrament.
4. Which of the two buildings is (more modern, most modern)?
5. Charles is (brighter, brightest) than Peter.
6. George is the (brighter, brightest) boy in our class.
7. Of the two girls, Barbara is the (better, best) musician.
8. I think this is the (shorter, shortest) route of the two.
9. Which city is (more progressive, most progressive), Montreal or Quebec?
10. Both boys are tall, but Paul is (taller, tallest).
11. Sin is the (worse, worst) evil that can befall us.
12. Who looks (happier, happiest), Jean or Anne?
13. Who did the (better, best) work, Mary, Alice, or Cecilia?
14. That was the (more exciting, most exciting) story of the two.
15. Football is the (more exciting, most exciting) sport of the year.

2. Fewer *and* Less

Use *fewer* when number is indicated. Use *less* when quantity is indicated.

In our class there are *fewer* girls than boys.
We have had *less* snow this winter than last winter.

EXERCISE 46

Fill in each blank with the correct form, *fewer* or *less:*

1. James has .... marbles than his brother.
2. Mr. Healey has .... cherry trees and .... corn than his neighbor.
3. There are .... books on the table than in the bookcase.
4. In our school we have .... time for lunch than in yours.
5. Since machinery has been invented, ... labor is needed.
6. Mexico has .... good harbors than the United States.
7. Canada mines .... coal than the United States.
8. There are .... accidents on the sea than on land.
9. There are .... flowers in our garden than in yours.
10. There were .... children at the party than were expected.
11. Marie spends .... money than her sister.
12. There is .... flour in the bin than there was last week.
13. This box contains .... cookies than that one.
14. Henry made .... mistakes today than he did yesterday.
15. A greater diligence will result in .... errors.

3. *The Repetition of the Article*

The repetition of the article changes the meaning of a sentence.

I know *the* president and *the* secretary.

Here the article is placed before both nouns to show that they are taken separately.

I know *the* president and secretary.

In this sentence the article is placed before the first noun *only* to show that both offices (president and secretary) are held by one individual.

EXERCISE 47

In the following sentences determine whether or not the articles in the parentheses are needed:

1. We had a plum and (a) peach for our lunch.
2. The Ohio and (the) Columbia are important rivers.
3. A blue and (a) yellow pencil are in the case.
4. The physician and (the) surgeon has opened a new office.
5. The president and (the) manager have sailed for Europe.
6. The secretary and (the) treasurer has written the report.
7. The sun and (the) planets that revolve around it belong to the solar system.
8. A canoe and (a) rowboat are on the lake.
9. A brown and (a) white dog were playing in the street.
10. The father and (the) mother of the priest were present at his ordination.
11. The captain and (the) pilot was speaking to the stewardess.
12. The Indians and (the) settlers made a treaty.
13. The aunt and (the) godmother of the baby is knitting a sweater for her.

THE CAPTAIN AND THE CENTER

THE CAPTAIN AND CENTER

4. *Demonstrative Adjectives*

The demonstrative adjectives *this* and *that* agree in number with the nouns they modify.

This book	*These* books
That kind of shoe	*Those* kinds of shoes

This and *these* denote objects that are near. *That* and *those* denote more distant objects.

EXERCISE 48

Fill in each blank space with the correct demonstrative adjective. Be sure that each agrees in number with the noun it modifies:

1. .... kind of picture is suitable for posters. *(Near)*
2. .... type of test is difficult. *(Near)*
3. Why doesn't he like .... kind of story? *(Distant)*
4. .... styles of hats are preferred by most girls. *(Distant)*
5. Is .... brand of flour satisfactory? *(Near)*
6. Use .... type of map. *(Distant)*
7. In my collection I have many of .... kinds of stamps. *(Distant)*
8. .... sort of game does not appeal to me. *(Distant)*
9. Do you like .... style of coat? *(Near)*
10. My uncle bought me .... skates. *(Near)*
11. Printers use .... kind of ink. *(Distant)*
12. Several of .... varieties were on display. *(Distant)*
13. My mother bakes .... kind of cake. *(Distant)*
14. Does your grandfather use .... brand of tobacco? *(Near)*
15. .... varieties of tulips are imported from Holland. *(Distant)*
16. .... shade of blue is attractive. *(Near)*
17. My father does not approve of .... manner of behavior. *(Distant)*
18. .... types of coats are warm. *(Distant)*
19. Mary wishes to purchase .... brand of soap. *(Near)*
20. The president will address .... group of students. *(Distant)*

5. *Words Used as Nouns and Adjectives*

The use of a word in the sentence determines the part of speech. Very frequently the same word may be used both as a noun and as an adjective.

A noun is a name word; an adjective describes or limits a noun.

The *iron* is very hot. *(Noun)*

An *iron* pot hung over the fireplace. *(Adjective)*

EXERCISE 49

Tell whether each word in italics is a noun or an adjective:

1. Christ observed a *fast* of forty days.
2. Did you see that *fast* train?
3. The *inside* cover was colorfully decorated.
4. Let me see the *inside*.
5. Mother has a new *brown* suit.
6. *Brown* predominates in that picture.
7. The *past* will never return.
8. His *past* acts of kindness will always be remembered.
9. Draw a *round* figure at the top of the page.
10. Yesterday was a *round* of excitement for us.
11. *March* is the first spring month.
12. *March* days are often windy.
13. George used a *rubber* hose to sprinkle the lawn.
14. *Rubber* has many uses.
15. That figure is a *solid*.
16. A *solid* wall surrounded the estate.
17. Mr. Hill was the first one called to the *witness* stand.
18. The *witness* arose and took the oath.
19. *Gold* is heavier than iron.
20. Mary broke the new *lamp* shade.
21. Do you like this *lamp*?
22. My father is a *custom* tailor in New Orleans.
23. That is an old Spanish *custom*.
24. Winifred plucked this *flower* from our garden.
25. Those *flower* seeds should be planted soon.

EXERCISE 50   [Test on Adjectives]

Read this selection very carefully and then answer the questions that follow:

[1] Have you ever considered what would happen to us if our American bird life became extinct? [2] To appreciate the dire consequences of such a misfortune we must be acquainted with the many ways in which these feathered friends help mankind. [3] The destruction of harmful insects is perhaps their most important work. [4] This constant war on one natural enemy of man makes the farmers' task easier. [5] The seed diet of some birds helps to keep the weed crop under control, while many of the larger birds prevent mice and rats from becoming intolerable pests. [6] What better reasons could we have for ranking these busy workers among our greatest benefactors?

1. Find a proper adjective in the paragraph.
2. Name the definite and the indefinite articles in the second sentence.
3. Find an interrogative adjective.
4. Select a numeral adjective.
5. What kind of adjective is *our* in the first sentence?
6. Find a singular and a plural demonstrative adjective.
7. Name an indefinite adjective in the fifth sentence.
8. How is the adjective *extinct* in the first sentence used?
9. Can the adjective *extinct* be compared?
10. What is the syntax of *easier* in the fourth sentence?
11. In the sixth sentence name adjectives in the positive degree, the comparative degree, and the superlative degree.
12. Write the positive and the comparative forms of *most important* in the third sentence.
13. Compare the adjective *harmful* in the third sentence.
14. Give the positive and the superlative forms of *larger,* an adjective in the fifth sentence.
15. Name the adjective which modifies the subject of the fifth sentence. Can this word be used as any other part of speech?

CHAPTER FOUR

Verbs

A verb is a word used to express action, being, or state of being.

Baptism *cleanses* us from original sin. *(Action)*
The pope *is* the visible head of the Church. *(Being)*
A large crucifix *hangs* on the wall. *(State of being)*

Without the verb there can be no sentence.

EXERCISE 51

Select the sentences from the following groups of words:

1. Listen.
2. Pray constantly for the grace of a happy death.
3. Skilled military leaders for the cause of the Confederacy.
4. The Holy Spirit is the third Person of the Blessed Trinity.
5. Roger B. Taney, our first Catholic chief justice of the Supreme Court.

6. See how these Christians love one another.
7. Many fine horses are raised in Argentina.
8. Close the door.
9. Saint Anne, the mother of the Blessed Virgin.
10. The United States is larger than Australia.
11. In place of the dilapidated chair.
12. Denver is the capital of Colorado.

VERB PHRASES

A verb phrase is a group of words used to do the work of a single verb.

Coal *is used* to furnish heat.
The name *has been pronounced* correctly.

Any verb used with the principal verb to form its voice, mood, and tense is called an auxiliary verb. The following are common auxiliary verbs:

be	are	do	has	will	might
am	was	did	had	may	could
is	were	have	shall	can	would

KINDS OF VERBS

1. *Division according to Form*

The principal parts of the verb are the present, the past, and the past participle because all other forms of the verb are determined from these.

REGULAR AND IRREGULAR VERBS

A regular verb is a verb that forms its past tense and its past participle by adding *d* or *ed* to the present tense.

An irregular verb is a verb that does not form its past tense and its past participle by adding *d* or *ed* to the present tense.

	PRESENT	PAST	PAST PARTICIPLE
Regular Verb:	pray	prayed	prayed
Irregular Verb:	rise	rose	risen

Review the principal parts of the following irregular verbs:

PRESENT	PAST	PAST PARTICIPLE
am (is, be)	was	been
*awake	awoke, awaked	awaked
*beat	beat	beat, beaten
begin	began	begun
bend	bent	bent
bet	bet	bet
bind	bound	bound
bite	bit	bitten
blow	blew	blown
break	broke	broken
bring	brought	brought
*build	built, builded	built, builded
*burn	burned, burnt	burned, burnt
burst	burst	burst
catch	caught	caught
choose	chose	chosen
come	came	come
creep	crept	crept
do	did	done
draw	drew	drawn
*dream	dreamed, dreamt	dreamed, dreamt
drink	drank	drunk
drive	drove	driven
*dwell	dwelt, dwelled	dwelt, dwelled
eat	ate	eaten
fall	fell	fallen
find	found	found
flee	fled	fled
fly	flew	flown
forget	forgot	forgotten
freeze	froze	frozen
give	gave	given
go	went	gone
grow	grew	grown

---

* If a verb has more than one form for its past tense or past participle, it is a redundant verb. The asterisk indicates redundant verbs.

PRESENT	PAST	PAST PARTICIPLE
hang	hung	hung
have	had	had
*hide	hid	hidden, hid
hold	held	held
hurt	hurt	hurt
keep	kept	kept
*kneel	knelt, kneeled	knelt, kneeled
*knit	knit, knitted	knit, knitted
know	knew	known
lay	laid	laid
lead	led	led
leave	left	left
lend	lent	lent
let	let	let
lie (recline)	lay	lain
*light	lighted, lit	lighted, lit
lose	lost	lost
make	made	made
mean	meant	meant
meet	met	met
read	read	read
ride	rode	ridden
ring	rang	rung
rise	rose	risen
run	ran	run
say	said	said
see	saw	seen
seek	sought	sought
set	set	set
shake	shook	shaken
*show	showed	shown, showed
sing	sang	sung
sink	sank	sunk
sit	sat	sat
sleep	slept	slept
*slide	slid	slid, slidden
*smell	smelled, smelt	smelled, smelt
*sow	sowed	sown, sowed

PRESENT	PAST	PAST PARTICIPLE
speak	spoke	spoken
spend	spent	spent
*spill	spilled, spilt	spilled, spilt
stand	stood	stood
steal	stole	stolen
stick	stuck	stuck
sting	stung	stung
stride	strode	stridden
swim	swam	swum
swing	swung	swung
teach	taught	taught
tear	tore	torn
throw	threw	thrown
*wake	waked, woke	waked, woken
wear	wore	worn
weave	wove	woven
win	won	won
wind	wound	wound
wring	wrung	wrung
write	wrote	written

Defective verbs are verbs that do not have all the principal parts. These are *shall, will, can, may, must, ought, beware.*

2. *Division according to Use*

TRANSITIVE VERBS

A transitive verb is a verb that expresses an action which passes from a doer to a receiver.

DOER	ACTION	RECEIVER
Christ	instituted	the sacraments.

Instituted is a transitive verb because the action passes from the doer, *Christ,* to the receiver, *sacraments.*

To determine the receiver of the action, ask the question *whom* or *what* after the verb. Christ instituted what? The answer to this question determines the receiver of the action.

The action may pass from the doer to the receiver in two different ways:

Christ *instituted* the sacraments.
The sacraments *were instituted* by Christ.

Christ is the doer of the action in both sentences, and *sacraments* is the receiver. Since the action passes from the doer to the receiver in each case, the verb *institute,* whether in the form of *instituted* or *were instituted,* is a transitive verb.

The doer is not always expressed when a transitive verb is used in the passive voice.

News *is broadcast* by many commentators. *(Doer expressed)*
News *is broadcast* every hour. *(Doer not expressed)*

INTRANSITIVE VERBS

An intransitive verb is a verb that has no receiver of its action.

DOER	ACTION	(NO RECEIVER)
The general	hastened away.	....

The action of the verb *hastened* begins and ends with the doer, or the subject of the verb. The question *whom* or *what* after the verb will receive no answer because there is no receiver.

Intransitive verbs are always in the active voice, since a verb is in the active voice when its subject is the doer of the action.

Some verbs may be transitive or intransitive according to their use in the sentence.

Experience *develops* character. *(Transitive verb)*
Manufacturing *developed* rapidly in the New England states. *(Intransitive verb)*
The sun *melted* the ice. *(Transitive verb)*
The ice *melted* slowly. *(Intransitive verb)*

A cognate verb is a verb whose object repeats the meaning implied by the verb itself.

The child *dreamed* a pleasant *dream.*

A cognate verb is usually an intransitive verb that becomes transitive by taking an object derived from the verb itself.

EXERCISE 52

Select the verbs in the following sentences and tell whether they are transitive, intransitive, or cognate:

1. Joseph Lister introduced antiseptics into surgery.
2. What mysteries are expressed by the sign of the cross?
3. Mother Katharine Drexel contributed large sums of money to charitable institutions.
4. At last the provisions arrived.
5. A bloody battle was fought there.
6. The Second Crusade was preached by Saint Bernard.
7. Marian smiled a pleasant smile.
8. The children scattered in all directions.
9. The altar is covered with three linen cloths.
10. Railroads aided greatly in the development of the West.
11. John, have you studied your lessons?
12. Those who live a life of virtue will sleep the sleep of the just.
13. Robert Louis Stevenson wrote stories of adventure.
14. Nothing remains of the old abbey but the ruins.
15. Multicolored pebbles were scattered along the beach.
16. Francis learns very quickly.
17. The first American flag was made by Betsy Ross.
18. The Holy Spirit filled the apostles with knowledge, grace, and strength.

COPULATIVE VERBS

A copulative verb is a linking verb. It links or couples with the subject a noun, a pronoun, or an adjective.

A word or a group of words used to complete the meaning of a copulative verb is called a *subjective complement*. If the complement is a noun or a pronoun, it is called a *predicate nominative;* if an adjective, it is called a *predicate adjective.*

SUBJECT	COPULATIVE	COMPLEMENT
Saul's Roman name	was	Paul.
I	am	she.
The room	seems	cold.

The verb *be* in its various forms is the most common copulative. Some other verbs which may be used as linking verbs are *appear, become, continue, feel, grow, look, remain, seem, smell, sound,* and *taste.*

EXERCISE 53

Select the copulative verb in each of the following sentences and tell whether this verb links to the subject a noun, a pronoun, or an adjective:

1. A good example is the best sermon.
2. We are God's children.
3. An encyclical is a papal letter to the bishops of the world.
4. The optic nerve is the nerve of sight.
5. Barbara and Helen are members of our club.
6. Jacob and Esau were brothers.
7. Saint John the Baptist was the cousin of our Lord.
8. Is that you, William?
9. Those violets smell fragrant.
10. The plan appears workable.
11. The Apostles' Creed is a summary of the principal truths of our faith.

12. God is merciful.
13. My hands feel chapped.
14. That gem seems valuable.
15. How high those mountains look!
16. Joseph has been present every day this year.
17. My brother has become a priest.
18. Our bodies are temples of the Holy Spirit.
19. The boy in that car may have been he.
20. Who is the winner?

ATTRIBUTES OR QUALITIES OF A VERB

1. *Voice*

Voice is that quality of a verb which shows whether the subject is the doer or the receiver of the action.

In the *active voice* the subject is the doer of the action. In the *passive voice* the subject is the receiver of the action.

Saint Patrick *converted* Ireland.
Ireland *was converted* by Saint Patrick.

In the first sentence the subject, *Saint Patrick,* is the doer of the action, *converted;* therefore *converted* is in the active voice. The receiver of the action is the direct object, *Ireland.* In the second sentence the subject, *Ireland,* is the receiver of the action, *was converted;* therefore *was converted* is in the passive voice.

Only transitive verbs are used in the passive voice. Intransitive verbs have no receivers of the action.

FORMATION OF THE PASSIVE VOICE

The passive voice is formed by using some tense of the verb *be* as an auxiliary with the past participle of the verb. Therefore the verb *be* (and its tenses), used before a past participle, is generally the sign of the passive voice.

was + called = passive voice

Two sentences may convey the same idea, the one expressing it by a verb in the *active voice,* and the other by a verb in the *passive voice.* When a verb in the active voice is changed to the passive voice, the subject of the active verb is usually made the object of a preposition, and the object of the active verb becomes the subject of the passive verb.

The brain *keeps* the body under control. *(Active voice)*
The body *is kept* under control by the brain. *(Passive voice)*

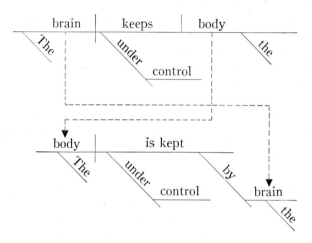

In each of these sentences the *brain* performs the action, and the *body* receives the action. In the first sentence *brain* is the subject of the verb *keeps;* in the second sentence it becomes the object of the preposition *by.*

Body, the receiver of the action, is the direct object of the active verb *keeps,* but in the second sentence it becomes the subject of the passive verb *is kept.*

EXERCISE 54

Rewrite the following sentences, changing active verbs to passive voice and passive verbs to active voice:

1. We help the souls in purgatory by prayers and good works.
2. The Panama Canal connects the Atlantic and the Pacific oceans. •

Act - Doer is Sub
Pas -   "   " D. O

3. Aggressive campaigns are frequently waged against forest fires.
4. Exercise strengthens the heart and the lungs.
5. The blue fox is highly prized for its fur.
6. The American Red Cross was founded by Clara Barton.
7. The will controls voluntary muscles.
8. Mince pie should be served hot.
9. Canadian wood pulp is exported to the United States.
10. Father Junipero Serra established many missions in California.
11. The incandescent lamp was invented by Edison.
12. Saint Augustine was converted by the prayers of his mother.

THE RETAINED OBJECT

When a verb in the passive voice "retains" the direct object it would govern if used in the active voice, this object is called a *retained object*.

The Negro was granted *freedom* by the Thirteenth Amendment.

Do not confuse the retained object with the predicate nominative. When the noun following the passive verb refers to the same person or thing as the subject, it is a *predicate nominative*.

Saint Joseph was appointed the *guardian* of the Christ Child. *(Predicate nominative)*

Saint Peter, the prince of the apostles, was given the *keys* to the kingdom of heaven. *(Retained object)*

EXERCISE 55

Select the retained objects and the predicate nominatives in the following sentences:

1. George was given a ticket for the football game.
2. John Quincy Adams was elected president by the House of Representatives.
3. David was anointed king.
4. The boys were refused admittance.
5. The baby was named Eleanor.

6. A baptized Christian who does not believe all the articles of faith is considered a heretic.
7. Artificial silk is called rayon.
8. Mr. Connors has been left a large estate.
9. The women of the country were granted suffrage by the Nineteenth Amendment.
10. Each pupil was assigned a place on the stage.

2. *Tense*

Tense is that quality of a verb which denotes the time of the action, the being, or the state of being.

SIMPLE TENSES

Present tense **signifies action, being, or state of being in present time.**

Past tense **signifies action, being, or state of being in past time.**

Future tense **signifies action, being, or state of being in future time.**

PRESENT: Regina *studies* diligently.
PAST: Regina *studied* diligently.
FUTURE: Regina *will study* diligently.

In the passive voice the tense is shown by the *auxiliary verb.*

PRESENT: The lesson *is studied.*
PAST: The lesson *was studied.*
FUTURE: The lesson *will be studied.*

EXERCISE 56

Give the tense and the voice of the verb in each of the following sentences:

1. Our class will present a radio program for Pan-American Day.
2. We lose sanctifying grace by mortal sin.
3. The expulsion of the Acadians was immortalized by Longfellow in his poem "Evangeline."

4. A new church will soon be built on this corner.
5. The first word of every sentence begins with a capital letter.
6. After her assumption Mary was crowned queen of heaven.
7. On feasts of our Lady the priest wears white vestments.
8. God will reward the good and will punish the wicked.
9. Opportunities never wait.
10. The scenery of the Swiss Alps attracted tourists from many countries.
11. Large quantities of butter and cheese are produced in Wisconsin.
12. Shall we leave now?

COMPOUND TENSES

Present perfect tense **signifies action, being, or state of being completed or perfected in present time.**

Past perfect tense **signifies action, being, or state of being completed or perfected before some definite past time.**

Future perfect tense **signifies action, being, or state of being that will be completed or perfected before some specified time in the future.**

ACTIVE VOICE

PRESENT PERFECT: Regina *has* always *studied* diligently.

PAST PERFECT: Regina *had studied* diligently before the examination.

FUTURE PERFECT: Regina *will have studied* diligently before the examination.

PASSIVE VOICE

PRESENT PERFECT: The lesson *has been studied.*

PAST PERFECT: The lesson *had been studied.*

FUTURE PERFECT: The lesson *will have been studied.*

EXERCISE 57

Give the tense and the voice of the verb in each of the following sentences:

1. Mary has purchased a statue of the Infant of Prague.
2. The letter will have been written before that time.

3. Railroads have been constructed through mountains in the West.
4. They will have returned from their trip before the end of March.
5. The bell had been rung early.
6. Have you read *Our Lady's Slave?*
7. A new airport has been built in Philadelphia.
8. Methods of farming have been greatly improved since colonial days.
9. I shall have completed my last assignment by Monday.
10. The United States has strictly limited immigration in recent years.
11. Throughout the ages the Catholic Church has been governed by one head.
12. Helen had misspelled the word three times.
13. Has Raymond followed your advice?
14. All the cakes have been sold. ᵗᵃˢᵗ Per.

3. *Mood*

Mood or mode is that attribute or quality of a verb that denotes the manner in which the action, the being, or the state of being is expressed.

INDICATIVE MOOD

The indicative mood is used to state a fact, to deny a fact, or to ask a question.

STATES A FACT: The population of Alaska *has increased* in recent years.
DENIES A FACT: It *is* not always cold in Alaska.
ASKS A QUESTION: When *was* the Alcan Highway *completed?*

All the six tenses are found in the indicative mood.

PRESENT: She *writes* letters.
PAST: She *wrote* the letters yesterday.
FUTURE: She *will write* the letters today.
PRESENT PERFECT: She *has written* many letters today.
PAST PERFECT: She *had written* the letters before noon.
FUTURE PERFECT: She *will have written* the letters before tomorrow.

PROGRESSIVE FORM OF THE INDICATIVE MOOD

The progressive form of the verb denotes an action as going on or in progress. In the active voice the various tenses of the verb *be* are used with the present participle of the main verb to form the progressive verb phrases.

PRESENT TENSE: She *is writing* letters.
PAST TENSE: She *was writing* letters yesterday.
FUTURE TENSE: She *will be writing* letters today.
PRESENT PERFECT TENSE: She *has been writing* letters this morning.
PAST PERFECT TENSE: She *had been writing* letters before noon.
FUTURE PERFECT TENSE: She *will have been writing* letters before the end of the day.

The present and the past tenses of the progressive form are the two tenses most frequently used in the passive voice.

PRESENT: The letter *is being written.*
PAST: The letter *was being written.*

EXERCISE 58

Select the progressive verb phrases and give the tense and the voice of each:

1. Robert is teaching his dog a new trick.
2. Numerous airplanes were flying back and forth over the field.
3. Hot chocolate was being served in the cafeteria.
4. The children were praying when our Lady appeared to them.
5. We have been resting for an hour.
6. The apostles had been fishing all night.
7. The prizes are being displayed in the library.
8. Marie has been checking the mistakes.
9. Where is your new home being built?
10. Dr. Ryan has been examining the pupils in our class.
11. Helen and Susan are washing the dishes.
12. The boys have been practicing for the game.
13. Who is preparing the lunch?
14. My sister has been teaching in that school for several years.
15. Had both of you been working on that puzzle?

EMPHATIC FORM OF THE INDICATIVE MOOD

The emphatic form is used to give emphasis to the verb.

Moral support *does lend* encouragement.
High ideals *did lead* him to the nobler things of life.

The emphatic form is used only in the present and the past tenses of the active voice. The auxiliary *do* before the present part of the verb forms the present tense, and the auxiliary *did* with the present part of the verb forms the past tense.

NOTE. In questions and in negative statements, *do* and *did* are not used emphatically.

EXERCISE 59

Select the emphatic verb phrases in the following sentences and give the tense of each:

1. I do see my mistake now.
2. I did try that key before.
3. Paul did deliver the telegram.
4. Lucille does study every night.
5. I did enjoy the first book, but I did not like the second one.
6. The secretary did submit the report on time.
7. Yes, our team did win the last game.
8. Did you receive Holy Communion this morning?
9. Eleanor and Clare do work well together.
10. My brother does sing in the choir.

POTENTIAL FORM OF THE INDICATIVE MOOD

The potential form of the indicative mood is used to express permission, possibility, ability, necessity, or obligation.

PERMISSION: You *may open* the box, Robert.
POSSIBILITY: Mother *might return* early.
ABILITY: My sister *can play* the violin.
NECESSITY: You *must wind* this clock every night.
OBLIGATION: We *should pray* frequently.

The auxiliary verbs *may, might, can, could, must, should,* and *would* are used in the potential form.

TENSES OF THE POTENTIAL FORM

The potential form is used in the present, the past, the present perfect, and the past perfect tenses, but not in the future tenses.

ACTIVE VOICE

PRESENT TENSE: We *must obey* all lawful authority.
PAST TENSE: I *could* not *find* the paper.
PRESENT PERFECT TENSE: He *may have broken* the chair.
PAST PERFECT TENSE: You *should have packed* the lunch last night.

PASSIVE VOICE

PRESENT TENSE: All lawful authority *must be obeyed.*
PAST TENSE: The paper *could* not *be found.*
PRESENT PERFECT TENSE: The chair *may have been broken.*
PAST PERFECT TENSE: The lunch *should have been packed* last night.

EXERCISE 60

Select the potential verb phrases and tell what idea is expressed by each:

1. Martin can swim better than any other boy in our class.
2. We should contribute to the church collections.
3. Ruth should have prepared the work yesterday.
4. Margaret can speak Spanish fluently.
5. The boys may have lost their way.
6. They could not sight the plane.
7. You may use my skates, Josephine.
8. This work must be completed immediately.
9. You should have answered the letter sooner.
10. You must take more outdoor exercise.
11. That fruit cannot grow in this soil.
12. Mother may take me with her.
13. Rose Marie could not accompany us.
14. John must have misunderstood your question.
15. The package may have arrived while we were gone.
16. The pilot could see the lights of the airport.
17. My father may go to Boston tomorrow.
18. Edward could have done the errand for you.

OUTLINE FOR DRILL ON SPECIAL FORMS OF THE INDICATIVE

	PROGRESSIVE	EMPHATIC	POTENTIAL
USE:	Denotes action in progress.	Lends emphasis to a statement.	Expresses permission, possibility, ability, necessity, obligation.
SIGN:	*ing* (present participle of the principal verb)	*Do* or *did* used as auxiliaries.	*May, can, must, might, could, should, would*
TENSE:	Present, past, future, present perfect, past perfect, future perfect	Present, past	Present, past, present perfect, past perfect
VOICE:	Active, passive	Active	Active, passive

EXERCISE 61

Give the special form, the tense, and the voice of each verb in the following sentences:

1. Our school is being painted.
2. The expressman may have left the package at your old address.
3. He did see Mr. Kennedy last night.
4. No one can disgrace us but ourselves.
5. The key must have been bent in the lock.
6. The boys did select the motto.
7. Daniel should have filled the gasoline tank yesterday.
8. British manufacturers have been making textile products for many years.
9. Mary does work perseveringly.
10. I do say the rosary every day.
11. My father had been working in a large department store.
12. Our exports do exceed our imports.
13. Who can solve this problem?
14. My parents are going to the seashore tomorrow.
15. Their house is being remodeled.
16. The speaker could not be heard in the back of the auditorium.

17. I have been making a novena for my grandparents.
18. You should have been more attentive.
19. Mary and Joseph had been looking for the Christ Child for three days.
20. She does understand the rules.
21. The boys may have been delayed by the storm.
22. We should have been more careful.
23. I did remind Mary of her appointment.
24. We were discussing plans for the picnic.
25. Lunch is being served in the cafeteria.

IMPERATIVE MOOD

The imperative mood is used to express a command in the second person. A mild command often takes the form of an entreaty or a request.

COMMAND: *Present* arms!
ENTREATY: *Have* pity on me, at least you, my friends.
REQUEST: *Close* the door quietly, Rose.

The present tense is the only tense in the imperative mood. The subject of a verb in the imperative mood is always in the second person, either singular or plural, and it is usually not expressed.

SUBJUNCTIVE MOOD

The subjunctive mood generally expresses a wish or desire, an uncertainty, or a condition contrary to fact.

The subordinate conjunctions *if, as if, provided, though, lest, whether, unless,* and some of the potential auxiliaries are sometimes used to introduce a verb in the subjunctive mood. A subordinate conjunction or an auxiliary verb, however, is not always necessary when the verb is in the subjunctive mood.

WISH: God *bless* you! *(No conjunction or auxiliary verb)*

UNCERTAINTY: Whether that *be* true or not, we have not changed our plans. *(With the subordinate conjunction* whether*)*

CONTRARY TO FACT: If she *were* a queen, she could not be more gracious. *(With the subordinate conjunction* if*)*

In the subjunctive mood there are four tenses: the present, the past, the present perfect, and the past perfect. Study the subjunctive mood in the conjugations of the verb *be* and the verb *teach* on pages 294-95 and 297-98.

EXERCISE 62

Name the verbs in the imperative and the subjunctive moods and explain the use of each:

1. Take off your boots, William.
2. Long live the king!
3. If my sister were here, she would play the piano.
4. May she be happy in her new work!
5. Heaven help you!
6. Whether he be honest or not, we do not know.
7. I wish it were warmer today.
8. Move to the rear of the bus, boys.
9. He looks as if he were ill.
10. Write your name on this sheet of paper, Martin.
11. Kindly fill out the enclosed application blank and return it as soon as possible.
12. Thy will be done.
13. If Uncle Robert had gone with us, we would not have lost our way.
14. Remember your prayers, Barbara.
15. If I were you, I should read that book.
16. May God grant us this favor.
17. Peace be to you!
18. Michael ran as if he were frightened.
19. Give us this day our daily bread.
20. Oh, that we were ready!

4. *Person and Number*

A verb may be in the first, the second, or the third person, and either singular or plural in number. Most verbs do not have a specific inflection or change in form for every person and number.

The present tense of the indicative mood of the verb *study* has the following forms:

	SINGULAR NUMBER	PLURAL NUMBER
FIRST PERSON:	I study	We study
SECOND PERSON:	You study	You study
THIRD PERSON:	He studies	They study

EXERCISE 63

Tell the person and the number of each verb:

1. Here come my brothers down the street.
2. This book doesn't interest me.
3. My chief concern is mistakes in English.
4. The bus leaves from this station.
5. Which one of the boys goes in my direction?
6. Were you at the football game yesterday?
7. The price of that radio seems too high.
8. On the next street lives my friend, George Gantz.
9. Many hands make light work.
10. This old trunk belongs to Grandmother.

CONJUGATION

Conjugation is the orderly arrangement of a verb according to voice, mood, tense, person, and number.

CONJUGATION OF THE VERB "BE"

	PRESENT	PAST	PAST PARTICIPLE
PRINCIPAL PARTS:	be	was	been

INDICATIVE MOOD

PRESENT TENSE

Singular	*Plural*
1. I am	We are
2. You are	You are
3. He is[1]	They are

---

[1] The subject in the third person singular may also be *she* or *it*.

PAST TENSE

Singular	*Plural*
1. I was	We were
2. You were	You were
3. He was[1]	They were

FUTURE TENSE

1. I shall be	We shall be
2. You will be	You will be
3. He will be	They will be

PRESENT PERFECT TENSE

1. I have been	We have been
2. You have been	You have been
3. He has been	They have been

PAST PERFECT TENSE

1. I had been	We had been
2. You had been	You had been
3. He had been	They had been

FUTURE PERFECT TENSE

1. I shall have been	We shall have been
2. You will have been	You will have been
3. He will have been	They will have been

SUBJUNCTIVE MOOD

PRESENT TENSE

1. If I be[2]	If we be
2. If you be	If you be
3. If he be	If they be

PAST TENSE

1. If I were	If we were
2. If you were	If you were
3. If he were	If they were

---

[1] The subject in the third person singular may also be *she* or *it*.

[2] May also be preceded by *provided, though, although, lest, unless,* and so forth.

PRESENT PERFECT TENSE

Singular	*Plural*
1. If I have been	If we have been
2. If you have been	If you have been
3. If he have been[1]	If they have been

PAST PERFECT TENSE

1. If I had been	If we had been
2. If you had been	If you had been
3. If he had been	If they had been

IMPERATIVE MOOD

PRESENT TENSE

Be (be you)   Be (be you)

INFINITIVES

PRESENT: To be   PRESENT PERFECT: To have been

PARTICIPLES

PRESENT: Being   PAST: Been   PERFECT: Having been

CONJUGATION OF THE VERB "TEACH"

	PRESENT	PAST	PAST PARTICIPLE
PRINCIPAL PARTS:	teach	taught	taught

INDICATIVE MOOD

Active Voice

PRESENT TENSE

1. I teach	We teach
2. You teach	You teach
3. He teaches	They teach

PAST TENSE

1. I taught	We taught
2. You taught	You taught
3. He taught	They taught

---

[1] *If he has been* is also accepted by some authorities.

FUTURE TENSE

Singular	*Plural*
1. I shall teach	We shall teach
2. You will teach	You will teach
3. He will teach	They will teach

PRESENT PERFECT TENSE

1. I have taught	We have taught
2. You have taught	You have taught
3. He has taught	They have taught

PAST PERFECT TENSE

1. I had taught	We had taught
2. You had taught	You had taught
3. He had taught	They had taught

FUTURE PERFECT TENSE

1. I shall have taught	We shall have taught
2. You will have taught	You will have taught
3. He will have taught	They will have taught

Passive Voice

PRESENT TENSE

1. I am taught	We are taught
2. You are taught	You are taught
3. He is taught	They are taught

PAST TENSE

1. I was taught	We were taught
2. You were taught	You were taught
3. He was taught	They were taught

FUTURE TENSE

1. I shall be taught	We shall be taught
2. You will be taught	You will be taught
3. He will be taught	They will be taught

PRESENT PERFECT TENSE

1. I have been taught	We have been taught
2. You have been taught	You have been taught
3. He has been taught	They have been taught

PAST PERFECT TENSE

Singular	*Plural*
1. I had been taught	We had been taught
2. You had been taught	You had been taught
3. He had been taught	They had been taught

FUTURE PERFECT TENSE

1. I shall have been taught	We shall have been taught
2. You will have been taught	You will have been taught
3. He will have been taught	They will have been taught

SUBJUNCTIVE MOOD

Active Voice

PRESENT TENSE

1. If I teach[1]	If we teach
2. If you teach	If you teach
3. If he teach	If they teach

PAST TENSE

1. If I taught	If we taught
2. If you taught	If you taught
3. If he taught	If they taught

PRESENT PERFECT TENSE

1. If I have taught	If we have taught
2. If you have taught	If you have taught
3. If he have taught[2]	If they have taught

PAST PERFECT TENSE

1. If I had taught	If we had taught
2. If you had taught	If you had taught
3. If he had taught	If they had taught

---

[1] May also be preceded by *provided, though, although, lest, unless,* and so forth.

[2] *If he has taught* is also accepted by some authorities.

Passive Voice

PRESENT TENSE

Singular	*Plural*
1. If I be taught	If we be taught
2. If you be taught	If you be taught
3. If he be taught	If they be taught

PAST TENSE

1. If I were taught	If we were taught
2. If you were taught	If you were taught
3. If he were taught	If they were taught

PRESENT PERFECT TENSE

1. If I have been taught	If we have been taught
2. If you have been taught	If you have been taught
3. If he have been taught[1]	If they have been taught

PAST PERFECT TENSE

1. If I had been taught	If we had been taught
2. If you had been taught	If you had been taught
3. If he had been taught	If they had been taught

IMPERATIVE MOOD

PRESENT TENSE

Active Voice	*Passive Voice*
Teach (teach you)	Be taught (be you taught)

INFINITIVES

PRESENT: To teach	To be taught
PERFECT: To have taught	To have been taught

PARTICIPLES

PRESENT: Teaching	Being taught
PAST: Taught[2]	Taught
PERFECT: Having taught	Having been taught

---

[1] *If he has been taught* is also accepted by some authorities.

[2] The past participle is essentially passive. In the case of intransitive verbs, however, it is in the active voice. (*Immersed* in his books, the boy did not hear my question.)

SYNOPSIS OF A VERB

A synopsis is an abbreviated conjugation. It is made by giving the form for one person and number of each tense in a designated mood or moods.

SYNOPSIS OF THE VERB "TEACH"

(Indicative mood, third person, singular number)

	Active Voice	*Passive Voice*
PRESENT TENSE	He teaches	He is taught
PAST TENSE	He taught	He was taught
FUTURE TENSE	He will teach	He will be taught
PRESENT PERFECT TENSE	He has taught	He has been taught
PAST PERFECT TENSE	He had taught	He had been taught
FUTURE PERFECT TENSE	He will have taught	He will have been taught

THE CORRECT USE OF VERBS

1. *Agreement of Verb with Subject*

The verb must always agree with its subject in person and number.

This agreement does not require a specific inflection in every person, number, and tense. In the present tense, for example, there is usually no change in the first and the second persons. In the third person of the present tense, however, the singular form ends in *s ;* the plural form does not.

Inflection is the grammatical change in the form of the verb. Observe the inflection of the verbs in the following sentences:

He speaks slowly.	They speak slowly.
The victory is ours.	The victories are ours.
She has answered.	They have answered.

Which verbs have singular subjects? Which have plural? From these examples you see that the finite[1] verb takes the *s* form in the third person, singular number of the present tense.

---

[1] A finite verb is one that may be used as the principal verb in a clause. *Finite* means "limited."

SIMPLE SUBJECTS

A singular subject requires a singular verb. A plural subject requires a plural verb.

When a sentence begins with the expletive *there* the verb must agree with the subject that follows.

Always use the forms *you are* and *you were* whether the subject is singular or plural.

Here (is, are) your books.

The correct form is: Here *are* your books.

EXERCISE 64

Rewrite the following sentences, using the correct form of the verb in each. Give the reason for your choice:

1. There (is, are) twenty children in the yard.
2. You (was, were) not at home when I called.
3. In the garden (is, are) many bright flowers.
4. There (was, were) only one man in the room.
5. The boys (likes, like) football.
6. The early American Indians (was, were) hunters and fishermen.
7. Smooth roads (makes, make) driving easy.
8. You (is, are) made to the image and likeness of God.
9. His friends (has, have) gone.
10. There (was, were) many toys in the playroom.
11. Grace (breaks, break) her glasses often.
12. Where (was, were) you this morning?
13. There (is, are) a new car in the garage.
14. (Was, were) you on the honor roll this month?
15. (Is, are) you going to camp this summer?
16. Why (is, are) crop rotation necessary?
17. You (has, have) come too early.
18. There (is, are) great natural forests in our country.
19. Against one wall of the library (stands, stand) two well-filled bookcases.
20. There (is, are) large sulphur deposits in Texas and Louisiana.

PHRASES AND PARENTHETICAL EXPRESSIONS

A phrase or a parenthetical expression between the subject and the verb does not change the number of the verb. If the subject is singular, the verb must be singular; if plural, the verb must be plural.

One of my sisters (goes, go) to high school.

The correct form is: One of my sisters *goes* to high school.

EXERCISE 65

Rewrite each of the following sentences, using the correct form of the verb indicated. Give the reason for your choice:

1. The delightful climate of the Hawaiian Islands (accounts, account) for the extensive tourist trade.
2. A plate of hot pancakes (was, were) placed before us.
3. His description of his journeys (was, were) most entertaining.
4. This statue, together with the pedestal, (was, were) donated to our class.
5. Marion, as well as her sisters, (is, are) very capable.
6. A shipment of citrus fruits (is, are) expected soon.
7. The construction of the bridges (seems, seem) slow.
8. The reference books, including a dictionary, (was, were) on the table.
9. The legends of that country (makes, make) interesting reading.
10. The second game of the series (was, were) played in Chicago.
11. The tuition, together with the cost of books, (has, have) been decreased.
12. The catalogue of pictures (has, have) a number of worth-while selections.
13. A complete list of the supplies (is, are) on the desk.
14. One of the men (has, have) applied for the position.
15. Edward, as well as Mary, (deserves, deserve) credit.

"DOESN'T" AND "DON'T"

If the subject of the sentence is in the third person, *doesn't* is the correct form in the singular; *don't* the correct form in the plural. In the first and the second persons the correct form is *don't,* whether the subject is singular or plural.

God (doesn't, don't) force His grace upon us.

The correct form is: God *doesn't* force His grace upon us.

EXERCISE 66

Supply the correct form, *doesn't* or *don't,* in each of the following sentences:

1. .... it seem quiet since Terence went away?
2. The librarian .... look well today.
3. The bus .... leave until four o'clock.
4. We .... begin class until the bell rings.
5. .... you understand the problem?
6. The cypress tree .... grow well in this region.
7. You .... seem to remember me.
8. .... the boy realize the value of money?
9. It .... pay to be dishonest.
10. My youngest sister .... resemble my mother or my father.
11. .... John know the answer?
12. He .... like the new arrangement.
13. Men .... pray enough.
14. Angels .... have bodies.
15. I .... disobey my father.
16. Why .... Geraldine help us?

COMPOUND SUBJECTS CONNECTED BY "AND"

Compound subjects connected by *and* require a plural verb unless the subjects refer to the same person or thing, or express a single idea.

Saint Peter and Saint Paul (was, were) martyred on the same day.
The writer and publisher of this book (is, are) well known.

The correct forms are:

Saint Peter and Saint Paul *were* martyred on the same day.
The writer and publisher of this book *is* well known.

EXERCISE 67

Rewrite each of the following sentences, using the correct form of the verb indicated. Give the reason for your choice:

1. John and Joseph (studies, study) together.
2. The president and manager (was, were) elected yesterday.
3. (Was, were) your father and mother with you last evening?
4. Elizabeth and her friend (is, are) expected soon.
5. Football and basketball (seems, seem) to be popular sports.
6. What (does, do) your parents and friends think of your new appointment?
7. Bread and butter (is, are) part of the ordinary diet.
8. My friend and classmate (writes, write) to me regularly.
9. Oranges and lemons (is, are) citrus fruits.
10. Here (comes, come) the president and the secretary together.
11. This is the second time that so many boys and girls (has, have) been on the honor roll.
12. His purpose and aim (is, are) to succeed.
13. The boys and the girls (agrees, agree) to help.
14. Michael and James (desires, desire) to enter the contest.
15. Bacon and eggs (was, were) served.

COMPOUND SUBJECTS PRECEDED BY "EACH" AND "EVERY"

Two or more singular subjects connected by *and* but preceded by *each, every, many a,* or *no* require a singular verb.

(Has, have) every pen and pencil been placed on the desk?

The correct form is: *Has* every pen and pencil been placed on the desk?

EXERCISE 68

Rewrite each of the following sentences, using the correct form of the verb indicated. Give the reason for your choice:

1. Many a man and woman (buys, buy) foolish things at times.
2. Every boy and girl (has, have) a desire to succeed.
3. Every town and borough (was, were) represented.
4. Many a boy and girl (has, have) tried to do the same thing.

5. Every door and window in the studio (is, are) closed.
6. Almost every man and boy (likes, like) to play ball.
7. Each boy and girl (is, are) to remain for the entertainment.
8. Many a soldier and sailor (risks, risk) danger.
9. Every city and village (was, were) destroyed by the flood.
10. Many a watch and clock (was, were) made by him.
11. Each day and hour (brings, bring) its duty.
12. Many a man and boy (is, are) familiar with camp life.
13. Each senator and representative (was, were) present.
14. No fortune and no position in life (makes, make) a guilty man happy.
15. Every woman and girl (likes, like) to look at styles.

COMPOUND SUBJECTS CONNECTED BY "OR" AND "NOR"

Singular subjects connected by *or* or *nor* require a singular verb. Plural subjects connected by *or* or *nor* require a plural verb.

Neither Walter nor James (is, are) ready.
Neither the boys nor the girls (is, are) ready.

The correct forms are:

Neither Walter nor James *is* ready.
Neither the boys nor the girls *are* ready.

When two or more subjects of different person or number are connected by *or* or *nor,* the verb agrees with the subject nearest it.

Neither he nor I (am, is, are) ready.

The correct form is: Neither he nor I *am* ready.

EXERCISE 69

Rewrite each of the following sentences, using the correct form of the verb indicated. Give the reason for your choice:

1. Neither history nor geography (is, are) difficult for me.
2. (Is, are) either Anne or Ellen going with you?
3. Neither the letter nor the post card (was, were) properly addressed.
4. Lilian or her sister (is, are) checking the list.

5. Neither Francis nor Mary (likes, like) the new schedule.
6. Neither the trunk nor the box (has, have) arrived.
7. (Has, have) either John or Robert been given a part in the play?
8. Neither Donald nor Edward (was, were) prepared.
9. Either the chairman or his secretary (is, are) in the office.
10. (Has, have) either Agnes or Kathleen returned?
11. Neither the tulips nor the daffodils (has, have) bloomed yet.
12. Either you or I (am, is, are) expected to answer.
13. Either you or he (has, have) lost the book.
14. Neither money nor worldly pleasures (satisfies, satisfy) man's desire for happiness.
15. Neither the coffee nor the sandwiches (is, are) ready.
16. Either you or your brother (is, are) to be chairman.
17. Neither the door nor the windows (was, were) bolted.
18. Neither Dolores nor I (was, were) inconvenienced by your action.
19. Either the meat or the potatoes (is, are) burning.
20. Neither Joan nor I (likes, like) peppermint candy.

COLLECTIVE NOUNS

A collective noun requires a singular verb if the idea expressed by the subject is thought of as a unit. A plural verb may be used if the idea expressed by the subject denotes separate individuals.

A flock of sheep (was, were) seen on the mountainside.
The flock of sheep (was, were) eating their food.

The correct forms are:

A flock of sheep *was* seen on the mountainside.
The flock of sheep (sheep in the flock) *were* eating their food.

EXERCISE 70

Rewrite each of the following sentences, using the correct form of the verb indicated. Give the reason for your choice:

1. The choir (is, are) singing "Panis Angelicus."
2. The committee (was, were) divided in the decision.

3. That team (displays, display) good sportsmanship.
4. (Has, have) the committee submitted its report?
5. That football team (is, are) the best in the city.
6. A flock of robins (was, were) scattered at the noise of the plane.
7. A tribe of gypsies (lives, live) along the banks of the river.
8. The herd of cattle (is, are) being taken to the stockyards.
9. (Is, are) the band ready to march?
10. The jury (has, have) reached a verdict.
11. The class (has, have) been dismissed.
12. The drove of horses (was, were) sold to the farmer.
13. The entire school (was, were) assembled in the auditorium.
14. The tribe of Indians (moves, move) slowly over the hill.
15. The congregation (was, were) addressed by a famous speaker.
16. A squadron of airplanes (has, have) just passed.
17. The audience (was, were) in their places early.
18. The troop (is, are) well trained.
19. Our club (has, have) its own constitution.
20. The crew (has, have) been paid their salaries.

DISTRIBUTIVE AND INDEFINITE PRONOUNS

The distributive pronouns *each, either, neither,* and the indefinite pronouns *one, anyone, no one, anybody, nobody, everyone, everybody, someone, somebody* are always singular and require singular verbs.

Each of the women (has, have) a new car.

The correct form is: Each of the women *has* a new car.

EXERCISE 71

Copy these sentences, filling in each blank with the correct form of the verb at the left. Give the reason for your choice:

was   1. Neither of the men .... at the baseball game.
like   2. Everybody .... to have his own way.
carry   3. Everyone in the procession .... a lily.
is   4. .... either of your brothers going on the hike?

have	5. Everybody .... been enrolled.
was	6. Neither of them .... noted for scholastic standing.
ride	7. Each of the boys .... a bicycle.
wear	8. Each of the pupils .... a class pin.
come	9. One of our most popular beverages .... from Brazil.
wish	10. Neither of the witnesses .... to be called.
want	11. Everybody in the class .... to take the part.
is	12. Everyone .... called for duty.
have	13. Somebody .... my fountain pen.
is	14. Somebody among our relatives .... sure to come.
have	15. Neither of the fliers .... been seen.
have	16. .... anyone taken my ticket ?

SPECIAL SINGULAR AND PLURAL NOUNS

Some nouns that are plural in form, but usually singular in meaning, require singular verbs. These include *aeronautics, athletics* (training), *civics, economics, mathematics, measles, molasses, mumps, news, physics.*

Other nouns are usually considered plural and require plural verbs. These nouns include *ashes, clothes, eaves, goods, pincers, pliers, proceeds, scales, scissors, shears, spectacles, suspenders, thanks, tongs, trousers, tweezers.*

Measles (is, are) a disease of the young
My scissors (has, have) been lost.

The correct forms are:

Measles *is* a disease of the young.
My scissors *have* been lost.

EXERCISE 72

Choose the correct verb form and give a reason for your choice:
1. Athletics (develops, develop) the muscles.
2. The molasses (has, have) stained the tablecloth.
3. His trousers (is, are) being pressed.

4. Measles (requires, require) careful nursing.
5. The ashes (is, are) still hot.
6. The news about their trip (was, were) very exciting.
7. Where (is, are) the pincers?
8. The proceeds from the party (was, were) greater than we had anticipated.
9. Mumps (is, are) an unpleasant illness.
10. These tongs (is, are) used to remove cinders.
11. Physics (is, are) a high-school subject.
12. The goods (was, were) not delivered on time.
13. The eaves of our house (has, have) been painted.
14. Mathematics (is, are) my brother's favorite subject.
15. These scissors (is, are) very sharp.
16. (Does, do) these pliers belong to you?
17. Many thanks (is, are) rendered to you for your kindness.
18. Aeronautics (claims, claim) the attention of most boys.
19. The old shears (is, are) rusted.
20. Economics (is, are) taught in college.

EXERCISE 73 [Oral Drill]

Read aloud each of the following sentences, choosing the correct verb form. Give the reason for your choice:

1. (Doesn't, don't) my brother drive his car well?
2. Everyone (was, were) happy when the home team won.
3. Each candidate (is, are) preparing for his campaign.
4. The news of the day (carries, carry) joy to many people.
5. (Has, have) everyone given a donation for the missions?
6. In our garden many beautiful tulips (blooms, bloom).
7. Aeronautics (has, have) been the man's chief interest.
8. Either Paula or she (is, are) sure to be there.
9. Coal and iron (is, are) our most valuable minerals.
10. Measles (causes, cause) skin eruption.
11. Either you or she (has, have) made a mistake.
12. His home, as well as his possessions, (was, were) saved from the fire.
13. Neither one of the pictures (is, are) very large.

14. The band (is, are) marching into the stadium.
15. Each of the boys (answers, answer) when the roll is called.
16. *The Adventures of Tom Sawyer* (is, are) very humorous.
17. The scissors (is, are) here, but not the paste.
18. My father (doesn't, don't) like mushrooms.
19. There (is, are) two motorboats on the river.
20. Both her conduct and her work (is, are) satisfactory.
21. One of the boys (is, are) painting the canoe.
22. There (is, are) several large buildings on our street.
23. There (was, were) no streamline trains or airplanes in Lincoln's day.
24. Several valuable pictures (was, were) shown at the exhibit.
25. Cattle and sheep (is, are) raised on our western ranches.

2. *Uses of* Shall *and* Will

To express simple futurity or expectation we use *shall* in the first person and *will* in the second and the third persons. To indicate an act of the will, promise, or determination on the part of the speaker, we use *will* in the first person and *shall* in the second and the third persons.

SIMPLE FUTURITY	DETERMINATION
I shall go tomorrow.	Indeed, I will go tomorrow.
You will go tomorrow.	You certainly shall go tomorrow.
He will go tomorrow.	He shall not go with that boy.

EXERCISE 74

Fill in each blank with the correct form, *shall* or *will*, to express future time:

1. My parents .... not be at home this evening.
2. All the schools .... be represented at the meeting.
3. My little sister .... be three years old tomorrow.
4. The bell .... be rung at four o'clock.
5. I must hurry or I .... be late.
6. We .... study the customs of the Chinese in our next lesson.

7. God .... reward or punish me according to my deeds.
8. You .... hear my sister sing at assembly this afternoon.
9. I .... be glad to go with you.
10. This class .... be in session until three o'clock.

EXERCISE 75

Fill in each blank with the correct form, *shall* or *will*, to express determination or promise on the part of the speaker:

1. That man .... not enter this house again.
2. I .... help you, Joan.
3. Thou .... not kill.
4. I .... study harder next month, Mother.
5. I .... carry the box for you.
6. He .... not go to the game until he has finished his work.
7. I .... wait for you.
8. Officers .... be elected by the members.
9. You .... rewrite that assignment.
10. I .... master this difficulty.

"SHALL" AND "WILL" IN QUESTIONS

To ask a question, use *shall* when the subject is in the first person. In the second and the third persons use the same word, either *shall* or *will*, that is expected in the reply.

QUESTION	EXPECTED REPLY
Shall we help him?	We shall.
Shall you see him?	Yes, I shall.
Will you help me?	Yes, I will help.
Will the concert begin soon?	It will.

EXERCISE 76

Fill in each blank with the correct form for each question:

1. .... somebody please carry this chair?
2. .... I meet you at three o'clock?
3. When .... the next bus leave?

4. Where .... I hang your coat?
5. .... you read us a story, Mother?
6. .... you walk to school with me?
7. For how many minutes .... he be permitted to speak?
8. What hymn .... we sing next?
9. .... you please sign my report card, Father?
10. Who .... write the answer on the blackboard?

"SHOULD" AND "WOULD"

The rules for *shall* and *will* also apply to *should* and *would*.

Thus, to express simple futurity, *should* is used in the first person and *would* in the second and the third persons.

To express determination, resolution, or promise on the part of the speaker, we use *would* in the first person and *should* in the second and the third persons.

Should is frequently used in all three persons to express obligation; that is, in the sense of *ought to*.

Would is used in all three persons to express a wish and to indicate customary action.

> I *should* like to help you. *(Simple futurity)*
> You *would* enjoy his company. *(Simple futurity)*
> We promised that we *would* help her. *(Promise)*
> Children *should* obey their parents. *(Obligation)*
> Every night Grandmother *would* tell us stories. *(Customary action)*

EXERCISE 77

Fill in each blank with *should* or *would*:

1. We .... prepare our lessons for class.
2. Mother said she .... meet you at the station.
3. We .... speak nothing but the truth.
4. The retired policeman .... often entertain us with his stories.
5. I promised Jane I .... go with her.
6. Children, you .... brush your teeth daily.
7. I .... like to discuss our plans with you.
8. You .... not skate on that thin ice.

9. The work .... have been completed by this time.
10. Mother .... always do the hardest work herself.

3. *Troublesome Verbs*

The verbs *lie* and *lay, sit* and *set, rise* and *raise, let* and *leave* are sometimes confused. Give special attention to these verbs when they are used in sentences.

Lie, lay, lain

This verb means to *rest or recline.* It is always intransitive.

Lay, laid, laid

This verb means to *put* or *place* in position. It is always transitive.

Sit, sat, sat

This verb means to *have* or *keep* a seat. It is always intransitive.

Set, set, set

This verb means to *place* or *fix* in position. It is always transitive.

Rise, rose, risen

This verb means to *ascend.* It is always intransitive.

Raise, raised, raised

This verb means to *lift.* It is always transitive.

Let, let, let

This verb means to *permit* or *allow.*

Leave, left, left

This verb means to *abandon* or *depart from.*

EXERCISE 78

Choose the correct verb form in each of the following:

1. The clerk (lay, laid) the package on the counter.
2. Who is that stranger (sitting, setting) over there?
3. Please (let, leave) Mary accompany you.
4. The boy has (lain, laid) under the tree for some time.

5. Vegetables are (risen, raised) on truck farms.
6. (Let, leave) John do the work in his own way.
7. May I (sit, set) with you at the concert?
8. Did she (rise, raise) when addressed?
9. The baby (lay, laid) gurgling there for hours.
10. The Scouts (sat, set) beside the brook.
11. We shall (let, leave) him know our answer in the morning.
12. The spectators became excited when a plane (rose, raised).
13. The carpet has been (lain, laid) on the stairs.
14. My sister (sit, set) the table for breakfast.
15. Do not (let, leave) him here by himself.
16. Robert (lay, laid) his books on the table and went out to play.
17. The temperature (rises, raises) very suddenly.
18. Daniel said he would (let, leave) the order at the door.
19. (Sit, set) the vase on the mantel.
20. The river (rose, raised) during the night.
21. My men have (lain, laid) concrete for a foundation.
22. The cat was (lying, laying) in the sun.
23. My fox terrier is (sitting, setting) on the step.
24. Her mother doesn't (let, leave) her travel alone.
25. My ring (lay, laid) hidden in the grass.
26. (Let, leave) me help you with the packages.
27. The little tin soldiers (lay, laid) where we placed them.
28. John's father would not (let, leave) him go.

EXERCISE 79 [Checking-up Exercises]

Test your knowledge of irregular verb forms by filling in the blanks with the past tense or the past participle of the verbs at the left:

take   1. He .... the book from the shelf.
begin   2. The storm .... early this morning.
ride   3. Have you ever .... in the subway?
steal   4. The cat .... into the room.
drive   5. My mother has never .... a car.
lose   6. I have .... my fountain pen.
sink   7. The enemy .... the ship.

see   8. Have you ever .... Saint Patrick Cathedral?

sell   9. He has .... the land by now.

go   10. Pope Pius has .... to his summer residence.

mean   11. My father .... every word he said.

tear   12. The men have .... down the old building.

forget   13. I have .... the date of my appointment.

freeze   14. They have .... the dessert for dinner.

be   15. We have .... friends for many years.

EXERCISE 80

Supply in the indicative mood the verb form called for in each of the following sentences:

write   1. The monks .... books on sheepskin. *(Past tense, active voice)*

convert   2. The barbarians .... by the early missionaries. *(Past tense, passive voice)*

build   3. A modern bridge .... over the lagoon. *(Present perfect tense, passive voice)*

toil   4. Saint Jerome .... for years translating the Bible. *(Past tense, active voice)*

visit   5. The Vatican .... yearly by pious Catholics. *(Present tense, passive voice)*

remodel   6. The old building .... *(Present perfect tense, passive voice)*

aid   7. Columbus .... by Queen Isabella. *(Past tense, passive voice)*

have   8. The monks .... a universal reputation for kindness. *(Past tense, active voice)*

shine   9. The moon .... on the water. *(Progressive form, present tense, active voice)*

finish   10. I .... the book this evening. *(Future perfect tense, active voice)*

choose   11. We .... Edwin president of the class. *(Past tense, active voice)*

see   12. You .... the picture before. *(Potential form, present perfect tense, active voice)*

present
13. "The Man without a Country" .... by the children of our school. *(Future tense, passive voice)*

destroy
14. The *Maine* .... in the harbor of Havana. *(Past tense, passive voice)*

consent
15. Our teacher .... to your plan. *(Future tense, active voice)*

break
16. The first Atlantic cable .... in midocean. *(Past tense, active voice)*

hear
17. .... you .... the news? *(Present perfect tense, active voice)*

sit
18. Grandfather .... there all morning. *(Progressive form, present perfect tense, active voice)*

be
19. The radio .... a bond between the inhabitants of Europe and the Americas. *(Present perfect tense)*

polish
20. I .... the furniture. *(Emphatic form, past tense, active voice)*

4. *Words Used as Nouns and Verbs*

A noun is a name word. A verb generally expresses action or being.

Sin is an *act* of disobedience to God. *(Noun)*
Always *act* according to your conscience. *(Verb)*

EXERCISE 81

Tell whether each word in italics is a verb or a noun:

1. *Drink* the milk slowly.
2. Chocolate is a nourishing *drink.*
3. *Stand* quietly.
4. Ferns and palms decorated the *stand.*
5. You may *sign* your name here.
6. The cross is the *sign* of our redemption.
7. That noise might *alarm* the children.

8. I was awakened by the sharp ring of the *alarm*.
9. Mother, *rest* for an hour.
10. After work we should take a *rest*.
11. The organ gave forth a beautiful *sound*.
12. *Sound* that note again for me.
13. There are three boys and four girls in the *cast*.
14. *Cast* all your care upon Him, for He has care of you.
15. *Love* of our neighbor is *love* of God.
16. We should *love* God with our whole heart.
17. *Laugh* a hearty *laugh*.
18. Who will carry the *crown?*
19. We shall *crown* Mary Queen of May.
20. We crossed the Great *Divide*.
21. *Divide* the apples among the three boys.
22. This *watch* came from Switzerland.
23. *Watch* and pray.
24. The card *catalogue* is an aid in locating books.
25. First, we must *catalogue* the books according to the authors.

EXERCISE 82   [Test on Verbs]

Read this selection very carefully and then answer the questions that follow:

¹ When Joan of Arc was brought for the first time into the camp of the French army, she found many abuses among the soldiers. ² They had been neglecting their religious duties and acting in a manner which she could hardly approve. ³ "Listen to me," she pleaded to the men who gathered around her. ⁴ "Our strength is in our faith; but if our faith is eaten away by the little things God hates, we shall be beaten back and die." ⁵ With military tactics and the strategy of war this new leader might have been unfamiliar. ⁶ This she did know, that the French could never gain victory until they had become good and pleasing in God's sight.

1. Is the first verb in the paragraph regular or irregular?
2. Find a regular verb in the fourth sentence.

3. Is the verb *is eaten* in the fourth sentence in the active or the passive voice?
4. Name the intransitive verbs in the third sentence.
5. Find a copulative verb in the last sentence.
6. In what mood is the verb *listen* in the third sentence?
7. Give the mood and the tense of the first verb in the fourth sentence.
8. Name a progressive verb phrase in the second sentence. In what tense is the verb in the progressive form?
9. Find an emphatic verb phrase in the paragraph. What is the tense of this verb?
10. What idea is expressed by the potential verb phrase in the fifth sentence?
11. Find a potential verb phrase in the last sentence.
12. What is the tense, the voice, the person, and the number of *shall be beaten* in the fourth sentence?

CHAPTER FIVE Participles,
Gerunds, Infinitives

A participle is a word that does the twofold work
of a verb and an adjective.

The children, *bearing* flags, marched into the classroom.
November is the month *dedicated* to the holy souls.

Bearing and *dedicated* are participles. Both words are derived
from verbs, for they express action. *Bearing* has a direct object
and *dedicated* is modified by the adverbial phrase *to the holy
souls*. The participles resemble adjectives in that they modify
nouns; *bearing* modifies *children* and *dedicated* modifies *month*.

1. *Properties of the Participle*

A participle has the properties of a verb and an adjective.

Properties of a Verb	Properties of an Adjective
1. It is derived from a verb.	1. It limits a noun or a pro-
2. It may take an object.	noun.
3. It may be modified by an adverb or an adverbial phrase.	

2. *Forms of the Participle*

A participle has voice and tense, but it does not have person and
number. The past participle is essentially passive. In the case of intransitive verbs, however, the past participle is in the active voice.

	Active	Passive
Present	seeing	being seen
Past	seen	seen
Perfect	having seen	having been seen

318

3. *Position of the Participle*

The participle may be placed after the noun or the pronoun it limits, or it may be used in an introductory phrase.

Morse, *having invented* the telegraph, asked the aid of Congress.
Having invented the telegraph, Morse asked the aid of Congress.

In both sentences the participle *having invented* modifies *Morse*. In the first sentence this participle follows the noun; in the second sentence it is used in the introductory phrase.

RESTRICTIVE AND NONRESTRICTIVE PHRASES. Note that the phrase *having invented the telegraph* is nonrestrictive in the two sentences given above. By this we mean that it is not a necessary part of the sentence and could be omitted. We show this by using commas to separate a nonrestrictive participial phrase from the rest of the sentence.

Some participial phrases are restrictive and cannot be omitted. Restrictive phrases are not set off by commas.

The man *asking aid from Congress* is Samuel Morse.

Here the phrase *asking aid from Congress* limits the word it modifies to a particular man. No commas are needed.

EXERCISE 83

Select the participles in the following sentences. Tell why each participle has the properties of a verb and an adjective:

1. The rivers flowing into the Pacific Ocean have little inland transportation.
2. The man driving that car is my uncle.
3. Cotton raised in Egypt has long, silky fibers.
4. The great oak, broken by the wind, fell against the building.
5. Seated upon a white horse, Saint Joan led the army to victory.
6. The child, having lost his way, sought the policeman.
7. A change made in a constitution is called an amendment.
8. Having crossed the Delaware, Washington baffled the British.
9. Carrying a cumbersome package, I entered the bus.
10. The missal is the book containing the prayers of the Mass.
11. The water, running slowly, wore away the stone.

12. Man is a creature composed of a body and a soul.
13. A miracle is a visible event surpassing all natural powers.
14. The rosary is a powerful prayer said in honor of our Blessed Lady.
15. We see God's goodness reflected in the lives of our fellow men.
16. The salesman showed us rugs brought from Persia.
17. They watched the boats sailing down the river.
18. Did you hear the carolers singing in the street?
19. Congress cannot make laws prohibiting the free exercise of religion.
20. Saint Patrick, preaching and baptizing, spread the faith throughout Ireland.
21. Shouting joyfully, they marched around the football field.
22. Oranges grown in California find a ready market in the East.
23. The man sitting on the park bench looks hungry.
24. The mail, locked in waterproof bags, was firmly strapped to the saddle.
25. Having discovered the hiding place, he showed it to all his companions.

4. *Participial Adjectives*

Do not make the mistake of thinking that all words derived from verbs and ending in *ing* or *ed* are participles. Note the use of the word *running* in the following sentence:

The *running* water wore away the stone.

Running is distinctly descriptive in character and has the usual position of an adjective—before the noun. This participial form is one of the types of descriptive adjectives; it is called a *participial adjective*. The following characteristics will help you to recognize a participial adjective:

1. It is descriptive in character.
2. It does *not* have the force of a verb.
3. It may *not* take an object.
4. It has the usual position of an adjective—before the noun or after a copulative verb.

EXERCISE 84

Select the participial adjectives and point out the word that each modifies:

1. The burning logs could be seen in the distance.
2. The girl told a touching story.
3. A searching party found the lost campers.
4. Smiling children appeal to everybody.
5. This book is very interesting.
6. An unopened letter lay on the desk.
7. Father's blazing eyes revealed his anger.
8. Her voice is very pleasing.
9. My father is a traveling salesman.
10. Is the United States the greatest manufacturing country in the world?
11. The governing body of the Church is called the hierarchy.
12. Experience is a trying teacher.
13. The boys on the basketball team look rested and refreshed.
14. Drifting snow blocked the highway.
15. The doctor rushed to the aid of the injured man.
16. Mother seems tired tonight.

5. *The Nominative Absolute*

A participle may be used with a noun or a pronoun in an independent adverbial phrase to express the time, the condition, the cause, or the circumstances of the action expressed by the main verb in the sentence. The noun or the pronoun used in this absolute construction is in the nominative case and the participle modifies it.

The war being over, the soldiers returned joyfully to their homes.

The introductory phrase in this sentence expresses the circumstances or the time when the soldiers returned. The participle *being* modifies *war,* the noun in the nominative absolute.

The noun in a nominative absolute is not the subject of any verb. It is part of an independent adverbial phrase and is modified by the participle.

Compare these sentences:

Having thrown the cowboy, the bull dashed madly across the field.
The cowboy having been thrown, the bull dashed madly across the field.

In the first sentence the participle modifies *bull*, the subject. In the second sentence the participle, *having been thrown,* is part of the nominative absolute. The participle in this sentence modifies *cowboy,* the noun in the nominative absolute.

EXERCISE 85

Point out the noun and the participle in each nominative absolute in the following sentences:

1. The door opening, the teacher entered the room.
2. The rain having ceased, the children continued on their trip.
3. Five days having passed without a reply, my mother became alarmed.
4. The rosary having been said, the children retired.
5. John having been elected, the meeting adjourned.
6. The gates having been opened, the crowd rushed into the arena.

nominative absolute

7. The armistice having been signed, fighting ceased.
8. The guests having arrived, dinner was served.
9. Spring coming on, the birds flew north.
10. Christ having risen, the apostles returned to Galilee.
11. The pipes having burst, the cellar was flooded.
12. The storm being over, the stars appeared.
13. The parade approaching, the crowd cheered wildly.
14. Years having passed, my father visited the scenes of his childhood again.
15. The address concluded, the speaker was applauded.

6. *The Correct Use of Participles*

TENSE OF PARTICIPLES

The present participle generally denotes action taking place at the same time as the predicate verb.

The perfect participle denotes action completed before the action of the predicate verb.

The children, (singing, having sung) merrily, skipped into the room.
(Finishing, having finished) their work, the pupils were dismissed.

The correct forms are:

The children, *singing* merrily, skipped into the room.
Having finished their work, the pupils were dismissed.

EXERCISE 86

Choose the correct form of the participle in each sentence:

1. (Waving, having waved) flags, the happy crowd marched down the street.
2. (Reading, having read) the article, Joan wrote a precis of it.
3. (Delivering, having delivered) the package, Michael went home.
4. I spent several hours (rambling, having rambled) through the woods.
5. (Studying, having studied) my lessons, I went for a ride.
6. (Resting, having rested), they continued their journey.

7. (Saying, having said) our prayers, we commenced our daily work.
8. (Riding, having ridden) in a new roadster, we admired the beauties of Yellowstone National Park.
9. (Opening, having opened) the door, he hurt his finger.
10. (Walking, having walked) to school, I meet many of my friends.

DANGLING PARTICIPLES

A participle does the work of a verb and an adjective. As an adjective the participle modifies a noun or a pronoun. When a sentence is written in such a way that the participle has no word to modify, we call it a dangling participle. Sentences must be re-written to avoid dangling participles.

Walking to school, the horse ran away.

In this sentence *walking* does not modify any noun. Who is walking to school? It cannot be the horse. We must have a word that the participle *walking* may limit. A dangling participle is corrected by supplying the missing noun or pronoun.

Walking to school, the *girl* saw the horse run away.

EXERCISE 87

Rewrite the following sentences to avoid dangling participles:
1. Having labored all morning, the work was completed.
2. Being careful, the room was left in order.
3. Sitting on the porch, the storm passed.
4. Going to school, the strap on my books broke.
5. Listening to the speaker, my chair suddenly collapsed.
6. Watching the animal, the accident happened.
7. Enjoying the game, the time passed swiftly.
8. Opening the window, the bird flew away.
9. Not knowing which road to take, the child directed me.
10. Standing beside Anne, the parade came into view.
11. Turning the corner, the store was seen.
12. Reading a book, the bus passed my stop.

EXERCISE 88

Select the participles in the following sentences and give the syntax of each:

1. Francis, whistling to himself, continued the work.
2. Colonies settled by the English were successful.
3. The old man telling the story amused the children.
4. Having been invited to the party, we accepted.
5. Helen, motioning to her father, attracted his attention.
6. The boys, hoping for success, played well.
7. We watched the boy playing the violin.
8. The Church is a perfect society instituted by Christ.
9. Curtains needed for the new house were purchased yesterday.
10. There goes John's canoe skimming across the lake.
11. The fire, spreading rapidly, caused great alarm.
12. We enjoyed a delicious dinner, cooked by an expert.
13. The bell, echoing through the quiet rooms, disturbed the entire household.
14. Helped by the tide, the boat made for shore.
15. Having been dismissed early, the boys hastened to the football field.
16. The road leading to the grotto has been repaired.
17. The birds, flying from tree to tree, sang merrily.
18. Miss Brown, recently appointed, gave the lectures.
19. Ground having been broken, work commenced immediately.
20. We watched the artist sketching the picture.
21. The boys, having been defeated, congratulated the victors.
22. We attended the musicale given by the children.
23. The map drawn by Catherine was the best in the class.
24. The sermon preached by Father Schmidt was very inspiring.
25. A sentence expressing sudden emotion is called an exclamatory sentence.
26. The house deserted by the owner fell into ruin.
27. Having enjoyed the party, the guests departed.
28. The Smiths own the house built of stone.
29. Christ, having risen from the grave, remained on earth forty days.

30. Father, pleased with our progress, gave us a reward.
31. Having hired a car, they set out for a day's ride.
32. Looking forward to a favorable reply, the firm made a generous concession.
33. New Orleans, situated on the Mississippi River, controls much trade.
34. Having sold their boat, the boys divided the profits.
35. The announcement made, the president left the room.
36. Preceded by his guards, the mayor approached the speakers' platform.
37. On the floor lay a rug covered with dust.
38. Mary, having told her mother, prepared for the journey.
39. Having been worn by use, the steps were repaired.
40. He saw the car coming toward him.

GERUNDS

A gerund is a verb form ending in *ing* that has the properties of a verb and a noun.

Reading good books is a profitable pastime.
Thinking quickly helped him out of his difficulty.

Reading and *thinking* are actions. These words have the force of verbs because *reading* takes the object *books* and *thinking* is modified by the adverb *quickly*. These words are also used as nouns. *Reading* is the subject of *is,* and *thinking* is the subject of *helped.*

1. *Properties of the Gerund*

A gerund has the properties of a verb and a noun. For this reason it is sometimes called a verbal noun.

PROPERTIES OF A VERB	PROPERTIES OF A NOUN
1. It is derived from a verb.	1. It is used as a noun.
2. It may take an object.	
3. It may be modified by an adverb or an adverbial phrase.	

2. *Uses of the Gerund*

As a noun a gerund may be used as the subject or the object of a verb, as a predicate nominative, as the object of a preposition, or as an appositive.

Traveling with my father is a joy. *(Subject)*
He enjoyed *skating* on the lake. *(Direct object)*
His favorite pastime is *reading* biographies. *(Predicate nominative)*
He began by *speaking* to the jury. *(Object of preposition)*
My appointed task, *opening* the door, kept me busy. *(Appositive)*

Name the verb from which each of these gerunds is derived and point out the adverbial modifier or the object of each gerund.

EXERCISE 89 [Gerunds Used as Subjects]

Select the gerunds in the following sentences and explain how each has the properties of a verb and a noun:

1. Saying the rosary is a praiseworthy habit.
2. Skating on the lake is forbidden.
3. Helping at home creates a happy family spirit.
4. Learning a new word every day increases one's vocabulary.
5. Assisting at Mass on Sundays is a positive duty of all Catholics.
6. Sleeping in a well-ventilated room is a good health habit.
7. Enforcing the laws is the duty of the executive department of the government.
8. Climbing mountains is dangerous.
9. In colonial days crossing the ocean took great courage.
10. Receiving Holy Communion frequently is a great aid to holiness.
11. Protecting our forests is the work of the forest rangers.
12. Controlling our tempers requires patient effort.
13. Mining coal is dangerous work.
14. Solving crossword puzzles is fun for me.
15. Seeing the mistakes of others is knowledge; seeing our own is wisdom.
16. Does his practicing in the room above disturb the pupils?

EXERCISE 90 [Gerunds Used as Direct Objects]

Select the gerunds in the following sentences and explain how each has the properties of a verb and a noun:

1. The Fifth Commandment forbids giving bad example.
2. My father dislikes driving in the dark.
3. Joan practiced talking before the microphone.
4. Courtesy demands answering an invitation promptly.
5. Catherine has just finished painting a picture of her mother.
6. Honesty requires paying our just debts.
7. Helen enjoys reading historical novels.
8. The gardener has finished planting the spring flowers.
9. Does he prefer going by airplane?
10. We should avoid running on the stairs.
11. Martin suggested fishing in the lake.
12. Have they begun erecting the monument?
13. Our opening exercises include singing the national anthem.
14. Do you enjoy riding in a roller coaster?
15. Mother proposed making our own favors for the party.

EXERCISE 91 [Gerunds Used as Predicate Nominatives]

Select the gerunds in the following sentences and explain how each has the properties of a verb and a noun:

1. An important industry of Australia is raising sheep.
2. My sister's work is teaching French.
3. His chief delight is camping in the woods.
4. The drawback will be finding the owner.
5. Leona's duty is answering the telephone.
6. My brother's hobby is collecting autographs of famous people.
7. Courtesy is considering the rights of others.
8. One of her most enjoyable tasks was cooking the meals.
9. Detraction is telling the hidden faults of another.
10. The most dangerous part of the journey was crossing the river.
11. My father's greatest pleasure has been listening to the radio.
12. One great power of a priest is administering the sacraments.

13. Perjury is taking a false oath.
14. His work is experimenting with coal tar.
15. Her most notable achievement was raising a Christian family.

EXERCISE 92   [Gerunds Used as Objects of Prepositions]

Select the gerunds in the following sentences and explain how each has the properties of a verb and a noun:

1. The United States has an excellent location for carrying on world trade.
2. Does your father have any objection to building the new garage now?
3. Christ honored Mary by choosing her for His Mother.
4. That will be an inducement for doing better work.
5. Albert earned money by selling magazines.
6. She followed carefully the directions for baking the cake.
7. He was commended for answering in a clear voice.
8. Immigrants played a large part in building the railroads of the West.
9. By consulting the dictionary we increase our vocabulary.
10. Christ sanctified marriage by making it a sacrament.
11. Saint Frances Cabrini spent her life in laboring for the salvation of souls.
12. Edward earned money for his school expenses by shoveling snow.
13. Do you find pleasure in sailing a boat?
14. We honor the saints by imitating their virtues.
15. Catholic schools furnish opportunities for developing the spiritual and mental powers of youth.

EXERCISE 93   [Gerunds Used as Appositives]

Select the gerunds in the following sentences and explain how each has the properties of a verb and a noun:

1. The chief industry of Brazil, raising coffee, is a profitable one.
2. Her problem, learning the language, was a difficult one.

3. Saint Patrick's mission, converting the Irish race, was given him by Pope Celestine I.
4. Michael will continue his present employment, operating an elevator.
5. The duty of the secretary, writing the minutes of the meeting, is very important.
6. Her favorite sport, playing tennis, keeps her in good physical condition.
7. Josephine likes her assignment, addressing the envelopes.
8. The most important part of the lesson, making an outline, was omitted.
9. He enjoys his daily exercise, walking to church.
10. The work of that old man, repairing watches, requires skill.
11. The children enjoyed their task, raking the leaves.
12. The work of the early missionaries, Christianizing the natives, was a great contribution to the development of our country.
13. The Crusades did not attain their immediate object, recovering the Holy Land from Mohammedan control.
14. My task, caring for the baby, is always pleasant.
15. The invalid's only recreation, reading books, occupies much of his time.

EXERCISE 94

Select the gerunds in the following sentences and give the syntax of each:
1. My father enjoys hunting in the woods.
2. Exploring the attic is rainy-day fun.
3. Praying to the saints is asking their help.
4. Mother has considered taking a trip to Europe.
5. Raising the lid was a difficult task.
6. Father Damien's work was caring for lepers.
7. Irrigation is a means of converting desert land into fertile fields.
8. Writing short stories is his favorite occupation.
9. Coasting down the mountains is an invigorating winter sport.
10. Jane helps her mother before going to school.

11. I remember writing that letter.
12. Singing merry songs made the peasants happy.
13. We prove our love for God by showing our love for our neighbor.
14. Your telling the story has created a genial atmosphere.
15. Marshal Foch's chief devotion was praying before the Blessed Sacrament.
16. Studying geography gives us a knowledge of the world in which we live.
17. Windmills are used for pumping water.
18. Making Swiss cheese requires special skill.
19. The children enjoyed riding in the bus.
20. Playing baseball is an American pastime.
21. Ralph's appointed task, directing traffic at the school, was pleasant for him.
22. Paul tried sketching the picture.
23. His position, tracing unclaimed packages, is interesting.
24. The process of developing pictures is taught in trade school.
25. Skating on the lake is winter fun.

3. Substantives Modifying Gerunds

A noun or a pronoun that modifies a gerund is usually in the possessive case.

Father approves of (us, our) joining the club.

The correct form is: Father approves of *our* joining the club.

EXERCISE 95

Rewrite each sentence, omitting the incorrect form:
1. There is no doubt of (she, her) being promoted.
2. Mother does not approve of (John, John's) going.
3. I have just heard of (you, your) winning the prize.
4. There is a rumor of Mr. (Egan, Egan's) being elected.
5. We could not prevent (them, their) moving to the country.
6. I have no objection to (you, your) helping them.
7. The news of (Albert, Albert's) coming reached us today.

8. What do you think about (me, my) forgetting the appointment?
9. This may lead to the (man, man's) securing a better position.
10. Father remembers (Joseph, Joseph's) speaking about the matter.
11. I object to a (person, person's) making a promise which he does not intend to keep.
12. We were surprised at (him, his) returning so soon.

4. "ing" Nouns

Many nouns end in *ing*. Some of these are formed from verbs and others are not.

> The *barking* of the dog aroused our attention.

Barking is a noun used as the subject of the verb *aroused*. It is modified by the article *the* and by an adjectival phrase, *of the dog*. The following characteristics will help you to recognize an *ing* noun:

1. It may not take an object.
2. It may not be modified by an adverb.
3. It is often preceded by the article *the* and followed by the preposition *of*.
4. It may have a plural form.

EXERCISE 96

Select the *ing* nouns and give the syntax of each:

1. We could hear the sighing of the wind in the trees.
2. He gave part of his earnings to the poor.
3. We were frightened by the screeching of the owl.
4. Have her paintings been on display yet?
5. The Chinese have many wise sayings.
6. The coming of the airplane has brought Alaska into prominence.
7. In all games the feelings of the defeated team should be respected.
8. God has bestowed upon us many blessings.

9. Suddenly our attention was attracted by the flashing of a bright light.
10. My brother is studying the writings of some of the early doctors of the Church.
11. My mother's washing hung on the line in neat, orderly rows.
12. Did you attend the meeting of the Catholic Action Club this morning?
13. Her timing was perfect.
14. There were flashes of lightning, rumblings and peals of thunder.
15. No smoking is permitted in this room.

RECOGNIZING NOUNS, GERUNDS, PARTICIPLES

Remember that not all words ending in *ing* are nouns or gerunds. They may be participles, participial adjectives, gerunds, *ing* nouns, or the progressive verb forms. Note the use of the word *singing* in the following sentences:

The *singing* of the birds brought joy to the children. *(*Ing *noun)*
The boy *singing* the solo is my cousin. *(Participle)*
Robert takes *singing* lessons. *(Participial adjective)*
We enjoyed *singing* that song. *(Gerund)*
The children had been *singing* for an hour. *(Progressive verb form)*

EXERCISE 97

Select the words ending in *ing* and tell whether they are participles, participial adjectives, gerunds, *ing* nouns, or verbs in the progressive form:

1. From the sufferings of Christ we learn His love for men.
2. We remember your being here last year.
3. We can help one another by performing the spiritual and corporal works of mercy.
4. Dropping the bone, the dog ran to his master.
5. Twinkling stars shone in the sky.
6. Saint Stephen, praying for his persecutors, was stoned to death.
7. The girls took whatever was necessary for the camping trip.

8. We were watching a broken fragment of rainbow after the storm.
9. Fording the river, they reached the other side.
10. Studying English increases one's opportunity for advancement.
11. A diligent studying of the classics improves one's art of speaking.
12. Cyrus Field encountered many obstacles in laying the Atlantic cable.
13. Field's persevering efforts finally brought him success.
14. We saw three airplanes flying high over our school.
15. When Fulton was building his steamboat, he received no encouragement.
16. Our earliest roads were foot trails connecting Indian settlements.
17. Good humor is a very effective aid in bearing annoyances.
18. We heard the birds singing in the trees.
19. The field being irrigated, the farmer planted sugar beets.
20. The boys enjoyed traveling by airplane.
21. My father, listening intently to the speech, did not hear us.
22. Running a locomotive is a responsible task.
23. We saw the soldiers marching down the street.
24. The tents are being constructed now.
25. The prayers of little children are pleasing to God.

INFINITIVES

An infinitive is a verb form, usually preceded by *to*, that may be used partly as a verb and partly as a noun, an adjective, or an adverb.

To read good books improves the mind.

I have planned *to leave* early.

The infinitives *to read* and *to leave* have the force of verbs because *to read* has the object *books* and *to leave* is modified by the adverb *early*. They are used as nouns, for the infinitive phrase *to read good books* is the subject of *improves* and the phrase *to leave early* is the object of *have planned*.

In the following sentences the infinitive is used as an adjective and as an adverb.

The florist has flowers *to sell. (Limits the noun* flowers)
The star sang *to please* the audience. *(Modifies the verb* sang)
I was pleased *to receive* your invitation. *(Modifies the adjective* pleased)

Infinitive means *not limited.* A finite verb changes form to agree with the subject in person and number. An infinitive does not.

FINITE VERB	INFINITIVE
I read.	They asked me to read.
He reads.	They asked him to read.

1. *Properties of the Infinitive*

An infinitive has the properties of a verb and those of a noun, an adjective, or an adverb.

PROPERTIES OF A VERB

1. It is derived from a verb.
2. It may take an object.
3. It may be modified by an adverb or an adverbial phrase.

OTHER PROPERTIES

1. It may be used as a noun.
2. It may limit a noun or a pronoun.
3. It may modify a verb, an adjective, or an adverb.

2. *Forms of the Infinitive*

The infinitive is used in the present and the perfect tenses, active and passive voices.

	ACTIVE	PASSIVE
PRESENT	to write	to be written
PERFECT	to have written	to have been written

3. *Uses of the Infinitive*

In a sentence the infinitive may do the work of a noun, an adjective, or an adverb.

INFINITIVES USED AS NOUNS

The infinitive is used as a noun when it does the work of a noun. It may be used as the subject or the object of a verb, the object of a preposition, a predicate nominative, or an appositive.

To win was their only thought. *(Subject)*
I should like *to live* in Boston. *(Direct object)*
He was about *to write* the letter. *(Object of preposition)*
The duty of every citizen is *to vote*. *(Predicate nominative)*
He had one desire, *to win* the race. *(Appositive)*

An infinitive is considered an appositive when it is used after the expletive *it*.

It is the president's duty *to enforce* the laws. *(Appositive)*

In this sentence the infinitive phrase *to enforce the laws* is the logical or real subject. Grammatically the expletive *it* is the anticipatory subject. The infinitive is in apposition with *it*.

EXERCISE 98 [Infinitives Used as Subjects]

Select the infinitives and the infinitive phrases in the following sentences. Show that the infinitives have properties of both verbs and nouns:

1. To refuse aid seems selfish.
2. To sketch that map was a difficult task.
3. To see snow in Australia is unusual.

4. To spread devotion to the Sacred Heart was the great desire of Saint Margaret Mary Alacoque.
5. To love our neighbor is a divine command.
6. To succeed was our only thought.
7. To feed the hungry is a corporal work of mercy.
8. To speak in public requires skill.
9. To skate is fun.
10. To make the honor roll requires perseverance.
11. To obey promptly is our duty.
12. To err is human.
13. To write an interesting letter is an accomplishment.
14. To be cheerful is a good health habit.
15. To be a pilot is Luke's present desire.

— EXERCISE 99 [Infinitives Used as Direct Objects]

Select the infinitives and the infinitive phrases used as direct objects in the following sentences:

1. Every girl should learn to cook.
2. Suddenly the band began to play.
3. My mother wishes to visit Rome.
4. We should try to imitate Christ more closely.
5. Do you like to dance?
6. He promised to be faithful to his duty.
7. Eleanor wants to work in the library.
8. I must remember to be a good Catholic always.
9. The boy undertook to find the lost dog.
10. Have you decided to move to the country?
11. We have planned to save stamps for the missions.
12. Joseph, try to be more careful.

EXERCISE 100 [Infinitives Used as Objects of Prepositions]

Select the infinitives in the following sentences and show that they have properties of verbs and nouns:

1. Abraham Lincoln desired nothing but to preserve the Union.
2. He could do nothing except to call for help.

3. He is about to write the letter now.
4. Theodore desires nothing but to be left alone.
5. The orchestra is about to begin.
6. We had no thought except to be of assistance.
7. They had no choice but to make a new model.
8. Father Ryan is about to talk.
9. The saints had no other aim but to serve God.
10. She made no other promise except to be punctual.

EXERCISE 101 [Infinitives Used as Predicate Nominatives]

Select the infinitives used as predicate nominatives:
1. Our first obligation is to recognize our duty to God.
2. The prime motive of a safety squad is to prevent accidents.
3. Leo's task was to set the scenery for the play.
4. The purpose of our club is to promote Catholic Action.
5. Saint Augustine's mission was to convert England.
6. Virginia's assignment was to design the costumes.
7. The work of a prospector is to search for minerals.
8. Mary's greatest desire is to visit Fatima.
9. The aim of every religious is to save souls for Christ.
10. The worst fault is to be conscious of none.
11. The duty of the governor is to enforce the laws of the state.
12. The joy of a priest is to bring sinners back to God.
13. A child's duty is to obey his parents.
14. Your best plan is to go by airplane.
15. Her most difficult problem was to interpret the directions.

EXERCISE 102 [Infinitives Used as Appositives]

Select the infinitives in the following sentences and show that they have properties of verbs and nouns:
1. The Little Flower had a fixed purpose, to serve God in her little way.
2. Mary's plan, to organize a speech club, succeeded.
3. The work of Saint Philip Neri, to instruct little children, is worthy of imitation.

4. The traffic officer has a responsible task, to protect lives.
5. It is sometimes difficult to locate mineral deposits.
6. It was a great feat of engineering to build the Panama Canal.
7. The work, to convert the heathens, was given to missionaries.
8. It is cowardly to tell a lie.
9. Martha's ambition, to be an accomplished musician, is her only thought.
10. Mr. Healy gave the final directions, to label the packages.
11. His vocation, to serve as a priest, was a free gift bestowed on him by God.
12. It is impossible to be good unless we pray.

EXERCISE 103

Select the infinitives used as nouns in the following sentences and give the syntax of each:

1. We should resolve to receive Holy Communion frequently.
2. It was fun to plan for the party.
3. To sort the papers required time.
4. Will you attempt to make the trip in that battered car?
5. God promised to send a Redeemer.
6. The soldiers could do nothing except to wait for orders.
7. To be courteous is a social asset.
8. I intend to study art this winter.
9. To develop good study habits is very important.
10. The house is completed except to paint the walls.
11. My father's chief delight is to read mystery stories.
12. Nothing seemed important to him except to save his soul.
13. To live on the frontier required courage.
14. In a paragraph the work of a beginning sentence is to arouse interest.
15. Joan refused to accept help.
16. The mission of the Church is to serve all men.
17. Would you like to try this trick?
18. The task, to decorate the auditorium, was given to the girls.
19. Joseph, always remember to bow your head at the name of Jesus.

20. We should learn to use the guide words in the dictionary.
21. That airplane is about to fly across the continent.
22. My little brother likes to look at pictures.
23. It is a privilege to be a godparent.
24. To travel is an education.
25. Fulton's dream, to move a boat by steam power, was finally realized.

INFINITIVES USED AS ADJECTIVES

An infinitive is used as an adjective when it does the work of an adjective; that is, when it modifies a noun or a pronoun.

This is a good place *to have* a picnic.
Saint Rose of Lima was the first American saint *to be canonized*.
She seems *to be* happy.

EXERCISE 104

Select the infinitive used as an adjective in each sentence and name the noun that it modifies:

1. Catholics have many opportunities to profess their faith.
2. A religious vocation is a special summons to serve God.
3. The lost regiment had no food to eat.
4. He is a boy to be trusted.
5. Every priest has the power to forgive sins.
6. Color blindness is inability to distinguish colors.
7. This is an occasion to be remembered.
8. Cherries to preserve are on sale here.
9. Health is a precious thing to have.
10. Failure to observe traffic regulations has resulted in many accidents.
11. A competent secretary must have the ability to write a good business letter.
12. There are several difficulties to be overcome.
13. The officer has a duty to perform.
14. The Constitution recognizes our right to worship as we please.
15. Have you time to see me now?
16. The president had several bills to sign.

INFINITIVES USED AS ADVERBS

Infinitives are used adverbially to express the purpose, the cause, or the result of an action. An infinitive is used as an adverb when it modifies a verb, an adjective, or an adverb.

Christ died *to redeem* the world. (*Modifies the verb* died)
The apprentice was quick *to learn*. (*Modifies the adjective* quick)
We arrived too late *to gain* admission. (*Modifies the adverb* too)

EXERCISE 105

Select the infinitive used as an adverb in each sentence and tell whether it modifies a verb, an adjective, or an adverb:

1. We eat to live.
2. The boys are ready to start the game.
3. Christ founded the Church to save all men.
4. We played hard to win the game.
5. They were anxious to return.
6. The cat ran to catch the mouse.
7. The modern artist is eager to show his ability.
8. A sower went forth to sow his seed.
9. The old man was surprised to see them.
10. We should practice to improve our skill.
11. The chalice is used to hold the precious blood.
12. My friends were delighted to see me.
13. His paragraph was written too carelessly to be accepted.
14. The mountain was not easy to climb.
15. Margaret came to greet us.
16. To write a good paragraph, a student must follow a definite plan.

4. *The Correct Use of Infinitives*

THE CORRECT TENSE OF THE INFINITIVE

The present infinitive is used when the action expressed by the infinitive takes place at the same time as the action of the main verb or after the time expressed by the main verb. The perfect infinitive is used only when the action has been completed at the time of the main verb.

I like *to write* letters. *(Same time as main verb)*

I had intended *to write* to you yesterday. *(Same time as main verb)*

I shall come *to see* you. *(After time of main verb; the* seeing *will take place after the* coming*)*

She seems *to have succeeded* in her work. *(Action completed before time of main verb)*

Both the present and the perfect infinitive may be used with the verb *ought*. The present infinitive indicates obligation or necessity; the perfect infinitive indicates that the action did not take place.

Joan ought *to call* immediately. *(Indicates duty or necessity)*

Joan ought *to have called*. *(Indicates that she did not call)*

EXERCISE 106

Select the correct tense of the infinitive in each sentence:

1. We are very eager (to see, to have seen) your new home.
2. The train was scheduled (to leave, to have left) early in the morning.
3. Mary intends (to apply, to have applied) for that position.
4. That man is said (to see, to have seen) every important city in Europe.
5. Did she mean (to do, to have done) that?
6. I was happy (to give, to have given) you the package.
7. Children ought (to obey, to have obeyed) their parents.
8. We ought always (to pray, to have prayed).
9. Joseph seems (to study, to have studied) his lesson.
10. Richard hopes (to go, to have gone) to the football game.
11. Mother will be delighted (to see, to have seen) you again.
12. You ought (to finish, to have finished) yesterday.

THE SUBJECT OF AN INFINITIVE

The infinitive may be used with a subject after such verbs as *want, wish, believe, know, think, consider,* and *expect*. An infinitive that has a subject may also be introduced by the preposition *for*.

Mother wants *Father* to take her to the store.

Sister Alice expects her *pupils* to be courteous.

It is impossible for *Joseph* to come.

If we ask the question *what* after the verb *wants,* the answer is the entire phrase—*Father to take her to the store.* The subject of *to take* is *Father.*

The subject of an infinitive is in the objective case.

The judge believed *him* to be guilty.

We consider *her* to be the best singer.

Our parents are anxious for *us* to succeed.

A noun or a pronoun after the infinitive *to be* is also in the objective case since it usually refers to the subject of the infinitive. If the infinitive does not have a subject, the pronoun following *to be* is in the nominative case, referring to the subject of the principal verb.

Helen thought (I, me) to be (she, her).

I was thought to be (she, her).

The correct forms are:

Helen thought *me* to be *her.*

I was thought to be *she.*

EXERCISE 107

Select the correct word in each sentence and give the reason for your choice:

1. Did Father expect (I, me) to be there?
2. The coach wishes (we, us) to report at nine o'clock.
3. Martha thought (she, her) to be the best speaker.
4. Father knew the lucky one to be (he, him).
5. Everyone believed Mary to be (she, her).
6. Rose expected (he, him) to be the winner.
7. Sister wants (we, us) to remain silent.
8. We all know Mr. Anderson to be (he, him).
9. The musician was believed to be (he, him).
10. (Who, whom) do they take us to be?
11. Uncle George wants (he, him) to help her.

12. I supposed (she, her) to be (he, him).
13. Mother thought the boy to be (I, me).
14. (Who, whom) did the teacher imagine him to be?
15. The best writer is supposed to be (she, her).
16. It is best for (we, us) to give in.
17. (Who, whom) am I supposed to be?
18. The librarian does not permit (they, them) to be taken from the library.
19. It was hard for (I, me) to understand the speaker.
20. I've never known (she, her) to neglect her work.

OMISSION OF THE INFINITIVE SIGN

The infinitive is used without the preposition *to,* often called the sign of the infinitive, in the following cases:

1. After verbs of perception, such as *hear, see, behold, know, feel,* and so forth:

We watched the great tree *fall.*
The boys heard the car *pass.*
The doctor felt the child *move.*

2. After the verbs *let, dare, need, make, bid,* and so forth:

The father made the boy *study.*
They dared the girls *jump* from the diving board.
You need not *go* to the library.

3. Frequently after the preposition *but* and the subordinate conjunction *than:*

The lions did nothing but *roar* for food.
It is more like him to write than *visit.*

EXERCISE 108

Find the infinitives hidden in these sentences:

1. The boys heard the whistle blow.
2. Let me help you carry the package.
3. I felt something sting me.
4. I saw Father sign the contract.
5. The story made the children laugh.

6. The Magi saw a bright star appear in the heavens.
7. He dared not show his fear.
8. We watched the canoe drift slowly down the stream.
9. My mother made me feel ashamed.
10. Bid him come quickly.
11. The children did nothing but play all day.
12. Let me help you carry the books.
13. Did you notice them leave?
14. She liked to write better than speak.
15. Bid the boys report at one o'clock.
16. The teacher's words made the pupils assume their tasks with enthusiasm.

SPLIT INFINITIVES

A word or a group of words used between *to* and the rest of the infinitive is said to split the infinitive. Care must be taken to avoid split infinitives.

I went (to merely see, merely to see) the picture.

The correct form is: I went *merely to see* the picture.

EXERCISE 109

Rewrite each of the following sentences, inserting the adverb at the left in the proper position:

not	1. Francis seemed to care very much.
already	2. The girls appear to have departed.
soon	3. They wish you to mention the fact.
thoroughly	4. Robert seemed to enjoy the play.
not	5. We expected to see you today.
easily	6. This is a task to be performed.
justly	7. To speak of others is our duty.
courageously	8. She learned to suffer.
efficiently	9. It requires much skill to handle an airplane.
rapidly	10. The candy seems to be disappearing.
eventually	11. She hopes to become a good actress.
quickly	12. Father Cody asked us to return.

EXERCISE 110 [Check on Uses of Infinitives]

Select the infinitives in the following sentences and give the syntax of each:

1. The best way to assist at Mass is to use the missal.
2. The good thief asked to be forgiven.
3. To escape was no easy matter.
4. Albert did not forget to do the errand.
5. It is too early to know the result.
6. To be childlike is to be Christlike.
7. Helen wishes to study French.
8. Most boys like to swim.
9. The Homestead Act was passed to develop the West.
10. My brother likes to read history.
11. These are the directions to be followed.
12. I have decided to go.
13. It is difficult to climb to the summit of success.
14. Her only aim was to serve God.
15. I like to watch the boat races.
16. Prayer is one way to help foreign missions.
17. Learn to study correctly.
18. To give is more blessed than to receive.
19. They have apples to sell.
20. William was about to jump on the train.
21. To solve the puzzle was almost impossible.
22. He is eager to hear your plans.
23. The artist tried to use bright colors.
24. Frances came to bring us the message.
25. Nothing remains but to go.

EXERCISE 111 [Test on Participles, Gerunds, Infinitives]

Read this selection very carefully and then answer the questions that follow:

[1] Standing in the raw winter wind had not been pleasant for the huge throng gathered before the Capitol to view the inauguration of a new president. [2] The prospect of witnessing so historic an

event, however, compensated the waiting crowd for the many hours of discomfort.

[3] A sudden burst of applause announced that the proceedings were about to begin. [4] A prayer having been offered, the president-elect stepped forward and, placing his hand upon the Bible, repeated in a firm voice the oath administered by the chief justice. [5] In the inaugural address which followed, the president assured the people of his determination to labor untiringly to justify the confidence they had placed in him.

1. Name a participle in the first sentence.
2. What noun does the participle in the first sentence modify?
3. The word *waiting* in the second sentence is what part of speech?
4. Give the tense and the voice of each participle in the fourth sentence.
5. Why is the noun *prayer* in the fourth sentence in the nominative case?
6. What part of speech is *proceedings* in the third sentence?
7. Find a gerund in the first sentence.
8. How is the gerund in the first sentence used?
9. In what respects does the word *witnessing* in the second sentence resemble a verb?
10. What is the syntax of the word *witnessing?*
11. Find an infinitive in the third sentence.
12. Is the infinitive in the third sentence used as a noun, an adjective, or an adverb?
13. Find an infinitive in the last sentence that is used as an adjective and name the noun that it modifies.
14. What word does the infinitive *to justify* in the last sentence modify?
15. Name an infinitive in the first sentence.
16. How is the infinitive in the first sentence used?

CHAPTER SIX

Adverbs

An adverb is a word that modifies a verb, an adjective, an adverb, a participle, a gerund, or an infinitive.

Mary walked *slowly*.
Mary's gait was *very* slow.
Mary walked *too* slowly.
Walking *slowly*, Mary sauntered down the street.
The art of writing *well* is not acquired without effort.
Children, try to come *early*.

CLASSIFICATION OF ADVERBS

1. *According to Meaning*

Adverbs of time answer the question *when* or *how often*. They include such adverbs as *again, before, early, frequently, now*.

Adverbs of place answer the question *where*. These are adverbs of place: *above, away, below, down, forward, overhead, upward*.

Adverbs of degree answer the question *how much* or *how little*. They include the following adverbs: *almost, barely, little, merely, quite, rather, very*.

Adverbs of manner answer the question *how* or *in what manner*. *Easily, fervently, quickly, thoroughly* are adverbs of manner.

Adverbs of affirmation and negation tell whether a fact is true or false. They include the adverbs *yes, no, indeed, doubtless, not*.

EXERCISE 112

Select the adverbs in the following sentences. Tell whether each adverb indicates time, place, degree, manner, affirmation, or negation and name the part of speech the adverb modifies:

1. Our Lord was exceptionally kind to the poor.
2. Breathlessly she pushed the curtains aside.
3. This task is rather difficult.

4. Walking confidently toward the group, John made the announcement.
5. The members of our class work well together.
6. We have been taught to obey cheerfully.
7. Having studied diligently, the children made rapid progress.
8. Our candidate was elected unanimously.
9. Yes, she completed the assignment promptly.
10. The bird was not in its cage.
11. Mary assisted at Mass almost every day.
12. The deer leaped forward.
13. I dislike rising early.
14. I shuddered excessively as I passed the haunted house.
15. The soul will live forever.

2. *According to Use*

SIMPLE ADVERBS

A simple adverb is an adverb used merely as a modifier.
Christ suffered *patiently.*

INTERROGATIVE ADVERBS

An interrogative adverb is an adverb used in asking questions. The interrogative adverbs are *how, when, where,* and *why.*
Why did Christ found the Church?

EXERCISE 113

Select the simple and the interrogative adverbs in the following sentences and tell what part of speech each adverb modifies:

1. A dilapidated roadster moved forward slowly.
2. When should we pray?
3. His answer was rather ridiculous.
4. Mary was always truthful.
5. Where is Leo going?
6. Spot barked frantically at the intruder.

7. Why was the message delayed?
8. I watched John peering eagerly at the sky.
9. How should we assist at Mass?
10. The spectators murmured discontentedly.
11. Did the boy answer correctly?
12. Where did you buy the book?

CONJUNCTIVE ADVERBS

A conjunctive adverb is a word that does the work of an adverb and a conjunction. The principal conjunctive adverbs are *after, as, before, since, until, when, where,* and *while.*

President Lincoln received no applause *when* he delivered the famous Gettysburg Address.

When is an adverb because it explains the time of the action. Because it connects the subordinate clause with the principal clause, *when* is also a conjunction. A conjunctive adverb usually modifies two verbs at the same time. In this sentence *when* modifies *delivered,* and the entire subordinate clause introduced by *when* modifies the verb *received* in the principal clause.

EXERCISE 114

Give the syntax of the conjunctive adverb in each of the following sentences:

1. The United States entered the First World War while Woodrow Wilson was president.
2. When snow falls the town presents a beautiful picture.
3. The class saluted as the flag was raised.
4. I have not seen him since the pictures were taken.
5. I shall remain here until you return.
6. We had completed the assignment before the bell was rung.
7. A ship anchors best where there is a deep harbor.
8. After many difficulties had been overcome, the Panama Canal was completed.
9. As the clock was striking twelve the princess fled.
10. The band played while the statue was being unveiled.

RELATIVE ADVERBS

A relative adverb is a word that does the work of an adverb and a relative pronoun. The principal relative adverbs are *when*, *where*, and *why*.

John returned to the room *where* he had left his hat.

Where explains the place of the action; hence it is an adverb. *Where* also does the work of a relative pronoun, for it joins the clause *where he had left his hat* to the principal clause.

NOTE. A relative adverb usually follows a noun of time or place. The test of a relative adverb is that it may be replaced by a prepositional phrase containing a relative pronoun.

John returned to the room *in which* he had left his hat.

EXERCISE 115

Give the syntax of each relative adverb in these sentences:

1. Winter is the time when the flowers sleep.
2. That is the reason why I like the story of Saint Joan of Arc.
3. This is the house where the first flag was made.
4. Rochester is the see where Saint John Fisher labored.

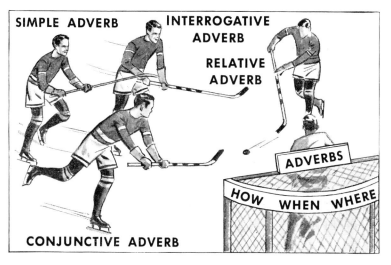

5. October is the month when the angels are honored.
6. They drove past an orchard where many peach trees were in bloom.
7. There are moments when all wish to be alone.
8. We discovered a field where beautiful violets grow.
9. Heaven is the place where we shall meet our own.
10. I visited Tower Hill, where Saint Thomas More was beheaded.
11. We left the village where our Lady had so often appeared.
12. Do you know the reason why the message was delayed?
13. We do not know the hour when God will call us.
14. The reason why I entered the contest is evident.
15. This is the field where the plane will land.

ADVERBIAL OBJECTIVES

An adverbial objective is a noun that expresses time, distance, measure, weight, value, or direction, and performs the function of an adverb.

James has attended this school eight *years*.

The word *years* is a noun. In this sentence it indicates time, a function usually performed by an adverb, by telling how long James has attended school.

Because an adverbial objective resembles an adverb, it may modify a verb, an adjective, or an adverb. Because it is a noun, the adverbial objective may be modified by an adjective. In the sentence above the adverbial objective *years* modifies the verb *has attended,* and it is modified by the adjective *eight.*

EXERCISE 116

Select the adverbial objectives and tell whether each expresses time, distance, measure, weight, value, or direction:

1. The session lasted three hours.
2. John remained a month at camp.
3. Mother waited all day for you.
4. This blanket cost fifteen dollars.
5. Our baby is one year old.

6. The stone dropped four feet.
7. Each streamer was three yards long.
8. The trip will cost ten dollars.
9. He moved three steps nearer to his goal.
10. The Bradleys live five miles from school.
11. A ton of coal weighs two thousand pounds.
12. Step this way, Mr. Curran.
13. Mount McKinley is about twenty thousand feet high.
14. The automobile traveled about twenty-five miles an hour.
15. The pool is twelve feet deep here.

COMPARISON OF ADVERBS

Many adverbs are compared. Like adjectives, they have three degrees of comparison: positive, comparative, and superlative.

1. *Regular Comparison*

Some adverbs form the comparative degree by adding *er* to the positive, and the superlative degree by adding *est* to the positive. Adverbs ending in *ly* generally form the comparative degree by prefixing *more* or *less* to the positive, and the superlative degree by prefixing *most* or *least* to the positive.

POSITIVE	COMPARATIVE	SUPERLATIVE
fast	faster	fastest
hastily	more hastily	most hastily

2. *Irregular Comparison*

Some adverbs are compared irregularly.

POSITIVE	COMPARATIVE	SUPERLATIVE
well	better	best
badly	worse	worst

Many adverbs denoting time and place *(here, now, then, when, where, again, always, down, above)* and adverbs denoting absoluteness or completeness *(round, eternally, never, universally)* cannot be compared.

Select the adverbs in the following sentences and state the degree of comparison of each adverb that can be compared:

1. Children are playing merrily in the street.
2. The man acted worse than a child.
3. The wind howled continuously.
4. The kitten purred more gently as we approached.
5. He listened most attentively.
6. Susan writes very well.
7. They gave it to the one who most deserved it.
8. Sound travels swiftly.
9. John has never spoken more sincerely.
10. The priest examined the manuscript closely.

THE CORRECT USE OF ADVERBS

1. *Distinguishing between Adjectives and Adverbs*

Adjectives modify nouns and pronouns. Adverbs modify verbs, adjectives, adverbs, participles, gerunds, and infinitives.

Predicate adjectives and adverbs are often confused. In order to determine whether a modifier is a predicate adjective or an adverb—that is, whether it completes a copulative verb and modifies the subject or whether it modifies a verb or an adjective—study each sentence carefully and ask yourself if the writer is trying to tell something about the subject, the verb, or an adjective.

The candy tasted *good*. (Candy *was* good; an adjective)
You may taste the candy *now*. (Tells *when* you may taste; an adverb)
Did the candy taste *exceptionally* good? (Tells *how* good; an adverb)

Select the correct word in each sentence:

1. The happy children sang (merry, merrily).
2. This chair seems (comfortable, comfortably).
3. The school bell sounds (harsh, harshly).
4. Our mother looks (beautiful, beautifully) today.

5. These violets smell (unusual, unusually) fragrant.
6. The dogs barked (fierce, fiercely).
7. This velvet feels (smooth, smoothly).
8. These cherries taste (tart, tartly).
9. That boy acted (courteous, courteously) today.
10. He seated himself (comfortable, comfortably) beside the radio.
11. Margaret is a (decided, decidedly) clever girl.
12. The soldiers appear (weary, wearily).
13. The stage looks (attractive, attractively).
14. The marine fought (gallant, gallantly).
15. The gardenias smell (fragrant, fragrantly).

2. Farther *and* Further

Farther refers to distance. *Further* denotes an addition. Both of these words may be used as adjectives and as adverbs.

I live *farther* than you.
I have nothing *further* to say.

EXERCISE 119

In the following sentences fill in each blank with the correct word, *farther* or *further:*

1. Anthony has received .... help from his father.
2. .... discussion on this matter is not necessary.
3. Pittsburgh is .... west than Harrisburg.
4. .... research will be required.
5. Angela lives .... from school than Joan.
6. We shall go without .... delay.
7. .... information will be given at the desk when someone calls for the book.
8. What .... proof has Matthew for his statement?
9. The soldiers under his command marched .... into the forest each day.
10. Is it .... to Ocean City than to Wildwood?
11. He has no .... use for this knife.
12. It is .... to town than I thought.

3. *Adverbs in Comparisons*

Use *as . . . as* when making comparisons that denote equality between persons or things. Use *so . . . as* in negative comparisons that deny equality between persons or things.

Albert is *as* tall *as* Edward.

I am not *so* old *as* you.

EXERCISE 120

Fill in each blank with *as* or *so :*

1. Mr. Carey's car is .... good as ours.
2. He is not .... clever with his hands as his friend.
3. The United States does not have .... much rain as Ireland.
4. He is .... good as he is brave.
5. Francis is .... eager to finish as Rose.
6. Frederick is not .... courageous as Thomas.
7. He is not .... kind as Mary.
8. It was .... dark as night.
9. Jane is .... pleasant as her sister.
10. Philadelphia is not .... large as New York.
11. He is .... happy as a lark.
12. My sister is not .... tall as I.

4. Equally *as an Adverb*

Equally means *as* when it modifies an adjective or an adverb. Practice using the correct forms *equally great, equally well, equally good*. Never use *as* between *equally* and the adjective or adverb.

Ruth and her sister are (equally as good, equally good).

The correct form is: Ruth and her sister are equally good.

EXERCISE 121

Select the correct form within the parentheses:

1. Agatha and Vera are (equally as proficient, equally proficient).
2. Webster and Calhoun were (equally as great, equally great).
3. Joan and Jane are (equally wise, equally as wise).

4. Gold and silver are (equally as useful, equally useful).
5. The radio and the telephone are (equally as important, equally important).
6. These two doctors are (equally as famous, equally famous).
7. Are Marie and Rose (equally talented, equally as talented)?
8. Were the Iroquois and the Hurons (equally as fierce, equally fierce) in warfare?
9. Were the French and the English (equally as active, equally active) in settling the New World?
10. My two brothers are (equally cheerful, equally as cheerful).

5. *Uses of* There

There is an adverb when used to denote place. *There* is an expletive when it introduces a sentence and does not form a necessary part of the sentence.

The book is *there* on the desk. *(Adverb)*
There are many duties in the home. *(Expletive)*

EXERCISE 122

In each sentence tell whether *there* is an adverb or an expletive:

1. There is my home.
2. There go the soldiers.
3. There are three boys absent from class today.
4. There stood my sister.
5. There are unknown heroes in every country.
6. There lie the child's toys, just as she left them.
7. There by the side of the road stands a beautiful tree.
8. There is a small sailboat on the lake.
9. There are many beautiful spring flowers in the woods.
10. There are many difficult problems to be solved.
11. There never was such a rush for tickets.
12. There on the desk is the letter.
13. There is a small stream which flows through the meadow.
14. There are some pupils without desks.
15. There are fifty pages in this book.

6. *Words Used as Adjectives and Adverbs*

An adjective describes or limits a noun or a pronoun. An adverb modifies a verb, an adjective, or an adverb.

Joseph had the *highest* mark in the class. *(Adjective)*
Of the three John tossed the football *highest*. *(Adverb)*

EXERCISE 123

Tell whether each word in italics is an adjective or an adverb:

1. The band marched *first*.
2. Is this the *first* day of the carnival?
3. *Little* acorns grow into great oaks.
4. The sick child plays *little*.
5. What do you mean by a *near* occasion of sin?
6. Come *near* and listen.
7. Helen is *well* today.
8. This meat is *well* cooked.
9. Follow exactly the *above* directions.
10. The airplane flew *above*.
11. The boys walked *farther* than the girls.
12. A man could be seen on the *farther* shore.
13. The eagle soars *high*.
14. The *high* hedge has been cut.
15. *Still* waters run deep.
16. Lie *still*, Chips.
17. Is your father *ill*?
18. You can *ill* afford to waste time.
19. This table has a *hard* surface.
20. Do you study *hard*?

EXERCISE 124   [Test on Adverbs]

Read this selection very carefully and then answer the questions that follow:

¹ The courage of the early martyrs has ever been an inspiration to the Church on earth. ² At a time when to be a Christian meant almost certain death, these intrepid men and women fearlessly

proclaimed their loyalty to Christ. ³ Undaunted by cruel torture and long imprisonment, they eagerly awaited the sentence which would send them home to heaven. ⁴ Those who saw them as they were led away declared that they could not have gone more joyfully to a wedding feast.

⁵ How were these defenders of the faith able to face danger and death so valiantly? ⁶ Our Lord was the source of their strength. ⁷ The thought of their Master's sufferings sustained them as it will always support most tenderly those who suffer for His sake.

1. Name an adverb in the first sentence and tell whether it modifies a verb, an adjective, an adverb, or a participle.
2. What part of speech does the adverb *almost* in the second sentence modify?
3. What adverb in the fifth sentence modifies another adverb?
4. Find an adverb of manner in the third sentence.
5. What kind of adverb is *away* in the fourth sentence?
6. Name an adverb of degree in the first paragraph.
7. Find an adverb of time in the second paragraph.
8. Name an interrogative adverb in the selection.
9. In what degree of comparison is the adverb in the third sentence?
10. The adverb *more joyfully* in the fourth sentence is in what degree of comparison?
11. Find an adverb in the superlative degree.
12. Write the positive and the comparative degrees of the adverb used in the superlative degree.
13. Can the adverb in the first sentence be compared?
14. Name an adverbial objective found in the selection.
15. Find a relative adverb in the first paragraph and name its antecedent.
16. Find a conjunctive adverb in the first paragraph.
17. Does the clause introduced by the conjunctive adverb express time, place, or manner?
18. What part of speech is *early* in the first sentence? Can this word be used as an adverb?

CHAPTER SEVEN

Prepositions,
Conjunctions, Interjections

A preposition is a word or a group of words that shows the relation between a substantive and some other word in the sentence.

The angels adore God *in* heaven.

The most commonly used prepositions are:

about	at	down	near	throughout
above	before	during	of	to
across	behind	except	off	toward
after	beside	for	on	under
against	between	from	over	until
among	beyond	in	past	up
around	by	into	through	with

1. *Forms of Prepositions*

The preposition may be a single word or a group of words used as one preposition.

A cry came *from* the woods.
The boat left *in spite of* the weather.

Groups of words that are considered one preposition when used with a substantive include the following:

on account of	in regard to	because of
instead of	in spite of	by means of
in addition to	in front of	for the sake of

2. *The Object of a Preposition*

The object of a preposition is a noun, a pronoun, or a group of words used as a noun. A noun or any word that takes the place of a noun is called a *substantive.*

We cannot succeed without God's *help. (Noun)*

Thomas gave the report to *him. (Pronoun)*

From *across the ocean* came the Pilgrims. *(Prepositional phrase)*

Don't go without *asking Mother. (Gerund phrase)*

Annette had no choice but *to accompany them. (Infinitive phrase)*

We could see the parade from *where we stood. (Clause)*

A preposition usually precedes its object.

EXERCISE 125

Point out the prepositions in the following sentences and name the object of each:

1. Which is the largest country in South America?
2. The policeman led the children across the street.
3. The team gave a report of how the victory had been won.
4. Bernard was rewarded for working hard.
5. The sun was hidden behind the clouds.
6. We were pleased with what we saw.
7. Give the book to me, Pauline.
8. From what we have heard, Raymond has been successful in his campaign.
9. We judge a person's character by what he says and does.
10. Easter time extends from the first Sunday in Lent to Trinity Sunday.
11. Many prayers ascend to heaven throughout the day.
12. The call came from behind the lighthouse.
13. He could do nothing except to answer the officer's questions.
14. Talking in the halls is prohibited.
15. John stood in front of Lucille.

3. *The Correct Use of Prepositions*

"BETWEEN" AND "AMONG"

Between is used in speaking of two persons or objects. *Among* is used in speaking of more than two.

He divided the money *between* Helen and Joan.

He divided the money *among* the four children.

"BESIDE" AND "BESIDES"

Beside means *at the side of* or *next to*. *Besides* means *in addition to*.

The shepherds knelt *beside* the manger.
Pierre speaks French and Latin *besides* English.

"IN" AND "INTO"

In denotes position within. *Into* denotes motion or change of position.

The papers are *in* the desk drawer.
The bird flew *into* its nest.

"FROM" AND "OFF"

From indicates the person from whom something is obtained. *Off* means *away from*.

We secured this paper *from* the newsboy.
The farmer hopped *off* the truck.

"BEHIND"

Use *behind* to indicate location at the rear of.
The barn is *behind* the house.

"DIFFER FROM" AND "DIFFER WITH"

Differ with denotes disagreement of opinion. *Differ from* denotes differences between persons or things.

I *differ with* you about the scoring of the game.
The ribbons *differ from* each other in width.

"DIFFERENT FROM"

After the adjective *different* use *from,* not *than.*
The writing is *different from* his.

"NEED OF"

Use *need of,* not *need for.*
We shall have no further *need of* you.

"WITHIN"

Use *within*, not *inside of*, to indicate the time within which something will occur.

I shall call for you *within* an hour.

"ANGRY WITH" AND "ANGRY AT"

Use *angry with* a person; *angry at* a thing.

I am *angry with* James.
We were *angry at* the result.

"AT" AND "TO"

At denotes presence in. *To* denotes motion toward.

The girls were *at* the children's party.
The man walked *to* the gate.

EXERCISE 126

Choose the correct preposition in each sentence:

1. The four girls had a secret (between, among) themselves.
2. The six boys divided the marbles (between, among) them.
3. He sat (between, among) Paul and Eugene.
4. My scrapbook is different (than, from) yours.
5. He threw the paper (in, into) the basket.
6. Mr. Cleary walked (in, into) the auditorium.
7. We bought these vegetables (off, from) our grocer.
8. They climbed (in, into) the car.
9. I am angry (at, with) my brother.
10. The tennis court is (in back of, behind) the barn.
11. We shall be in the hall (inside of, within) an hour.
12. Mrs. Mahan was angry (at, with) her servant.
13. We have no need (of, for) a car.
14. Have you any books (beside, besides) those I have read?
15. Four members of the family (beside, besides) the father were honored by the society.
16. Do you think he has need (of, for) a doctor?
17. How does this material differ (from, with) yours?

18. John laughed when the clown fell (off, from) the horse.
19. The old man divided his fortune (between, among) his two daughters.
20. The boy dived (in, into) the lake.
21. The messenger should come (inside of, within) an hour.
22. This bottle of medicine is different (than, from) the last bottle.
23. Robert borrowed the books (off, from) his cousin.
24. The playground is (in back of, behind) the courthouse.
25. We planted ivy (beside, besides) the grotto.

4. *Words Used as Adverbs and Prepositions*

An adverb tells *how, when,* or *where.* A conjunctive adverb does the work of an adverb and a conjunction. A preposition shows the relation between its object and some other word in the sentence.

Have you ever visited Washington *before? (Simple adverb)*
We make an outline *before* we write a paragraph. *(Conjunctive adverb)*
Christ stood *before* Pilate. *(Preposition)*

EXERCISE 127

Tell whether each word in italics is a preposition, a simple adverb, or a conjunctive adverb:

1. *Down* splashed the rain.
2. The child crawled *down* the stairs.
3. She waited *outside.*
4. There is a rug *outside* the door.
5. *Since* you left we have purchased a new car.
6. I have not seen Thomas *since* last Tuesday.
7. Do not walk *on* the grass.
8. "March *on!*" he cried.
9. Suddenly the door opened and *in* rushed Michael.
10. Is your father *in* his den?
11. *After* the storm had ceased, we started on our journey.
12. We left immediately *after* the game.
13. He led the dog *about* on a leash.
14. My friend was *about* to enter the plane.

15. He carries every project *through*.
16. *Through* the window we viewed the parade.
17. Everybody answered *but* Josephine.
18. I *but* touched her.
19. Put the doll in the box *beneath*.
20. Mary stood *beneath* the cross.

CONJUNCTIONS

A conjunction is a word used to connect words, phrases, or clauses in a sentence.

Saint Peter *and* Saint Paul suffered martyrdom. *(Connects words)*
Sugar cane grows in the Philippines *and* in Hawaii. *(Connects phrases)*
Although we are tired, we are not discouraged. *(Connects clauses)*

1. *Kinds of Conjunctions*

COORDINATE CONJUNCTIONS

A coordinate conjunction is a conjunction that connects words, phrases, or clauses of equal rank.

Richard made one error, *but* Kathleen had a perfect paper.

The most common coordinate conjunctions are *and, or, nor, but,* and *yet*.

The words *however, moreover, nevertheless, also, therefore,* and *consequently* are also used to link independent clauses. A clause introduced by one of these connectives is grammatically independent of, but logically dependent on, what has gone before.

He was poor; *therefore* he worked after school.

EXERCISE 128

Name the coordinate conjunctions in the following sentences and tell whether they connect words, phrases, or clauses:

1. The United States and Canada are in North America.
2. Shall I meet you in Harrisburg or in Scranton?
3. They called us, but we did not hear them.

4. Man cannot replace minerals, nor can he increase their amount.
5. The children are poor, yet they are happy.
6. Slowly and sadly the bell tolled.
7. Columbus was courageous and persevering.
8. The water was warm, but they drank it.
9. Honors were given for scholastic and athletic achievements.
10. Margaret is not going nor am I planning to go.
11. That pupil is obedient and cooperative.
12. The ship passed through the canal and into the ocean.
13. The prophets foretold the time and the place of Christ's birth.
14. The early Christians suffered and died for Christ.
15. The Crusades strengthened the influence of the Church and of the Holy See.

CORRELATIVE CONJUNCTIONS

Correlative conjunctions are coordinate conjunctions used in pairs.

Neither silk *nor* hemp is produced in the United States.

The most frequently used correlative conjunctions are:

neither . . . nor   not only . . . but also
either . . . or   both . . . and

EXERCISE 129

Select the correlative conjunctions in the following:

1. They traveled not only in Mexico but also in Brazil.
2. Margaret reads both history and fiction.
3. Elizabeth plays either the piano or the violin.
4. Pennsylvania mines both hard and soft coal.
5. Not only men but also women have the right to vote.
6. Demetrius Gallitzin was both priest and prince.
7. We could find neither Mary nor her brother.
8. Either James or John may go.
9. Both honesty and truthfulness are admirable traits.
10. The Holy Eucharist is both a sacrifice and a sacrament.

SUBORDINATE CONJUNCTIONS

A subordinate conjunction is a conjunction that connects clauses of unequal rank.

I will tell you *because* you ask me.

In this sentence there are two clauses. The first, *I will tell you,* is the principal or independent clause. It does not depend upon any other part of the sentence and forms a complete idea. The second clause, *because you ask me,* is a dependent clause answering the question *why* and modifying the verb *will tell.* The subordinate conjunction *because* joins the dependent or subordinate clause to the independent clause in the sentence.

The most common subordinate conjunctions are:

although	for	since	that
as	if	so	then
because	provided	than	unless

The conjunctive adverbs—words that do the work of an adverb and a conjunction—are likewise considered subordinate conjunctions. *After, as, before, since, until, when, where,* and *while* are conjunctive adverbs.

Very often groups of words are used as subordinate conjunctions. Learn these groups:

as well as	in order that	provided that
as if	inasmuch as	so that

NOTE. Relative adverbs and relative pronouns are also used to connect clauses of unequal rank.

They showed us the room *where* he slept. *(Relative adverb)*
Here are some books *which* you may read. *(Relative pronoun)*

EXERCISE 130

Name the principal clause, the subordinate clause, and the subordinate conjunction in each of the following sentences:

1. You must study hard if you seek success.
2. Since Brazil is a large country, it has a varied climate.
3. We practice that we may become proficient.
4. The family was happy, for peace reigned in the home.

5. Rose Marie sings better than I sing.
6. Although Saint Paul was not one of the Twelve, he is called an apostle.
7. We shall go picnicking provided the weather is clear.
8. We obeyed Sister as if she were our mother.
9. Since that is your wish, it shall be done.
10. Although he is young, he is wise.
11. Because they could find no room in the inn, Mary and Joseph went to an abandoned stable.
12. The farmer tilled the soil so that he could plant his seeds.
13. We cannot move the box unless you help us.
14. If wishes were horses, beggars would ride.
15. He practiced every day in order that he might win.
16. Inasmuch as they did not approve of his conduct, the boys left immediately.

2. *The Correct Use of Conjunctions and Prepositions*

Prepositions are often carelessly used as conjunctions. The following prepositions and conjunctions require special study.

Without is a preposition and introduces a *phrase*. *Unless* is a conjunction and introduces a *clause*.

Do not come *without your textbook.* (*Phrase*)
Do not come *unless you bring your textbook.* (*Clause*)

Like is a preposition and introduces a *phrase*. *As* and *as if* are conjunctions and introduce *clauses*.

John looks *like his father.* (*Phrase*)
John writes *as his father writes.* (*Clause*)

EXERCISE 131

Rewrite the following sentences, selecting the correct word in each sentence:

1. I may not go (without, unless) I receive permission from my father.
2. He did that work (like, as if) he were accustomed to it.
3. Make this cake (like, as) the recipe directs.

4. The battle will be lost (without, unless) they receive reinforcements.
5. Grandmother will be unhappy (without, unless) her grandchildren.
6. (Like, as) his father, David is very ambitious.
7. Theresa went out in the rain (without, unless) her umbrella.
8. Do not come (without, unless) you bring your camera.
9. (Like, as) Mary's gloves were soiled, she did not wear them to church.
10. Helen looks very much (like, as) her mother.
11. She looked (like, as if) she had discovered a fortune.
12. We started on a hike (like, as) the sun was rising.
13. He will be here (without, unless) you cancel the appointment.
14. (Without, unless) you work harder, your father will be disappointed.
15. Do not go (without, unless) you take your raincoat.
16. Abraham did (like, as) God commanded him.

INTERJECTIONS

An interjection is a word that expresses some strong or sudden emotion.

Hurrah! Here comes our captain.
Ouch! I hurt my arm.

An interjection may express *delight, disgust, contempt, pain, assent, joy, impatience, surprise, sorrow, wonder, regret.* It is generally set off from the rest of the sentence by an exclamation point. If the entire sentence is exclamatory, however, the interjection may be followed by a comma, and the exclamation point placed at the close of the sentence.

Ah, how beautifully those children sing!

The most common interjections are:

Ah!	Good!	Hush!	Oh!
Alas!	Hark!	Indeed!	Pshaw!
Beware!	Hello!	Listen!	Shh!
Bravo!	Hurrah!	Lo!	What!

"O" AND "OH"

The interjection *O* is used before a noun in direct address and is not directly followed by an exclamation point. *Oh* expresses such emotion as surprise, sorrow, or joy. It is followed by an exclamation point unless the emotion continues throughout the sentence. In this case *Oh* is followed by a comma, and the exclamation point is put at the end of the sentence.

O Marie! I wish I could go to the beach with you. *(Direct address)*
Oh! The man was injured. *(Emotion does not continue)*
Oh, how surprised I am! *(Emotion continues)*

EXERCISE 132

Select the interjections in the following sentences and tell what emotion is expressed by each interjection:

1. Pshaw! I am sorry to hear that.
2. Look! Here comes the sergeant.
3. Oh, how the sun is shining!
4. Alas! The goblet overflowed.
5. Hush! The baby is sleeping.
6. Good! Charles gained the reward.
7. Oh, how pleased I am!
8. What! Is everybody leaving?
9. Hurrah! Here comes the train.
10. Hark! What is that I hear?
11. O Agnes! Have you seen my new coat?

EXERCISE 133 [Test on Prepositions, Conjunctions, and Interjections]

Read this selection very carefully and then answer the questions that follow:

[1] Less than a minute remained in the final Catholic League basketball game of the season. [2] The contest had been an exciting, hard-fought battle between our Aquinas team and the De Sales boys. [3] Everything depended on what we did in the next few seconds, for De Sales held a one-point lead. [4] In spite of close guard-

ing, one of our players made a clever one-hand shot from under the basket. ⁵ Good! The spectators cheered loudly as two precious points put us in the lead. ⁶ De Sales, now in possession of the ball, made a desperate attempt to score. ⁷ The ball, however, sailed harmlessly through the air and across the basket. ⁸ It fell into eager hands as a loud blast from a horn announced, not only the end of the game, but also a glorious victory for Aquinas.

1. Name the prepositions in the last sentence.
2. In what case are nouns used as objects of prepositions?
3. Find a phrase that is used as the object of a preposition.
4. Is the group of words used as the object of the preposition *on* in the third sentence a phrase or a clause?
5. Pick out a group of words used as a single preposition.
6. Find a coordinate conjunction in the second sentence and tell what words this conjunction connects.
7. Name two phrases that are connected by a coordinate conjunction.
8. Name two correlative conjunctions in the paragraph.
9. What two words do the correlative conjunctions connect?
10. What word used in the third and the eighth sentences is a preposition in one of the sentences and a subordinate conjunction in the other sentence?
11. Find a conjunctive adverb in the last sentence.
12. What part of speech is the first word in the fifth sentence?

EXERCISE 134 [Review of Parts of Speech]

Test your knowledge of parts of speech by telling the part of speech of each italicized word in the following sentences:

1. This morning the temperature was *below* zero.
2. *Advanced* countries use modern means of transportation.
3. Can you *fashion* a castle out of this clay?
4. We bought two pounds of *ground* beef.
5. Put the toy *down* now, Timothy.
6. We export a variety of *wood* products.
7. They waited *below* for an hour.

8. The army *advanced* rapidly.
9. The tulip *blossoms* in early spring.
10. They took the *sign* down.
11. Children will remember these stories in *after* years.
12. Dorothy has a pretty tea *rose.*
13. The *ground* is cold and damp.
14. *That* is my favorite radio program.
15. The United States is rich in *mineral* deposits.
16. Mother will *sign* for the telegram.
17. Uranium is a radioactive *mineral.*
18. The airplane *rose* gradually.
19. Did our team make a first *down* on that play?
20. Mahogany is a valuable *wood.*
21. The delicate *blossoms* swayed in the breeze.
22. What does *that* picture represent?
23. He will write to his father *after* he has seen you.
24. You must have good brakes when you go *down* that hill.
25. Opinion sways *fashion.*

EXERCISE 135 [Test on Parts of Speech]

Read this selection very carefully and then answer the questions that follow:

¹ Above the confessional in a secluded corner of our church is a stained-glass window which depicts a touching and familiar scene. ² The prodigal son, who has been so long absent from home, kneels humbly at his father's feet. ³ The older man embraces him tenderly and assures the boy of his forgiveness. ⁴ Ah, how encouraging to poor sinners is this glowing reminder of the mercy of God as it sheds down its spirit, as well as its light, on the sacred tribunal of penance!

1. Select a proper noun. In what case is this noun?
2. What kind of noun is *mercy* in the last sentence?
3. Select a common noun in the first sentence that is used as a direct object.
4. Name a predicate adjective found in the paragraph.

5. In what degree of comparison is the descriptive adjective in the third sentence?

6. Is *his* in the second sentence used as an adjective or as a pronoun?

7. What is the case of the pronoun *him* in the third sentence? Why?

8. Name a relative pronoun in the first sentence and tell how it is used.

9. What is the antecedent of the relative pronoun in the second sentence?

10. What is the syntax of the relative pronoun in the second sentence?

11. Find a regular verb and an irregular verb in the first sentence.

12. Is the verb *sheds* in the last sentence transitive or intransitive? Why?

13. Name the verbs in the second sentence and give the tense of each.

14. Name an adverb of degree in the second sentence.

15. What kind of adverb is *down* in the last sentence?

16. What part of speech is *encouraging* in the last sentence? How is it used?

17. Name a coordinate conjunction in the third sentence and tell what words it connects.

18. Select an interjection in the paragraph. What emotion do you think it expresses?

19. What part of speech is the first word in the paragraph?

20. Name a group of words used as a conjunction.

CHAPTER EIGHT

Phrases, Clauses,
Sentences

A phrase is a group of related words used as a
single part of speech.

Rugs *from Persia* are expensive.

1. *Division according to Form*

A prepositional phrase is a phrase introduced by a preposition.

A participial phrase is a phrase introduced by a participle.

An infinitive phrase is a phrase introduced by an infinitive.

A gerund phrase is a phrase introduced by a gerund.

Fairmount Park is *in Philadelphia. (Prepositional phrase)*
The boy *riding the bicycle* works for my father. *(Participial phrase)*
To succeed in school is our aim. *(Infinitive phrase)*
Writing correct English is a pleasure. *(Gerund phrase)*

2. *Division according to Use*

An adjectival phrase is a phrase used as an adjective.

An adverbial phrase is a phrase used as an adverb.

A noun phrase is a phrase used as a noun.

There are nine choirs *of angels. (Adjectival phrase)*
The children went *to the circus* today. *(Adverbial phrase)*
"To the Airport" was the sign they read. *(Noun phrase)*

Adjectival phrases modify nouns or pronouns. Adverbial phrases
modify verbs, adverbs, adjectives, participles, gerunds, or infinitives. Noun phrases may serve as the subject of the sentence, the
direct object, the predicate nominative, the object of a preposition, and an appositive.

EXERCISE 136

Select the phrases in the following sentences and classify each according to form and use:

1. The Eskimos live in little villages in the North.
2. Edward Dormer works on a cattle ranch in Arizona.
3. The picture called "The Last Supper" is painted on the wall of a convent in Milan.
4. Many Japanese ride in odd little carts called jinrikishas.
5. "To the Right" was written on the sign.
6. The United States purchased Alaska from Russia.
7. Cotton is packed in bales and sent to the mills.
8. The Lincoln Highway extends across the United States.
9. Having said their prayers, the boys retired.
10. The aviation industry has expanded with great rapidity.
11. Rubber is produced in many tropical countries.
12. In 1807 Fulton made his first trip on the *Clermont*.
13. I enjoyed the exhibitions at the fair.
14. Letters of earlier times are often extremely interesting.
15. We should always have kind thoughts about others.
16. Helen likes to read poetry.
17. John, having explained the problem well, was commended by his teacher.
18. Losing that game was a hard blow.

CLAUSES

A clause is a part of a sentence containing a subject and a predicate.

A *principal clause* is one that expresses a complete thought.

A *subordinate clause* is one that does not express a complete thought and that cannot stand alone.

Saint Isaac Jogues, *who was a Jesuit,* labored among the Mohawks.
Saint Isaac Jogues labored among the Mohawks. *(Principal clause)*
who was a Jesuit *(Subordinate clause)*

Subordinate clauses are classified as adjectival, adverbial, or noun clauses.

1. *Adjectival Clauses*

An adjectival clause is a subordinate clause used as an adjective.

An *ambitious* boy usually succeeds.
A boy *with ambition* usually succeeds.
A boy *who has ambition* usually succeeds.

In the first sentence the adjective *ambitious* modifies the noun *boy;* in the second sentence *boy* is modified by the adjectival phrase *with ambition;* in the third sentence the modifier is a group of words, *who has ambition.* This group of words contains a subject and a predicate and is therefore a clause. Since the clause does the work of an adjective, it is an adjectival clause.

Some adjectival clauses are nonrestrictive; others are restrictive. A nonrestrictive clause is one that may be omitted from the sentence without changing its meaning. It is separated from the rest of the sentence by commas. A restrictive clause is one that is a necessary part of the sentence because it points out or identifies a particular person or object. No punctuation is required for restrictive clauses.

Aunt Margaret, who lives in Boston, is my godmother. *(Nonrestrictive clause)*

My aunt who lives in Boston is my godmother. *(Restrictive clause)*

Adjectival clauses are usually introduced by *relative pronouns* or *relative adverbs.*

EXERCISE 137

Point out the adjectival clauses in the following sentences and tell what noun or pronoun each clause modifies:

1. Happy is the man who finds wisdom.
2. Mr. Graham, who is our coach, gave a pep talk.
3. All things come to him who waits.
4. Ellen Ewing, who became the wife of General Sherman, was a fervent Catholic.
5. The farm where he once lived is now deserted.
6. Gertrude is a girl in whom I have great faith.

7. The income which supports our club comes from our handicraft.
8. He is never alone who is accompanied by noble thoughts.
9. Susan brought fruit which she distributed to the children.
10. The man who is last in that line is the captain.
11. The factory where my father worked has been closed.
12. We did not know the hour when the train would arrive.
13. The museum is a place where I enjoy many happy hours.
14. I know of no reason why he should not come.

EXERCISE 138

Rewrite the following sentences, changing the italicized adjectives to adjectival phrases and adjectival clauses:

1. The *courageous* soldier faced the cannon.
2. A *beautiful* red rose grew on the bush.
3. The *worthy* girl was rewarded.
4. They purchased a *powerful* engine.
5. They read a *mystery* story.
6. We crossed a *wooden* bridge.
7. A *shady* place was sought by the picnickers.
8. A *quiet* resort will satisfy my mother.
9. We gazed at the *colossal* statue.
10. *Scientific* books give him pleasure.

2. *Adverbial Clauses*

An adverbial clause is a subordinate clause used as an adverb.

The boy acted *courageously*.
The boy acted *with courage*.
The boy acted *as if he had courage*.

In the first sentence the adverb *courageously* modifies the verb *acted;* in the second sentence the adverbial phrase *with courage* modifies the verb *acted;* in the third sentence the clause *as if he had courage* modifies the verb *acted*. Since this clause does the work of an adverb, it is an adverbial clause.

Adverbial clauses are usually introduced by *conjunctive adverbs* or *subordinate conjunctions*. These clauses may tell time, place, degree, manner, cause, or purpose.

In adverbial clauses of degree (those that answer the questions *how much* or *how little*) there is often an omission of words.

Peter jumped higher than he [*jumped*].

I admire him more than [*I admire*] her.

EXERCISE 139

Select the adverbial clauses in the following sentences and tell what word each clause modifies:

1. Strike while the iron is hot.
2. Go when you are told.
3. We saw them when we were in New York.
4. Theodore Roosevelt learned the value of outdoor exercise when he lived in the West.
5. The plant flowered, for it received good care.
6. The rabbit ran faster than we could run.
7. An honest man speaks as he thinks.
8. He saved his money that he might attend college.
9. As the twig is bent the tree is inclined.
10. Texas is larger than California.
11. I will give you the money if you need it.
12. John is more devoted to his sister than his brother.
13. When an infant is in danger of death, he may be baptized without parental consent.
14. When the Japanese attacked Pearl Harbor, the people of the United States clamored for war.
15. While laws are in existence they must be obeyed.

EXERCISE 140

Rewrite the following sentences, changing the italicized adverbs to adverbial phrases and adverbial clauses:

1. The children answered *correctly*.
2. My sister writes *carefully*.

3. The boy sang *merrily*.
4. John studied *diligently*.
5. The teacher dismissed her class *promptly*.
6. Listen *attentively* to me.
7. He gave the donation *generously*.
8. They worked *willingly*.
9. The train is entering the station *now*.
10. The messenger ran *swiftly*.

3. *Noun Clauses*

A noun clause is a subordinate clause used as a noun.

Robert's *defeat* was unfortunate.
That Robert was defeated was unfortunate.

In the first sentence the noun *defeat* is the subject; in the second sentence the clause *That Robert was defeated* is the subject. Since this clause does the work of a noun, it is a noun clause.

NOUN CLAUSES USED AS SUBJECTS

A noun clause may be used as the subject of a sentence. In sentences containing noun clauses the entire sentence is considered the principal clause. The noun clause is the subordinate clause.

That the Panama Canal benefits many nations has been proved. *(Principal clause)*

That the Panama Canal benefits many nations *(Noun clause used as subject)*

EXERCISE 141

Name the subject clause in each of the following sentences:
1. That she was late for the party surprised me.
2. That there are three Persons in God is a mystery.
3. What we should do next was the question.
4. That McCormick invented the reaper is a fact.
5. Whether he will be elected is doubtful.
6. That we must all die is certain.
7. Why I did not receive a reply to the letter disturbed me.

8. How leather is tanned is explained in that book.
9. That he overcame the difficulty is proof of his perseverance.
10. When they will return has not been decided.
11. That the earth is round is evident.
12. Why they took that path puzzled me.
13. "Always be prepared" is a good motto.
14. That our national resources should be conserved is a wise policy.
15. How she bakes such delicious pies has always interested me.
16. Where she went is not known.

NOUN CLAUSES USED AS DIRECT OBJECTS

A noun clause may be used as the object of a verb.

We know *that the Panama Canal benefits many nations.*

It is easy to recognize a subordinate clause, but we must remember that the entire sentence is the principal clause.

We know that the Panama Canal benefits many nations. *(Principal clause)*

that the Panama Canal benefits many nations *(Noun clause used as object)*

Quotations, both direct and indirect, are considered noun clauses in such sentences as these:

John said, *"I have finished my paragraph." (Direct quotation)*
Mother asked *who spilled the milk. (Indirect quotation)*

EXERCISE 142

Name the object clause in each of the following sentences:

1. You may appoint whoever is capable.
2. The Church teaches that Christ died for all.
3. The paper announced that the president had signed the bill.
4. We asked how she made the dress.
5. Have you heard when the boat will dock?
6. I recall that I delivered that package.
7. God promised that He would send a Redeemer.
8. Everybody admits that television is a great invention.

9. Can you explain how this machine is operated?
10. The Our Father tells us that God is our Father in heaven.
11. Alexander Bell proved that the human voice could be heard over a wire.
12. John did what he was told.
13. Christ said, "I thirst."
14. I do not know whether my answer is correct.
15. Have you found what you lost?

NOUN CLAUSES USED AS OBJECTS OF PREPOSITIONS

A noun clause may be used as the object of a preposition.

He spoke of *how the Panama Canal benefits many nations.*

He spoke of how the Panama Canal benefits many nations. *(Principal clause)*

how the Panama Canal benefits many nations *(Noun clause used as object of a preposition)*

EXERCISE 143

Name the noun clause used as the object of a preposition in each of the following sentences:

1. The president addressed the people from where he stood.
2. The captain had no thought but that his team would win.
3. That man cannot live on what he earns.
4. God will reward us for whatever good we do.
5. We are studying about how sugar cane grows.
6. Give the basket to whoever comes first.
7. The children were edified by what they saw.
8. Have you ever read about what Father Damien did for the lepers?
9. We know all the details except how it was planned.
10. The missionary converted many by what he taught.
11. Our Lord gives His graces to whoever asks for them.
12. We could not see the announcer from where we sat.
13. Many people will be affected by what he has written.
14. We should make use of what we have.
15. Our teacher is always interested in what we do.

NOUN CLAUSES USED AS PREDICATE NOMINATIVES

A noun clause may be used as a predicate nominative. We remember that the predicate nominative follows a linking verb and completes its meaning.

The fact is *that the Panama Canal benefits many nations.*

The fact is that the Panama Canal benefits many nations. *(Principal clause)*

that the Panama Canal benefits many nations *(Noun clause used as predicate nominative)*

EXERCISE 144

Name the noun clause used as a predicate nominative in each of the following sentences:

1. My hope is that we finish this work soon.
2. The truth is that John is not fitted for the position.
3. One of the requirements is that the secretary must write legibly.
4. The general opinion was that the army would invade from the south.
5. The fact is that Saint Francis Xavier did not reach China.
6. The greatest proof of Christ's divinity is that He arose from the dead.
7. The mystery to me is how she finished the work so quickly.
8. Regina's chief concern was what she would wear to the party.
9. A qualification for the presidency is that the candidate must be a natural-born citizen.
10. The decision is that we should start early in the morning.
11. A favorite exhortation of Saint John was that Christ's followers should love one another.
12. The greatest advantage of the team is that the members are unselfish.
13. His most admirable characteristic is that he helps everybody.
14. His favorite saying is that haste makes waste.
15. The general's order was that the army should surrender unconditionally.

NOUN CLAUSES USED AS APPOSITIVES

A noun clause may be used as an appositive. An appositive clause explains or describes the noun or the pronoun which precedes it.

The fact *that the Panama Canal benefits many nations* cannot be denied.

A noun clause is considered an appositive when it follows and explains the expletive *it*.

It is a fact *that the Panama Canal benefits many nations*.

Do not confuse appositive clauses with adjectival clauses. An appositive clause is a noun clause and takes the place of a noun; an adjectival clause modifies a noun or a pronoun.

The notice *that we would have a holiday* caused great joy. *(Noun clause)*
The notice *that she posted* was read by everybody. *(Adjectival clause)*

EXERCISE 145

Name the noun clauses used as appositives:

1. The fact that these volcanoes are active is well known.
2. He forgot his promise that he would take us for a boat ride.
3. It is my hope that they will return before dark.
4. It is evident that experience is the best teacher.
5. Have you heard the news that a new stadium will be erected here?
6. It is generally known that many minerals have been discovered by chance.
7. It cannot be denied that prayer is necessary to salvation.
8. The saying that many hands make light work is familiar to all.
9. Her wish that she might visit Rome was realized last summer.
10. The belief that good health promotes happiness is encouraging.

EXERCISE 146

Select the noun clauses and tell how each is used:

1. Matthew showed us where the camp was located.
2. My only hope is that Henry reaches home soon.
3. That he meant what he wrote was plain.

4. I cannot say that you are correct in your statement.
5. I know that I answered the letter.
6. Do you believe the report that the ship has docked?
7. What they told you may be untrue.
8. The birds could not fly from where they had built their nests.
9. Do you know who rang the bell?
10. The fact that he was honest could not be denied.
11. We have no idea of when he painted the portrait.
12. He told us why he liked chemistry.
13. Vincent's only excuse was that he had been delayed.
14. Catholics believe that Christ is present in the Blessed Sacrament.
15. The trouble is that the message was misunderstood.

EXERCISE 147

Tell whether the clauses in the following sentences are adjectival, adverbial, or noun clauses:

1. Uneasy lies the head that wears the crown.
2. I was pleased when I heard the news.
3. The man who visited us promised me a silver coin.
4. He realized that he had made a mistake.
5. Bruce read the article which Rose had written.
6. It's a long road that has no turning.
7. The lady was not at home when we called.
8. Bernard was delighted because he won the scholarship.
9. The room has a window that faces west.
10. It is true that the child is very ill.
11. Matthew won because he played a good game.
12. The man who wrote the book addressed the class.
13. What can't be cured must be endured.
14. Monticello is the name of the estate where Thomas Jefferson lived.
15. We die in the friendship of God if we are free from mortal sin.
16. That we should obey our parents is a divine command.
17. We cannot see God because He is a pure spirit.
18. Make hay while the sun shines.

19. Mary Magdalene proved in many different ways that she loved her Master.
20. Dr. Smith, can you tell me where the office of the chief surgeon is located?
21. In the Epistle to the Philippians Saint Paul said, "Rejoice in the Lord always."
22. The upright man speaks as he thinks.
23. Saint Paul tells us that we should rejoice in the Lord always.
24. We know that the Catholic Church is the one true Church.
25. The ciborium is a gold vessel in which the small hosts are kept in the tabernacle.

SENTENCES

A sentence is a group of words expressing a complete thought.

Sanctifying grace makes us temples of the Holy Spirit.

1. Essential Elements of a Sentence

No sentence is complete without a *subject* and a *predicate*.

The subject is that part of the sentence which names a person, a place, or a thing about which a statement is made. The predicate is that part of the sentence which tells something about the subject.

The subject with all its modifiers is called the *complete subject*. The predicate with all its modifiers and complements is called the *complete predicate*.

COMPLETE SUBJECT	COMPLETE PREDICATE
We	cannot see our guardian angels.
Our guardian angels	watch over us.
Dear Guardian Angels, [you]	watch over us.

EXERCISE 148

Decide which of the following groups of words are sentences:

1. Sitting on the floor.
2. Laughs merrily.
3. Stand.
4. Give it to me.
5. Knowledge is power.
6. The boy who saw the boat race.
7. Riding on a bicycle through the city streets.
8. Smooth seas make poor sailors.
9. Houses beautifully constructed.
10. During the night the boat drifted out to sea.
11. Into the burning house dashed the fireman.
12. On the auditorium platform stood the guest speaker.
13. General MacArthur, who was in command in the Philippines.
14. Beside the river stood their tiny cottage.
15. Where have you been?
16. As soon as I received the small package.
17. Heavy footsteps made the man start in surprise.
18. The boys whom we treated as friends.
19. The cathedral choir, singing beautifully.
20. You may sit here.

EXERCISE 149

Select the subject and the predicate in each sentence:

1. Spanish missionaries labored in the southwestern states.
2. There was a storm on the lake last evening.

3. Around the field galloped the excited horses.
4. Over the house flew the airplane.
5. The *Titanic* struck an iceberg.
6. God be with you.
7. In Italy was born Marconi, a Catholic scientist.
8. One of the greatest of our daily needs is light.
9. Report at nine o'clock.
10. At the Centennial Exposition of 1876 the telephone was exhibited.
11. Ireland was converted to Christianity by Saint Patrick.
12. Have you corrected all the errors in your arithmetic paper?
13. The United States leads in the production of petroleum.
14. Mother of Perpetual Help, pray for us.
15. Always be prompt.

2. *Natural and Transposed Order in Sentences*

Whenever the complete predicate follows the complete subject, a sentence is in the natural order.

Whenever the complete predicate or part of the predicate is placed before the subject, a sentence is in the transposed order.

The wild flowers bloom in the spring. *(Natural order)*
In the spring wild flowers bloom. *(Transposed order)*

EXERCISE 150

Name the subjects and the predicates in the following sentences. Rewrite each sentence, changing those in natural order to transposed order, and those in transposed order to natural order:

1. Beyond the distant mountains lay the little Indian village.
2. Lincoln's statue was placed at the far end of the bridge.
3. Under the great arch passed many pilgrims.
4. In the rear of the hall a man rose quietly.
5. The children rushed to the lake at the first sound of the whistle.
6. The milk flowed from the overturned can like a white waterfall.

7. Into the corner of the luxurious car crept the tired child.
8. From behind the trees and bushes came the fatal shots.
9. There were about two thousand men in the army.
10. In the hotels were found all sorts of people.
11. Admiral Penn was among the officers of King Charles.
12. From the new West came the great leader, Andrew Jackson.
13. Down from the sky came the fluttering flakes of snow.
14. The trees in their autumn colors were beautiful.
15. At the head of the parade marched the band.

3. *Division of Sentences according to Use*

A *declarative sentence* is a sentence that states a fact.

An *interrogative sentence* is a sentence that asks a question.

An *imperative sentence* is a sentence that expresses a command.

An *exclamatory sentence* is a sentence that expresses strong or sudden emotion.

The first American see was established in Baltimore. *(Declarative)*
Who was the first American bishop? *(Interrogative)*
Read the life of Saint Thomas Aquinas. *(Imperative)*
How generous you are! *(Exclamatory)*

EXERCISE 151

Classify the following sentences according to use and tell what punctuation should be placed at the end of each sentence:

1. With God's grace we supernaturalize our ordinary actions
2. What beautiful flowers these are
3. What is actual grace
4. Who painted "By the River"
5. What a great inventor Edison was
6. Chicago is one of the largest cities in the world
7. Bring the report to me at once
8. Samuel F. B. Morse invented the telegraph
9. Elizabeth was chosen secretary of the club
10. Saint Augustine is the oldest city in the United States

11. Who promoted the laying of the first Atlantic cable
12. Put your desks in order before you leave
13. See the hydroplane
14. From whom were the Virgin Islands purchased
15. Who was the first chief justice of the Supreme Court

4. *Division of Sentences according to Form*

According to form, sentences are divided into simple, compound, complex, and compound-complex sentences.

SIMPLE SENTENCES

A simple sentence is a sentence containing one subject and one predicate, either or both of which may be compound.

Saint Dominic taught the use of the rosary.

If the subject of a sentence consists of more than one noun or pronoun, it is said to be a *compound subject*. If the predicate consists of more than one verb, it is said to be a *compound predicate*.

A sentence may have a compound subject, a compound predicate, or a compound subject and a compound predicate.

Saint Dominic and *Saint Bernard* had great devotion to our Blessed Mother. *(Compound subject)*

Saint Dominic *taught* and *preached* about our Blessed Mother. *(Compound predicate)*

Saint Dominic and *Saint Bernard taught* and *preached* about our Blessed Mother. *(Compound subject and compound predicate)*

EXERCISE 152

Show that each of the following sentences is simple by selecting the subject and the predicate:

1. Missionaries go to China every year.
2. From the church came the sound of celestial music.
3. Did Alice and Louise invite you to the party?
4. In October the leaves change color and fall from the trees.
5. Singing and whistling, the boys marched steadily forward.

6. There are many fish in the waters of Alaska.
7. Children should belong to the Holy Childhood Association.
8. Many aids have been given to the missionaries in Asia.
9. Father Schulte and his assistants read and graded all the religion papers.
10. The next morning the landscape was covered with snow.

EXERCISE 153

Make a complete sentence of each expression by supplying a compound subject or a compound predicate:

1. .... and .... are large cities of the United States.
2. _Tom_ ...., _Mark_ ...., and _Steve_ .... are playing together. *squeers!*
3. The boys and the girls in our classroom .... and ....
4. .... and .... brought flowers to school.
5. The children either .... a letter or ....
6. Joseph ....*has*.... nuts and *plays with* them.
7. .... and .... expect to visit Mexico this summer.
8. Mother .... and .... our clothes.
9. Christ .... and .... for us.
10. To gain the happiness of heaven we must ...., and .... God in this world.

COMPOUND SENTENCES

A compound sentence is a sentence that contains two or more independent clauses.

Saint Dominic had great devotion to our Blessed Mother, and he taught the use of the rosary in her honor.

This sentence contains two complete statements (simple sentences) which are connected by the conjunction *and*.

Saint Dominic had great devotion to our Blessed Mother. He taught the use of the rosary in her honor.

Coordinate conjunctions are used to connect the clauses of a compound sentence because these clauses are of equal rank. Sometimes the clauses of a compound sentence have no connecting word. The connection is then indicated by the use of the semicolon.

EXERCISE 154

Analyze by diagram or otherwise each of the following compound sentences:

1. The day for the picnic finally arrived and everybody was happy.
2. I cannot tell you now; I will explain the matter later.
3. Class was dismissed and the children went home.
4. The home of the pope is at the Vatican, but in summer he resides at Castel Gandolfo.
5. George received the award, and his class was proud of him.
6. The boys were enthusiastic, yet their plans failed.
7. The orchestra is the best in the city; it is directed by Mr. Bryson.
8. The harvest is great, but the laborers are few.
9. Rose is reading, and her sister is practicing her music lesson.
10. Watch the traffic light, or you may meet with an accident.
11. Walter walked to the field, and the players cheered him wildly.
12. Be mission-minded, and you will help the missions.
13. I am the vine; you are the branches.
14. I read *The Adventures of Tom Sawyer,* but I did not see the motion-picture version of it.
15. God made us; we belong to Him.

EXERCISE 155

Combine each group of simple sentences into one compound sentence:

1. In Christ there is one Person. There are two natures.
2. I watched. I did not see him again.
3. In the mountains the summer days are warm. The nights are cool.

4. The Holy Ghost missionaries labor in Africa. The Maryknoll missionaries labor in China.
5. The crucifix has a figure of Christ on it. The cross has no figure on it.
6. The Council of Trent lasted eighteen years. The Council of Trent condemned the heresies of the Protestant reformers.
7. Ichabod Crane was tall and lanky. His whole frame was loosely hung together.
8. Synonyms are words of similar meanings. Antonyms are words of opposite meanings.
9. Good words cost nothing. Good words are worth much.
10. James Madison was president during the War of 1812. Abraham Lincoln was president during the Civil War. William McKinley was president during the Spanish-American War.

COMPLEX SENTENCES

A complex sentence is a sentence that contains one principal clause and one or more subordinate clauses.

Saint Dominic, who was the founder of the Dominicans, taught the use of the rosary.

This is a complex sentence because it contains one principal clause, *Saint Dominic taught the use of the rosary,* and one subordinate clause, *who was the founder of the Dominicans.*

SUBORDINATE CLAUSE   **PRINCIPAL CLAUSE**

Subordinate clauses may be adjectival, adverbial, or noun clauses, according to their use in the sentence.

Adjectival clauses are generally introduced by relative pronouns *(who, which, what, that, but, as)* or relative adverbs *(when, where, why)*. They are discussed on page 376.

Adverbial clauses are generally introduced by subordinate conjunctions *(as, that, since, because, for, if, then, than, provided, so, though, unless)* or conjunctive adverbs *(after, when, before, since, where, until, while)*. An explanation of these clauses may be found on pages 377-78.

Noun clauses are usually introduced by the introductory conjunction *that*. Refer to pages 379-83 for a discussion of the various types of noun clauses.

EXERCISE 156

Point out the principal and the subordinate clauses in each of the following complex sentences. Tell whether each subordinate clause is an adjectival, an adverbial, or a noun clause:

1. I rejoice when I see a rainbow in the sky.
2. Monte Cassino was a famous Benedictine monastery which was destroyed in World War II.
3. He who avoids the temptation avoids the sin.
4. Although Paris and Vienna had their charms, Mary longed for home.
5. When a man is in earnest, his work is half done.
6. The child came when he was called.
7. Father Donovan, who was a Maryknoll missionary, died in China.
8. If you can't help, don't hinder.
9. The general opinion is that they are in Mexico.
10. Father teaches us that we must obey.
11. When the result of the Battle of Gettysburg was announced, the northerners rejoiced.
12. Until you see Yellowstone National Park, you cannot fully appreciate its beauty.
13. When Father returns, we shall go for a ride.

14. Newfoundland, which lies at the mouth of the St. Lawrence River, is a rugged land.
15. Our Holy Father, who is Christ's representative, is the successor of Saint Peter.
16. Interesting and delightful was the trip which we made to California.
17. The books that were sent to the invalid cheered his lonely hours.
18. We admire a person who is sincere.
19. We enjoyed many pleasant days on my uncle's farm when we visited it last year.
20. The last book of the Bible, which is called the Apocalypse, was written by Saint John.
21. I will always obey when my parents command.
22. The grotto of Lourdes now stands where our Lady appeared to Saint Bernadette.
23. Peter was talking about what had been accomplished by the club.
24. Philadelphia, which is the largest city of Pennsylvania, is located on the Delaware River.

EXERCISE 157

Make one complex sentence from each of the following groups of simple sentences:

1. Saint Helena discovered the true cross. She was the mother of Constantine.
2. Mary Magdalene followed Christ to Calvary. She stood beneath His cross.
3. President Monroe issued the Monroe Doctrine. He was our fifth president.
4. The Egyptians made paper from the papyrus plant. This plant grew along the banks of the Nile.
5. Sacagawea was an Indian woman. She helped the explorers Lewis and Clark.
6. The knight wore a coat of mail. It had a hood of steel to protect his head.

7. Charlemagne was the grandson of Charles Martel. Charles Martel defeated the Moors at Tours.
8. Saint Francis Xavier is called the Apostle of the Indies. He belonged to the Jesuit order.
9. Theodore Roosevelt was leader of the Rough Riders. He was also president of the United States.
10. I studied the lesson. The lesson was assigned yesterday.
11. I looked up the river. I saw a beautiful boat sailing. The boat was sailing toward me. The boat was sailing swiftly.
12. The Panama Canal was begun by a French company. The Panama Canal was completed by the United States. The Panama Canal connects the Atlantic Ocean with the Pacific.

COMPOUND-COMPLEX SENTENCES

A compound-complex sentence is a sentence that contains two or more principal clauses and one or more subordinate clauses.

General Sherman had an austere manner, but he was always kind to the men who were under his charge.

EXERCISE 158

Check on your knowledge of sentences by telling whether the following are simple, compound, complex, or compound-complex:

1. We should cultivate confidence in God and faith in the power of prayer.
2. Many decorative and useful articles are made from copper.
3. Do you know the reason why he did not leave the package?
4. The policeman mounted his horse and rode away.
5. The material that was ordered for the building has not arrived, but we shall continue the work without it.
6. Is there a child here who does not enjoy reading about the adventures of Robin Hood?
7. When a pupil understands his work, then it interests him.
8. We should be proud of our many Catholic heroes.
9. Shylock is a character in *The Merchant of Venice*.

10. The Statue of Liberty, which is located on Bedloe's Island, is the largest metal statue in the world.
11. Do you know a brief biography of Benjamin Franklin?
12. The windowpane was broken, but the boys who were playing ball offered to pay for it.
13. Every pupil should have a portfolio in which he can file his daily work.
14. In penmanship the wrist should not be tilted more than forty-five degrees.
15. If you go, you must return early.
16. Do you know that Portland, Oregon, received its name by the toss of a coin?
17. The United States has some outlying possessions that are rich in natural resources.
18. The Appalachian Mountains are in the East, and the Rocky Mountains are in the West.
19. On the table near the tree were many packages wrapped in tissue paper and tied with gay ribbons.
20. A travel club is an interesting way in which one can take imaginary trips to various countries.
21. When Rosa Bonheur was nineteen, she sent her first picture to an art exhibition.
22. Opening the old album, she showed us many pictures of her ancestors.
23. Sir Joshua Reynolds painted many pictures, but I prefer "Angels' Heads."
24. He stood on the bank of the river and watched the boat race.
25. The Pilgrims sailed from England on a small ship called the *Mayflower*.
26. The dog ran up and down the path and barked at the mailman.
27. Our American Indians made light, swift canoes of birch bark, which they paddled about the lakes and streams.
28. Francis remembered that no one was allowed to ride the pony.
29. Mother asked what I had done.
30. President Garfield appointed Clara Barton the first president of the American Red Cross.

EXERCISE 159 [Test on Phrases, Clauses, Sentences]

Read this selection very carefully and then answer the questions that follow:

[1] What are the factors which determine the occupations of those who live in certain localities? [2] To answer this question, consider carefully the physical features of the region. [3] If the climate, soil, and rainfall favor the raising of crops, the people turn to farming. [4] The fact that they live near the sea moves others to make fishing their work. [5] Inhabitants of districts having rich mineral deposits find employment in the mines. [6] In thickly populated areas many workers are available, and good transportation facilities make raw materials available. [7] If power resources are sufficient, manufacturing becomes important in such sections. [8] Since the other occupations are similarly controlled by natural environment, we see that man's choice of a life's work is limited greatly by the conditions under which he lives.

1. How is the phrase *having rich mineral deposits* in the fifth sentence classified according to form?
2. What is the form of the phrase *to answer this question* in the second sentence?
3. Name a prepositional phrase in the seventh sentence.
4. Is the phrase *of a life's work* in the last sentence adjectival or adverbial?
5. Name an adverbial phrase in the fourth sentence.
6. Name two adjectival clauses in the first sentence.
7. Find an adverbial clause in the seventh sentence. What verb does the clause modify?
8. What kind of clause is *that they live near the sea* in the fourth sentence? Give the syntax of this clause.
9. Name an adjectival clause in the last sentence. What noun does this clause modify?
10. Find a compound sentence in the paragraph. Is it a declarative or an interrogative sentence?
11. Are there any complex sentences? If so, name one.
12. Find one simple sentence in the natural order.

Model Diagrams

By means of diagrams we show in a graphic manner the relationships that exist among the various words that make up a sentence. As we have seen, there are simple, compound, and complex sentences. Since sentences of all types may contain modifiers, no one form of diagram will serve for every kind of sentence. The diagrams given here are those that should help us in our work. When asked to diagram a sentence, look here for one of the same kind and see how the diagram is made.

The diagraming of sentences should serve a double purpose. First, it should make it easier for us to understand the complete meaning of every sentence we read. Secondly, it should help us to write effectively and to avoid the use of faulty sentences. If we keep these purposes before our mind, diagraming will improve our English. It will not become a mechanical exercise which does not help us to read more intelligently nor to write more correctly.

SIMPLE SENTENCES

NOMINATIVE CASE

Subject: Into the fort stumbled the exhausted *messenger*.

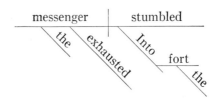

Predicate Nominative: The child was named *John*.

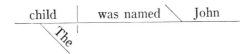

Apposition: Basil, the *blacksmith*, was the father of Gabriel.

Address: *Mary*, be our guide through life.

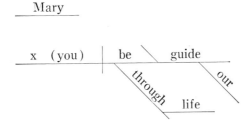

Exclamation: *Action!* The play needs action.

Action

Absolute: *Mary* being our model, we pattern our lives on hers.

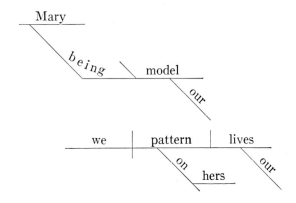

OBJECTIVE CASE

Direct Object: Christ instituted seven *sacraments.*

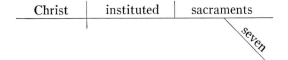

Indirect Object: The teacher told the *children* a story.

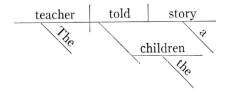

Apposition: We honor Mary, our *Queen.*

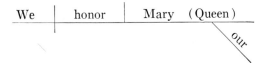

Object of Preposition: Washington performed his duties with great *courage*.

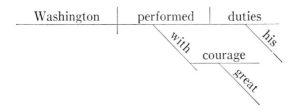

Adverbial Objective: This *morning* the ground was covered with frost.

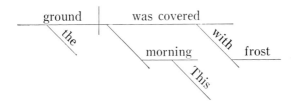

Objective Complement: My father appointed Joseph *guardian*.

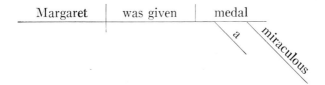

Retained Object: Margaret was given a miraculous *medal*.

COMPOUND ELEMENTS

Compound Predicate: Joseph *gathered* nuts and *ate* them.

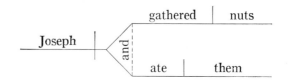

COMPOUND SENTENCE

The harvest is great, but the laborers are few.

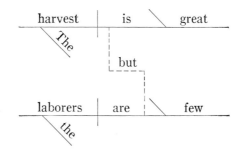

COMPLEX SENTENCES

ADJECTIVAL CLAUSES

This is the spot where the treaty was signed.

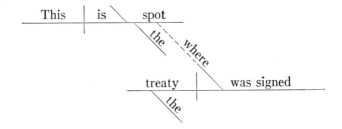

Mary gave her the picture that she had brought from Rome.

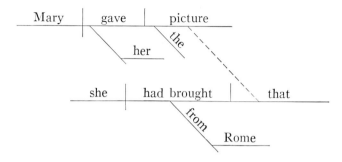

This is the man whose horse won the prize.

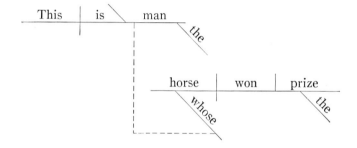

ADVERBIAL CLAUSES

Mary came because you sent for her.

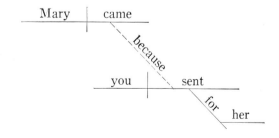

When snow falls the town presents a beautiful picture.

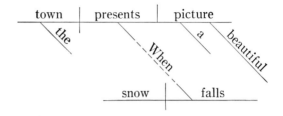

NOUN CLAUSES

Subject: That the earth is round is evident.

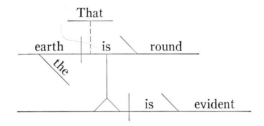

Predicate Nominative: My hope is that we finish the work soon.

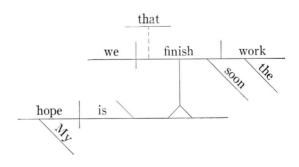

Direct Object: He realized that he had made a mistake.

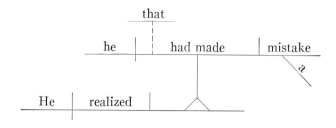

Object of Preposition: The boys could see the town from where they had camped.

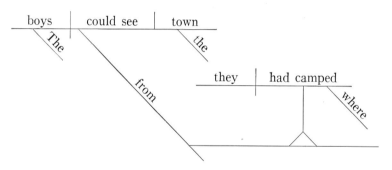

Apposition: The fact that he was honest could not be denied.

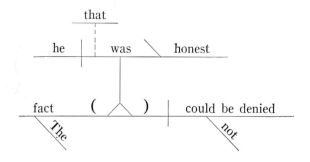

INFINITIVES

Subject: *To win* was their only thought.

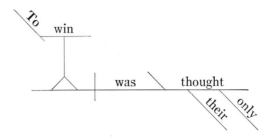

Predicate Nominative: Augustine's mission was *to convert* England.

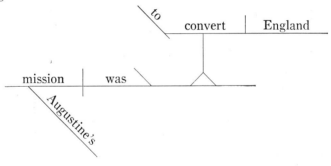

Object: I like *to read* good books.

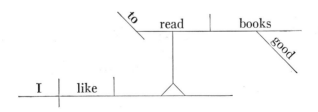

Object of Preposition: He was about *to write* the letter.

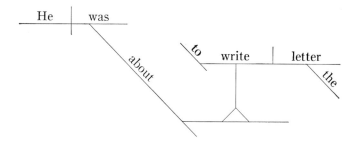

Apposition: It is the president's duty *to enforce* the laws.

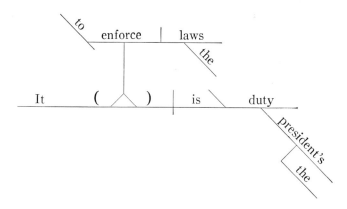

Adjective: Catholics have many opportunities *to profess* their faith.

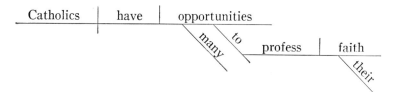

Adverb: Christ died *to redeem* the world.

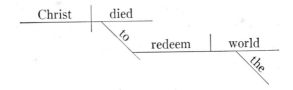

They were anxious *to return.*

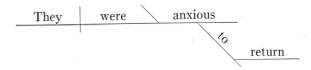

The king is powerful enough *to gather* an army.

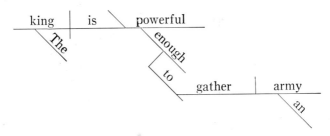

PARTICIPLES

The children, *bearing* flags, marched into the classroom.

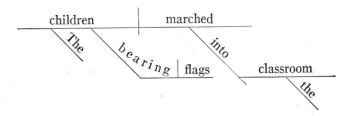

Shouting joyfully, they marched around the football field.

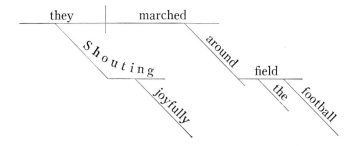

PARTICIPIAL ADJECTIVE

The *running* water wore away the stone.

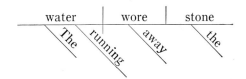

GERUNDS

Subject: *Painting* pictures is my favorite hobby.

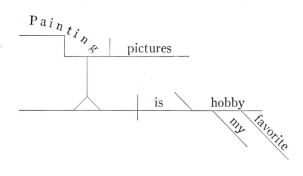

Direct Object: I remember *writing* that letter.

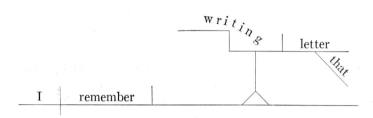

Object of Preposition: Windmills are used for *pumping* water.

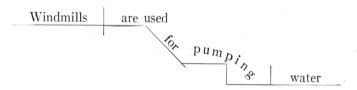

Predicate Nominative: My favorite pastime is *reading* biographies.

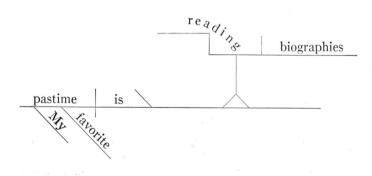

Punctuation

The purpose of punctuation is to make clear the meaning of what is written. In speaking, the inflection of our voice enables the listener to understand our thoughts. In writing, there are different kinds of punctuation marks—the period, comma, semicolon, colon, exclamation point, interrogation point, quotation marks, apostrophe, hyphen, and dash—which enable the reader to interpret our thoughts. The same marks must be used for similar constructions at all times. The following rules are the ones which we shall need in our writing.

THE PERIOD

Use a period:

1. At the end of a declarative or an imperative sentence.

   Saint Isaac Jogues was tortured by the Mohawks.
   Come here, John.

2. After an abbreviation and an initial.

   D.D.S.   James A. Garfield

THE COMMA

Use a comma:

1. To separate words or groups of words used in a series.

   Faith, hope, and charity are divine virtues.
   On the streets, in the shops, and at the lake the father searched for his little boy.

2. To separate independent elements and words of direct address.

   Yes, Saint Frances Cabrini was the first canonized American citizen.
   Bless me, Father.

3. To set off a short direct quotation and the parts of a divided quotation, unless an interrogation mark or an exclamation point is required.

"I shall be glad to come," answered Mary.

"We must all die," reminded the priest, "but we do not know the day nor the hour."

"Have you ever read *Uncle Tom's Cabin?*" asked the boy.

4. To set off the parts of dates, addresses, or geographical names.

The Japanese bombed Pearl Harbor, Hawaii, on December 7, 1941.

5. To separate nonrestrictive phrases and clauses from the rest of the sentence.

The boat, crowded with people, sailed away.

My father, who has been to Boston, returned last night.

NOTE. A nonrestrictive phrase or clause is one that may be omitted from the sentence without changing the meaning. Some phrases and clauses are necessary in the sentence, and cannot be omitted without changing the meaning. They are called *restrictive* phrases or clauses and are not separated by commas.

Truth crushed to earth shall rise again.

The evil that men do lives after them.

6. After long introductory phrases and clauses and when needed to make the meaning clear.

Seated in the midst of a group of enthusiastic spectators, Michael clapped and cheered.

If you had stopped, John would have followed.

7. To set off an appositive that is not part of the name or that is not restrictive.

Lincoln, the Great Emancipator, was loved by all.

William the Conqueror became king of England in 1066.

8. To set off a parenthetical expression; that is, a word or a group of words inserted in the sentence as a comment or an explanatory remark, and one that is not necessary to the thought of the sentence.

You are, indeed, an industrious pupil.

Columbus was, without a doubt, a courageous man.

9. To separate the clauses of a compound sentence connected by the conjunctions *and, but, or, nor, yet*. If the clauses are short and closely connected, the comma may be omitted.

Your team won two games, but ours won three.
The door opened and he entered quietly.

10. After the salutation in a social letter and after the complimentary close in all letters.

Dear Maureen,   Dear Mrs. Ryan,   Sincerely yours,

EXERCISE 1

Study the following sentences. Give reasons for the punctuation:

1. Lucy went to the fair, but Mary stayed at home.
2. When gold was discovered in California in 1848, there was a rush of people to the West.
3. Christ converted Mary Magdalene, a notorious sinner.
4. Mary, we are told, excelled in English and history.
5. "Come and see my new canoe," said Judith.
6. The cities that ship wheat to the East are Duluth, Chicago, Superior, and Kansas City.
7. Mr. Jamison, who is the coach, was pleased with the result of the game.
8. On August 17, 1807, Robert Fulton made his first successful trip in the *Clermont*.
9. Listen and you will learn.
10. While Matthew was reading, his dog lay at his feet.
11. Yes, Teresa has written to me.
12. I am ready now, Father.

EXERCISE 2

Copy the following sentences, inserting the proper punctuation marks where necessary:

1. Answer all questions truthfully, completely and courteously
2. Come over Thomas and see my new skates
3. Francis parked his car a green coupe in front of the school

4. Italy surrendered on September 8,1943 but Germany did not capitulate until May 8,1945

5. The boys watching their opponents carefully caught them off guard and won the game

6. The setting, for example should be carefully arranged

7. Dorothy brought business letters from home from her father's office and from her uncle's store .

8. If you had called Mother would have told you where I was

9. Although Philip and Thomas are no longer together they keep up a frequent and fervent correspondence

THE SEMICOLON

Use a semicolon :

1. To separate the clauses of a compound sentence when they are not separated by a coordinate conjunction.

Peter did not go to the football game; he went on a hike instead.

2. To separate the clauses of a compound sentence that are connected by such words as *nevertheless, moreover, therefore, then, thus.*

He was a good worker; therefore his name was added to the list.

3. Before *as* and *namely* when these words introduce an example or an illustration.

There are two kinds of indulgences; namely, plenary and partial.

4. To separate the members of a series when a comma alone would not separate them clearly.

That Jesus Christ is the promised Savior can be proved from the prophecies of the Old Testament that are fulfilled in Him; from His own testimony, which is worthy of belief; and from the miracles He worked in proof of His divine mission.

EXERCISE 3

Insert semicolons and commas where they are needed :

1. There did not seem to be room for another person in the car nevertheless Mary and I squeezed into it.

2. Leonard has more than repaid Austin for his kindness he has become one of his best friends.
3. There are four officers in our club namely the president the vice-president the secretary and the treasurer.
4. In writing a paragraph we must select and limit the subject build a vocabulary make an outline follow the outline in writing beginning middle and ending sentences select a good title for the paragraph.
5. Just leave it to me I'll have it arranged in the morning.

THE COLON

Use a colon:

1. After the salutation of a business letter.

Dear Miss Graves: Gentlemen:

2. Before a list or enumeration of items.

They ordered the following: a desk, a chair, a bookcase, and a table.

3. Before a long direct quotation.

Pope Pius XI in his encyclical on education states: "But nothing discloses to us the supernatural beauty and excellence of the work of Christian education better than the sublime expression of love of our Blessed Lord, identifying Himself with children, 'Whosoever shall receive one such child as this in My name, receiveth Me!'"

THE EXCLAMATION POINT

Use an exclamation point:

1. After an exclamatory sentence.

What a gorgeous scene lay before us!

2. After an exclamatory word, phrase, or clause.

"Silence!" called the teacher.

THE INTERROGATION POINT

Use an interrogation point:

1. At the end of every question.

Where is my camera?

QUOTATION MARKS

Use quotation marks:

1. Before and after every direct quotation and every part of a divided quotation.

> "Give me liberty, or give me death!" said Patrick Henry.
> "I would rather be right," said Henry Clay, "than be president."

NOTE. Sometimes a quotation includes another quotation. Such an included quotation is known as a *quotation within a quotation* and is marked with single quotation marks.

> Helen replied, "Christ said to the grateful leper, 'Arise, go thy way, for thy faith hath saved thee.'"

2. To enclose titles of stories, poems, magazine articles, newspaper articles, and works of art.

> The best number on the program was Kilmer's "Trees."

NOTE. Titles of books, magazines, and newspapers are usually printed in italics, although some writers quote them.

> *The Call of the Wild* is an interesting book.
> "The Call of the Wild" is an interesting book.

EXERCISE 4

Insert colons, exclamation points, interrogation points, and quotation marks where they are needed in the following sentences:

1. Where is the schedule inquired Madeline.
2. We visited the Sistine Chapel, where we saw Michelangelo's Last Judgment.
3. Do you know, asked Father, who wrote *The Last of the Mohicans*
4. The Gift of the Magi was written by O. Henry.
5. Brutus explained his actions in these words As Caesar loved me, I weep for him; as he was fortunate, I rejoice at it; as he was valiant, I honour him; but, as he was ambitious, I slew him.
6. Hurrah Our band won the contest.
7. Did Father promise to take us to the circus

8. Shall we leave early inquired John.
9. What a becoming dress you are wearing
10. The following are included among the important industrial cities of the South Savannah, Georgia; New Orleans, Louisiana; Houston, Texas; Oklahoma City, Oklahoma.
11. Patrick Henry said, If this be treason, make the most of it.
12. The following are some of Christ's miracles He restored sight to the blind, cured lepers in an instant, walked on the waters of the sea, multiplied the loaves and fishes, raised the dead to life, and rose from the dead Himself by His own power.

THE APOSTROPHE

Use an apostrophe:

1. To show possession.

   Children's hats are sold here.

2. With *s* to show the plural of letters, figures, and signs.

   i's   4's   ?'s

3. To show the omission of a letter, letters, or figures.

   didn't   I'll   class of '52

THE HYPHEN

Use a hyphen:

1. To divide a word at the end of a line whenever one or more syllables are carried to the next line.

2. In compound numbers from twenty-one to ninety-nine.

   She is twenty-five years old.

3. To separate the parts of some compound words.

   self-respect   son-in-law

THE DASH

Use a dash:

1. To indicate a sudden change of thought.

   I suddenly turned—I am still surprised at my action—and left the room.

EXERCISE 5

Rewrite the following sentences, inserting the proper punctuation marks:

1. Make your *m*s more plainly
2. Mother bought twenty five acres of land
3. When you play play hard when you study study hard
4. James laughed and said Ill stay home
5. Father Tabb a southern poet wrote many beautiful nature poems
6. I cannot find Mothers sewing basket
7. Have you ever seen the picture Angels Heads by Reynolds
8. What is her name her age her address
9. Oh what a pleasant sight exclaimed Aunt Helen
10. Donald wont give me his toy cried the baby
11. Yes your answer is correct
12. My father worked faithfully therefore he was rewarded
13. It taught him the value of honesty sympathy and kindness
14. Good morning called Francis
15. It was early when we arrived the shops were not even open
16. Ouch I cut my finger
17. No Ellen I did not see your book
18. John asked Do you know who wrote that note
19. Mary wrote her 5s her 8s her 9s illegibly
20. O Lord have mercy on me
21. My friends address was changed to 453 Abbott Street Lansford Ohio
22. Lincolns Gettysburg Address begins with these words Four score and seven years ago
23. Father Flanagan the founder of Boys Town died in Germany in 1948
24. The cross examination lasted three hours
25. The teacher made the following suggestions test for clearness diction and spelling
26. The library is open on Monday Wednesday and Friday
27. The work had to be done Anne was the one to do it
28. Cinderella lived an unhappy life but her sisters lived in luxury

CAPITAL LETTERS

Use a capital letter for:

1. The first word in a sentence.

    In many Catholic families the rosary is recited daily.

2. The first word of every line of poetry.

    Mother! Whose virgin bosom was uncrost
      With the least shade of thought to sin allied;

3. The first word of a direct quotation.

    Jane cried, "Come quickly!"

4. Proper nouns and proper adjectives. These include particular persons or groups of persons, months of the year, days of the week, holidays, religious denominations, political parties, institutions, buildings, cities, states, and streets.

    Joseph, March, Armistice Day, Democrats, Catholic, Empire State Building, the American flag, Republican party

5. Titles of honor and respect when preceding the name.

    Bishop O'Hara   Queen Elizabeth

    NOTE. Do not capitalize any title not followed by a proper noun unless it is used in direct address as a substitute for the name.

    The judge has entered the courtroom.
    Not guilty, Your Honor.

6. *North, east, south,* and *west* when they refer to sections of a country.

    He comes from the West.

7. All names referring to the deity, the Bible, or parts of the Bible.

    Holy Scripture is a collection of sacred books composed by authors under the inspiration of God.

8. The principal words in the titles of books, plays, poems, and pictures.

    The Little Shepherd of Kingdom Come

9. The pronoun *I* and the interjection *O.*

    O Father! forgive them.

10. Abbreviations when capitals would be used if the words were written in full.

Gen.   St.

Do not capitalize:

1. The seasons of the year.

fall   winter

2. The articles *a, an, the,* conjunctions, or prepositions in titles, unless they are the first words.

   Two Years before the Mast
   Fra Angelico painted "The Coronation of the Virgin."

3. The names of studies, unless they are derived from proper nouns.

history   geography   English

4. The words *high school, college,* and *university,* unless they are parts of the names of particular institutions.

   My brother goes to high school in Dayton.
   My sister is a senior at the University of Southern California.

5. Abbreviations for the time of day.

a.m.   p.m.

EXERCISE 6

Divide the following two selections into sentences, using the necessary capitals and inserting the proper punctuation marks in each selection:

I

my father as i said was greatly delighted if my teacher had compared me to william shakespeare or had exclaimed he is a genius he could not have felt better he called me into the living room and with a face beaming with smiles said

there is no need for me to say that i was pleased when your teacher said henry is a boy who always tries to do his duty i am not going to spoil this achievement by giving you any reward the best reward for virtue is the testimony of a good conscience

II

a merry christmas uncle god save you cried a cheerful voice it was the voice of scrooges nephew who came upon him so quickly that this was the first intimation he had of his approach

bah said scrooge humbug

he had so heated himself with rapid walking in the fog and frost this nephew of scrooges that he was all in a glow his face was ruddy and handsome his eyes sparkled and his breath smoked again

christmas a humbug uncle said scrooges nephew you dont mean that i am sure

i do said scrooge merry christmas what right have you to be merry if i could work my will every idiot who goes about with merry christmas on his lips should be boiled with his own pudding and buried with a stake of holly through his breast

—From *A Christmas Carol*, by Charles Dickens

Calendar

THE MONTH OF SEPTEMBER

PATRON: Mary, Queen of Martyrs

LITURGICAL FEASTS: *September 3*, Saint Pius X, pope who encouraged frequent Communion. *September 8*, Birthday of Our Lady. *September 9*, Saint Peter Claver (d. 1654), Apostle of the Negroes. *September 10*, Saint Nicholas of Tolentino (d. 1306), member of the Order of Saint Augustine. *September 12*, Feast of the Holy Name of Mary, to commemorate the salvation of Europe from the Turks at the Battle of Vienna, September 12, 1683. *September 14*, Exaltation of the Holy Cross, celebrated to honor the recovery of the cross from the infidels. *September 15*, Feast of the Seven Dolors of Mary. *September 21*, Saint Matthew, one of the apostles, author of the first Gospel. *September 24*, Feast of Our Lady of Ransom. *September 26*, Saint Isaac Jogues (d. 1646), Saint Jean de Brébeuf (d. 1649), and other Jesuit martyrs of North America. *September 28*, Saint Wenceslaus (d. 935), patron of Bohemia. *September 29*, Saint Michael the Archangel. *September 30*, Saint Jerome (d. 420), doctor of the Church, author of Vulgate version of the Bible.

CIVIL HOLIDAYS AND BIRTHDAYS OF FAMOUS MEN: *First Monday (movable)*, Labor Day, inaugurated by Knights of Labor in 1882. *September 3*, Eugene Field (1850-1895), poet and journalist. *September 5*, Meeting of First Continental Congress, Philadelphia, 1774. *September 6*, Marquis de Lafayette (1757-1834), French statesman and soldier who helped the United States in the Revolutionary War. *September 14*, Writing of the "Star-Spangled Banner" by Francis Scott Key, 1814. *September 15*, James Fenimore Cooper (1789-1851), novelist. *September 17*, Constitution Day, completion of the writing of the Constitution of the United States, 1787. *September 19*, Washington's Farewell Address, 1796; Charles Carroll (1737-1832), signer of the Declaration of Independence. *September 21,* Louis Joliet (1645-1700), explorer, companion of Father Marquette. *September 22,* Emancipation Proclamation issued by President Lincoln, 1862. *September 24,* John Marshall (1755-1835), chief justice of the Supreme Court. *September 29,* Leif Ericson Day, Norsemen reached American continent, 1000.

THE MONTH OF OCTOBER

PATRON: The Guardian Angel

LITURGICAL FEASTS: *October 2,* Feast of the Guardian Angels. *October 3,* Saint Thérèse of Lisieux (d. 1897), known as the Little Flower. *October 4,* Saint Francis of Assisi (d. 1226), founder of the Franciscans. *October 6,* Saint Bruno (d. 1101), founder of the Carthusians. *October 7,* Feast of the Most Holy Rosary, instituted in thanksgiving for delivery of Christian world at Battle of Lepanto, 1571. *October 8,* Saint Bridget of Sweden (d. 1373). *October 10,* Saint Francis Borgia (d. 1572), noble Spanish Jesuit. *October 11,* Feast of the Maternity of Mary. *October 13,* Saint Edward the Confessor (d. 1066), king of England. *October 15,* Saint Theresa of Avila (d. 1582), Carmelite nun. *October 17,* Saint Margaret Mary (d. 1690), spread devotion to the Sacred Heart. *October 18,* Saint Luke, disciple of Saint Paul, author of the third Gospel. *October 24,* Saint Raphael the Archangel. *Last Sunday in October (movable),* Feast of Christ the King.

CIVIL HOLIDAYS AND BIRTHDAYS OF FAMOUS MEN: *October 7,* James Whitcomb Riley (1849-1916), poet. *October 9,* Fire Prevention Day, anniversary of the great Chicago fire, 1871. *October 10,* Benjamin West (1738-1820), first great painter born in America. *October 12,* Columbus Day, commemorates the landing of Columbus at San Salvador, 1492. *October 14,* William Penn (1644-1718), founder of Pennsylvania. *October 16,* Noah Webster (1758-1843), publisher of dictionaries. *October 27,* Theodore Roosevelt (1858-1919), president of United States; Navy Day. *October 31,* All Hallows' Eve or Halloween.

THE MONTH OF NOVEMBER

PATRON: The Holy Souls

LITURGICAL FEASTS: *November 1,* Feast of All Saints, honors all the heroes of the Church Triumphant. *November 2,* All Souls' Day, established by Saint Odilo and the monks of Cluny, 998. *November 4,* Saint Charles Borromeo (d. 1584), archbishop of Milan. *November 5,* Saint Elizabeth, mother of Saint John the Baptist; Blessed Martin de Porres, Dominican lay brother of Peru. *November 11,* Saint Martin of Tours (d. 397), noted for charity to the poor. *November 13,* Saint Stanislaus Kostka (d. 1568), patron of youth. *November 16,* Saint Gertrude (d. 1302), famed for supernatural visions. *November 19,* Saint Elizabeth of Hungary (d. 1231), devoted to the poor and needy. *November 21,* Presentation of Blessed Virgin. *November 22,* Saint Cecilia (d. 230), patroness of music. *November 25,* Saint Catherine of Alexandria (d. 313), patroness of teachers. *November 30,* Saint Andrew, apostle, brother of Saint Peter.

CIVIL HOLIDAYS AND BIRTHDAYS OF FAMOUS MEN: *Tuesday after first Monday (movable),* Election Day. *November 2,* Daniel Boone (1734-1820), American pioneer. *November 3,* William Cullen Bryant (1794-1878), poet and editor. *November 4,* Will Rogers (1879-1935), humorist and lecturer. *November 6,* John Philip Sousa (1854-1932), bandmaster and composer. *November 11,* Armistice Day, World War I came to an end on November 11, 1918. *November 13,* Edwin Booth (1833-1893), Shakespearean actor, foremost American tragedian. *November 14,* Robert Fulton (1765-1815), inventor of the steamboat. *November 19,* Lincoln's Address at Gettysburg, 1863; George Rogers Clark (1752-1818), frontier leader in American Revolution. *November 22,* Robert Cavelier, Sieur de La Salle (1643-1687), French explorer, claimed Mississippi Valley for France. *November 24,* Junipero Serra (1713-1784), Franciscan missionary in California. *November 29,* Louisa May Alcott (1832-1888), author of *Little Women. November 30,* Cyrus W. Field (1819-1892), promoted laying of first Atlantic cable; Samuel Clemens (1835-1910), used name of Mark Twain, author of *Tom Sawyer* and *Huckleberry Finn*. *Fourth Thursday of November (movable)*, Thanksgiving Day.

THE MONTH OF DECEMBER

PATRON: The Infant Jesus

LITURGICAL FEASTS: *December 3*, Saint Francis Xavier (d. 1552), Apostle of the Indies, patron of missions. *December 6*, Saint Nicholas (d. fourth century), patron of children. *December 7*, Saint Ambrose (d. 397), bishop of Milan and doctor of the Church. *December 8*, Feast of the Immaculate Conception, patroness of the United States. *December 12*, Our Lady of Guadalupe, patroness of Mexico. *December 13*, Saint Lucy (d. 304), virgin-martyr. *December 21*, Saint Thomas the Apostle. *December 22*, Saint Frances Xavier Cabrini (d. 1917), foundress of the Missionary Sisters of the Sacred Heart. *December 25*, Feast of the Nativity, Christmas Day. *December 26*, Saint Stephen, the first martyr. *December 27*, Saint John the Evangelist, the Beloved Disciple, author of the fourth Gospel and the Apocalypse. *December 28*, Feast of the Holy Innocents, children murdered by Herod in the hope of doing away with the Messias. *December 29*, Saint Thomas of Canterbury (d. 1170), murdered in cathedral of Canterbury, England.

CIVIL HOLIDAYS AND BIRTHDAYS OF FAMOUS MEN: *December 3*, Gilbert Charles Stuart (1755-1828), portrait painter. *December 6*, Joyce Kilmer (1886-1918), Catholic poet killed in World War I. *December 7*, Attack on Pearl Harbor by Japanese, 1941. *December 8*, World War II declared, 1941; Eli Whitney (1765-1825), inventor of the cotton gin. *December 11*, Pilgrims landed at Plymouth, 1620. *December 17*, John Greenleaf Whittier (1807-1892), poet, author of "Snow-Bound"; anniversary of the first successful flight of Wright brothers at Kitty Hawk, North Carolina, 1903. *December 18*, Edward A. MacDowell (1861-1908), American composer. *December 22*, Demetrius Gallitzin (1770-1840), early Catholic missionary in Pennsylvania. *December 24*,

Kit Carson (1809-1868), scout and Indian agent. *December 25,* Christmas Day; Clara Barton (1821-1912), founder of American Red Cross. *December 27,* Louis Pasteur (1822-1895), founder of preventive medicine. *December 29,* Charles Goodyear (1800-1860), discovered vulcanization of rubber. *December 30,* Rudyard Kipling (1865-1936), English poet and story writer. *December 31,* New Year's Eve.

THE MONTH OF JANUARY

PATRON : Holy Name of Jesus

LITURGICAL FEASTS : *January 1,* Feast of the Circumcision, holyday of obligation. *Sunday between the Circumcision and Epiphany (movable),* Feast of the Holy Name of Jesus. *January 6,* Feast of Epiphany, commemorates the visit of the wise men. *Sunday after Epiphany (movable),* Feast of the Holy Family. *January 18,* Saint Peter's Chair at Rome, commemorates the transfer of the papacy to Rome. *January 21,* Saint Agnes, patroness of young girls. *January 25,* Conversion of Saint Paul. *January 27,* Saint John Chrysostom (d. 407), patron of orators. *January 29,* Saint Francis de Sales (d. 1622), founder of the Visitation Order. *January 31,* Saint John Bosco (d. 1888), founder of the Salesians.

CIVIL HOLIDAYS AND BIRTHDAYS OF FAMOUS MEN : *January 1,* New Year's Day; Paul Revere (1735-1818), American patriot. *January 5,* Stephen Decatur (1779-1820), American naval hero. *January 8,* John Carroll (1735-1815), first Catholic bishop in the United States. *January 10,* Ethan Allen (1738-1789), American patriot and soldier. *January 11,* Alexander Hamilton (1757-1804), first secretary of the treasury. *January 12,* John Hancock (1737-1793), president of Continental Congress and first signer of the Declaration of Independence. *January 17,* Benjamin Franklin (1706-1790), statesman, scientist. *January 18,* Daniel Webster (1782-1852), statesman, lawyer, orator. *January 19,* Robert E. Lee (1807-1870), commander in chief of the Confederate army; Edgar Allan Poe (1809-1849), poet and story writer.

January 20, Inauguration Day, president of United States inaugurated on this date every four years. *January 25,* Robert Burns (1759-1796), Scottish poet. *January 29,* Thomas Paine (1737-1809), author of *Common Sense,* pamphlet urging independence; Albert Gallatin (1761-1849), statesman, financier, secretary of the treasury; William McKinley (1843-1901), president of the United States. *January 30,* Franklin Delano Roosevelt (1882-1945), president of the United States.

THE MONTH OF FEBRUARY

PATRON: The Boy of Nazareth

LITURGICAL FEASTS: *February 1,* Saint Ignatius (d. 107), bishop of Antioch, martyr. *February 2,* Feast of the Purification, Candlemas Day. *February 3,* Saint Blaise (d. 316), invoked by those suffering from throat ailments. *February 4,* Saint Andrew Corsini (d. 1373), bishop of Fiesole. *February 5,* Saint Agatha (d. 251), virgin and martyr. *February 11,* Feast of Our Lady of Lourdes, anniversary of first apparition of our Lady to Saint Bernadette at Lourdes in 1858. *February 14,* Saint Valentine (d. 270), martyr. *February 24,* Saint Matthias, apostle elected to take the place of Judas.

CIVIL HOLIDAYS AND BIRTHDAYS OF FAMOUS MEN: *February 2,* Fritz Kreisler (1875-   ), violinist and composer. *February 11,* Thomas Edison (1847-1931), scientist, inventor of incandescent lamp and phonograph. *February 12,* Abraham Lincoln (1809-1865), statesman, Civil War president; Peter Cooper (1791-1883), philanthropist and reformer, builder of first locomotive in America. *February 22,* George Washington (1732-1799), first president of the United States; James Russell Lowell (1819-1891), poet, critic, and editor. *February 26,* William F. Cody (1846-1917), American scout and showman known as Buffalo Bill. *February 27,* Henry Wadsworth Longfellow (1807-1882), author of "Evangeline," "The Courtship of Miles Standish," and many other poems. *February 29,* Louis Montcalm (1712-1759), French general, mortally wounded in the Battle of Quebec.

THE MONTH OF MARCH

PATRON: Saint Joseph

LITURGICAL FEASTS: *March 4,* Saint Casimir (d. 1484), patron of Poland. *March 6,* Saints Perpetua and Felicitas (d. 203), martyrs. *March 7,* Saint Thomas Aquinas (d. 1274), the Angelic Doctor. *March 8,* Saint John of God (d. 1550), patron of the sick and of hospitals. *March 9,* Saint Frances of Rome (d. 1440), foundress of the Oblates of Saint Benedict. *March 12,* Saint Gregory the Great (d. 604), doctor of the Church, father of the Gregorian chant. *March 17,* Saint Patrick (d. 493), Apostle of Ireland. *March 19,* Saint Joseph, patron of the universal Church. *March 21,* Saint Benedict (d. 543), founder of the Benedictines. *March 24,* Saint Gabriel the Archangel. *March 25,* Feast of the Annunciation of Our Lady.

CIVIL HOLIDAYS AND BIRTHDAYS OF FAMOUS MEN: *March 1,* Augustus Saint-Gaudens (1848-1907), sculptor. *March 2,* De Witt Clinton (1769-1828), influential in building Erie Canal; Samuel Houston (1793-1863), Texas statesman. *March 3,* Alexander Graham Bell (1847-1922), inventor of the telephone and early teacher of the deaf. *March 7,* Luther Burbank (1849-1926), botanist and plant breeder. *March 13,* Joseph Priestley (1733-1804), chemist, clergyman, discoverer of oxygen. *March 15,* Andrew Jackson (1767-1845), hero of Battle of New Orleans, president of the United States. *March 17,* Roger B. Taney (1777-1864), chief justice of Supreme Court. *March 22,* John B. Tabb (1845-1909), priest and poet. *March 23,* John Bartram (1699-1777), first native American botanist. *March 25,* Maryland Day, Mass celebrated for the first time in English colonies, 1634.

THE MONTH OF APRIL

PATRON: The Risen Christ

LITURGICAL FEASTS: *April 11,* Saint Leo the Great (d. 461), saved Rome from Attila. *April 14,* Saint Justin (d. 165), martyr, patron of Catholic philosophy. *April 21,* Saint Anselm (d. 1109), archbishop of Canterbury. *April 23,* Saint George (d. 303), martyr, patron of England. *April 25,* Saint Mark, disciple of Saint Peter, author of second Gospel. *April 26,* Feast of Our Lady of Good Counsel. *April 27,* Saint Peter Canisius (d. 1597), Jesuit preacher and writer. *April 30,* Saint Catherine of Siena (d. 1380), instrumental in bringing the popes from exile in Avignon to Rome. *Friday in Passion Week (movable),* Feast of the Seven Dolors of the Blessed Virgin. *Holy Thursday (movable),* Institution of the Holy Eucharist. *Good Friday (movable),* The Crucifixion. *Easter Sunday (movable),* The Resurrection of Our Lord.

CIVIL HOLIDAYS AND BIRTHDAYS OF FAMOUS MEN: *April 2,* Hans Christian Andersen (1805-1875), Danish writer of fairy tales and folk tales. *April 3,* Washington Irving (1783-1859), author. *April 5,* Booker T. Washington (1856-1915), Negro educator. *April 6,* Army Day. *April 12,* Henry Clay (1777-1852), American statesman. *April 13,* Thomas Jefferson (1743-1826), author of the Declaration of Independence, president of the United States. *April 14,* Pan-American Day. *April 19,* Patriots Day, anniversary of Battle of Lexington and Concord, 1775. *April 23,* William Shakespeare (1564-1616), dramatist and poet; Stephen A. Douglas (1813-1861), political leader, engaged in series of debates with Abraham Lincoln. *April 26,* John James Audubon (1785-1851), naturalist, author and designer of *Birds of America. April 27,* Samuel Morse (1791-1872), inventor of the telegraph, artist; Ulysses S. Grant (1822-1885), Civil War general, president of the United States. *April 30,* Washington inaugurated first president of the United States, New York, 1789.

THE MONTH OF MAY

PATRON: Our Lady, Queen of the May

LITURGICAL FEASTS: *Forty days after Easter (movable),* Ascension Thursday. *May 1,* Feast of Saint Joseph the Worker. *May 3,* Finding of the Holy Cross, 325. *May 4,* Saint Monica (d. 387), mother of Saint Augustine. *May 11,* Saints Philip and

James the Less, apostles. *May 13,* Saint Robert Bellarmine (d. 1621), doctor of the Church. *May 15,* Saint John Baptist de la Salle (d. 1719), founder of the Christian Brothers. *May 16,* Saint Simon Stock (d. 1265), received Scapular of Mount Carmel from Blessed Virgin. *May 20,* Saint Bernardine of Siena (d. 1444), began the devotion to the holy name of Jesus. *May 22,* Saint Rita of Cascia (d. 1456). *May 25,* Saint Madeleine Sophie Barat (d. 1865), foundress of the Society of the Sacred Heart of Jesus. *May 26,* Saint Philip Neri (d. 1595), founder of the Oratorians. *May 27,* Saint Bede (d. 735), doctor of the Church. *May 28,* Saint Augustine of Canterbury (d. 604), Apostle of England. *May 29,* Saint Mary Magdalen of Pazzi (d. 1607), Carmelite nun and mystical writer. *May 30,* Saint Joan of Arc (d. 1431), savior of the French. *May 31,* Feast of the Blessed Virgin Mary the Queen.

CIVIL HOLIDAYS AND BIRTHDAYS OF FAMOUS MEN : *Second Sunday in May,* Mother's Day. *May 1,* May Day, of old English origin ; Child Health Day, established by President Hoover in 1930. *May 4,* Horace Mann (1796-1859), educator. *May 12,* Florence Nightingale (1820-1910), English war nurse. *May 13,* Settlement of Jamestown, Virginia, 1607. *May 18,* World Goodwill Day, anniversary of the opening of the first Hague Peace Conference, 1899. *May 21,* American Red Cross founded in 1881. *May 25,* Ralph Waldo Emerson (1803-1882), poet and essayist. *May 27,* Julia Ward Howe (1819-1910), author, composer of "Battle Hymn of the Republic." *May 28,* Louis Agassiz (1807-1873), zoologist, teacher. *May 29,* Patrick Henry (1736-1799), colonial statesman, lawyer, orator. *May 30,* Memorial Day, designated for the decoration of graves of Union soldiers and exercises in their honor, 1868; observed in southern states on April 26 or May 10.

Index

Nor, subjects connected by, 304
Noun clauses, 379-83, 393, 404-05
Noun phrases, 374
Nouns, 215-33
  abstract, 216
  case of, 223-31, 321, 331
  collective, 216, 305
  common, 215
  ending in *ing,* 332-33
  gender of, 222-23
  gerunds used as, 326-27, 409-10
  in direct address, 370
  infinitives used as, 334, 336
  kinds of, 215-16
  number of, 218-21, 307
  person of, 217-18
  proper, 215
  test on, 232-33
  words used as adjectives and, 271
  words used as verbs and, 315
Number
  of nouns, 218-21, 307
  of pronouns, 235-36, 255-56, 306
  of verbs, 292-93, 299-307
  plural, 218-21, 256, 292-93, 299-302, 304-05, 307
  singular, 218, 255-56, 292-93, 299-307
Numeral adjectives, 261

O, correct use of, 370
Object
  cognate, 231
  direct. *See* Direct object
  gerund as, 327, 409
  indirect, 229, 234, 248, 400
  infinitive as, 334, 336, 406
  of preposition, 230, 234, 249, 254, 282, 327, 336, 360, 364, 381, 401, 405, 407, 410
  retained, 230, 283, 401
Objective case, 229-31, 234, 248-49, 253, 283, 343, 400-01
Objective complement, 230, 263, 401
Objectives, adverbial, 230, 352, 401
Off, correct use of, 362
Oh, correct use of, 370
Open forums, 170-75

Or, subjects connected by, 304
Order, natural and transposed, 109, 387
Outlines
  for compositions, 86
  for formal talks, 15
  for paragraphs, 71, 79
Ownership, joint and separate, 228

Panel discussions, 193-97
Paragraphs
  class, 69-74
  coherence in, 51-53, 58-59, 61, 69, 81
  definition of, 35
  disorderly, 52-53
  in letters, 127, 129
  in longer compositions, 84-86
  outlines for, 71, 79
  parts of, 35-45
  polishing, 97-117
  rules for form of, 117
  steps in writing, 70-81
  study of, 35-61
  subject of, 42, 70, 75-76
  titles for, 73-74, 81
  topic of, 35, 40, 42, 48-49, 52, 61, 69, 70, 75-76, 81
  types of, 55-61
  unity in, 48-49, 58, 61, 69, 81
  writing of, 69-86
Parenthetical phrases, 301
Parliamentary procedure, 18-21, 23-26
Participial adjectives, 260, 320, 333, 409
Participial phrases, 224-25, 319, 321-22, 374
Participles, 318-24, 408-09
  correct use of, 323-24
  dangling, 324
  forms of, 318
  position of, 319
  properties of, 318
  recognition of, 333
  tense of, 318, 323
  test on, 346-47
Parts of speech, 274-77, 371-73
Passive voice, 278, 281-82, 283, 284, 285, 287, 289, 318, 336